Mystic Sails, Texas Trails

by Robert Davant
with Mickey Herskowitz

Texas Review Press
Huntsville, Texas

FIRST EDITION

Requests for permission to acknowledge material from this work should be sent to:

Permissions
    Texas Review Press
    English Department
    Sam Houston State University
    Huntsville, TX 77341-2146

Library of Congress Cataloging-in-Publication Data

Names: Davant, Robert, 1932- author. | Herskowitz, Mickey, author.
Title: Mystic sails, Texas trails / Robert Davant, Mickey Herskowitz.
Description: Huntsville, Texas : Texas Review Press, [2016]
Identifiers: LCCN 2016015498 (print) | LCCN 2016020096 (ebook) | ISBN
    9781680031133 (hardback : alk. paper) | ISBN 9781680031140 (e-book)
Subjects: LCSH: Grimes family. | Texas--History--19th century. |
    Pioneers--Texas--Biography. | Frontier and pioneer life--Texas. |
    Coastwise shipping--United States--History--19th century. |
    Ranching--Texas--History--19th century. | Cattle
    drives--Texas--History--19th century
Classification: LCC F385 .D26 2016 (print) | LCC F385 (ebook) | DDC
    976.4/05--dc23
LC record available at https://lccn.loc.gov/2016015498

*This book is dedicated to the memory of Thomas Jefferson Poole, Jr.,
who returned to the WBG Ranch in 1899 to continue cattle ranching
on the ranch started by his grandfather William Bradford Grimes; to
the memory of my mother Fannie Louise Davant, and to the memory
of my daughter Jessica who rests with the Captain in
the WBG Ranch cemetery.*

Contents

PROLOGUE

Master and Commander Richard Grimes, the "Captain," stood at the helm of the schooner *Henry* where he had been for three days and three nights, battling a fierce hurricane in the Gulf of Mexico. Fortified by alternating shots of coffee and whiskey, the seasoned old sea captain made the choice to hold a course away from the mainland rather than seeking the closest port as the other ships in his convoy did. One by one his companion ships perished. It was a pivotal decision, for had the Captain and his family died in the storm, the rich Grimes legacy in Texas history would have been lost forever beneath the waves.

The Captain's story began at an inland seaport on the Connecticut River where sailing ships were built and sailed by men who produced the vessels that would participate in wars and trade in the West Indies. This is the port the Captain sailed from as a young man, and where he began a long voyage to the new Republic of Texas. There he and his son Bradford invested in the beginnings of the cattle industry, and where Bradford engaged in a range war with Shanghai Pierce and herded cattle up the Chisholm Trail to Dodge City, Kansas.

In 1836, during the Texas War for Independence and within the time frame covering both the Battle at the Alamo and the Battle at San Jacinto, the Captain, in command of his schooner *Henry*, delivered gunpowder, troops, palm leaf hats and whiskey at the Port of Matagorda. The following year, as the new Republic was coming to life, the Captain returned to Connecticut to collect his wife and young daughter and return to the excitement that was Texas to pursue maritime trading from his new home and make a gradual transition from a life at sea to that of a land baron. When Bradford came to join him after years of schooling in the North, they began to gather and put the Grimes brand on wild cattle and to transport them by land and by sea to markets in New Orleans, Havana and beyond.

Bradford established the legendary WBG ranch and assumed the mantle of leadership as a Texas cattleman. During the Civil War, Union gunboats denied Texans access to traditional markets, but after the war, a bourgeoning cattle market created the legendary cattle drives out of Texas to meet the railroads pushing south from the Missouri River and across the plains of Kansas. The era of the cattle drives began with its combination of hardship, danger and romantic excitement created by cowboys driving cattle "up the trail." The memoir of Bradford's oldest son Bradford Robbins, included herein in its entirety, is a firsthand account of one of these legendary trail drives. That same 1876 drive became the basis for one of the earliest and best known western novels by Charles Siringo.

After the death of his wife in 1876, and after continuing territorial disputes over range lands with his former employee, Shanghai Pierce, Bradford moved with his young children to Kansas City, Missouri. There, in a quieter and more sophisticated environment, his children grew and were educated and he started a second career in business as a Kansas City banker and merchant. His eldest son BR continued the annual trail drives to Kansas from his WBG ranch in Texas while Bradford continued his ranching operations in the Indian Territory and the Dakotas.

Grimes became a prominent figure in Kansas as a rancher, banker, and owner of the "Grimes Block," a multi-story building in downtown Kansas City from which he conducted a dry goods business. In 1881, upon the marriage of his oldest daughter Fannie Louise to Thomas Jefferson Poole, Grimes gave the WBG ranch in Texas to her as a wedding gift. Upon her death in 1888, Fannie Louise's two young children, Irene and Tom Jr., inherited the WBG and Bradford's grandson Tom, Jr., continued the Grimes legacy expanding the family's Texas cattle business to its zenith.

Over the years, Tom Poole, Jr., the great grandson of Captain Grimes, shipped thousands of Texas steers by rail to the Osage prairies of Oklahoma and the Flint Hills of Kansas to fatten on strong summer ranges. His death in 1969 closely coincided with the end of the era of gathering large cattle herds to graze on Kansas prairies. Tom's daughters continued to ranch into the 1980s as did Grimes descendants in Kansas. All of them owe their legacy to their early cattlemen ancestors who rounded up mavericks on the open range and drove them "up the trail."

Mystic Sails, Texas Trails

CHAPTER ONE

A Godly Massacre

When the English Reformation produced the Anglican church, there were those seeking even more reform and distance from the Catholic church and to remove every vestige of Catholicism from their midst including the clergy's vestments and Catholic liturgy. Because of their fervor and continuing clamor for purification, they began to annoy both the King and the Archbishop of the Anglican church who began referring to them in the pejorative sense as Puritans. They preferred to refer to themselves as "Godly." Under King James I, they were forced to either stay and suffer punishment for their tiresome provocations or separate and find somewhere else to clamor for radical change.

To encourage their departure they were granted a charter which permitted colonization in parts of several New England states but primarily in Massachusetts where the immigrating group became the Massachusetts Bay Colony. In the governance of their members, the Puritans established rules and regulations so rigidly enforced, especially around Salem, that some members seeking to govern themselves began to drift away into Connecticut and Rhode Island.

One splinter group traveled south from Watertown to explore the outskirts of their surroundings and in their wanderings, came across a settlement of Pequot Indians. As they became better acquainted with the Pequot they realized that the village encampment and surrounding tribal lands were in a valley with choice soils, an abundance of wild game and all of the natural resources they needed to sustain their group; and, with total disregard for the rights of the tribe living peacefully there for generations, they summarily laid claim to it.

The valley, six miles long and eight miles wide, was bounded on the north by a sharp bend in the Connecticut River and on the south by the southern border of the Hartford Colony. Once the best lands for their crops were clearly defined, a wave of immigrants from the colonies, England and Scotland began to arrive and the settlers who took from the Pequot began to survey and sell plantation land to the newcomers.

When the Pequot realized that their ancient homeland was vanishing, they made an effort to reclaim it and attacked and killed nine of the settlers working in their fields. Armed men from Wethersfield and two other river plantations were quickly organized and a brutal, murderous assault was made upon the Mystic River village. The Indians, armed with primitive weapons, were easily overwhelmed and the assault ended with the merciless killing of hundreds of men, women and children and the pitiful handful of survivors sold into slavery. The Wethersfield men that joined in the massacre then formed a Commonwealth and having made the land safe from the original owners, drew up "Fundamental Orders" by which they were thereafter governed.

Among the immigrants was a Scotsman named Henry Grihmes, the first identifiable ancestor of the Captain. His surveying skills got him the job of Chief Surveyor of Highways, and allowed him to purchase the lands where his son, Joseph, now spelling his surname *Grimes*, settled in 1705. There in the Parish of Stepney Joseph helped construct the Stepney Parish Meeting House and there his son, Hezekiah, would marry Abigail Smith, a prosperous descendant of one of the founders of Wethersfield. This fortuitous union brought prosperity to Grimes descendants for the next one hundred years. Their youngest son, Alexander, fathered Captain Richard Grimes in 1790 at a time when the Parish of Stepney had become a center of Connecticut River ship building. It had become a community where everyone owed their livelihood to the construction, outfitting and command of sailing ships. So began the plantation known as Wethersfield, birthplace of the ship captain whose life would inspire this story.

The Old Town Shipyard

Stepney was officially founded in 1636 and is one of the earliest towns in New England. On an easterly bend in the river, its long, flat shoreline was a natural site for a ship yard. Proceeding further upstream under sail from that point meant the risk of running aground on dangerous, shallow shoals and a sand bar. These natural advantages made Stepney a thriving port and in 1672 its governors set aside five acres in the bend as a "common" landing dedicated to the building of ships.

Early ship building began with the construction of small sloops and ketches and due to an abundance of accessible timber, they designed and built vessels cheaper than those being built in England. By 1750 they began to produce two-masted schooners and brigs and the landing became a bustling ship yard with the entire village becoming a workforce engaged in the art of ship building. The construction of sailing ships brought with it a high level of commercial activity as the rigging and finishing of sailing ships gave birth to all the attendant industries. Men were crafting pumps, blocks, halyards, sheets and winches while the smithies shaped and hammered out nails, spikes, bolts and pins to complement the needs of the ships' carpenters and architects. The masts and spars to carry the sails aloft were crafted locally and the yard also had rope walks, a sail loft and a pit where men could stand and saw timbers for the keels and ribs.

The Stepney docks were connected to the stores and warehouses necessary for the ships outfitted for departing voyages and for the sale of goods from those returning from the West Indies and other foreign ports of call. The upstream shoals and sand bars impeding passage to Hartford worked to Stepney's advantage for years and made her naturally *the* port of the Hartford Township.

During the Colonial years after 1750, large, two-masted ships were built here with as many as nine ships in the stocks at any one time. Trades in support of the carpenters created a large force of workmen and a village where everyone was engaged in one form or another in ship building. During the crucial years of Revolutionary War, building was heightened as the need arose for larger, faster ships that could carry men and cannon. Many of the schooners and brigs built for the West Indies were easily adapted to fighting ships. There was great admiration for these ships by the British Admiralty as they learned from the few that were captured and studied, that American schooners and brigs were much faster than those of English design.

Fighting ships built here for the Revolution were the *Ann,* the *Revenge,* the brig *Minerva* and the brigantine *Hornet.* Others built during this period were owned and commanded by privateers. Among those were the *Drake,* the sloop *Here* commanded by Justice Riley, the schooner *Humbird* commanded by Ozais Goodwin, the schooner *Experiment* commanded by Joseph Combs and Captain Samuel Stillman's brig the *Jason.* Captain William Griswold of Stepney owned the brig *Minerva,* 108 tons chartered by the Navy and fitted with 16 guns and a crew of 100; the armament put on her made her a vessel of war.

Many of the owners and Captains were members of the seafaring families living in the village of Stepney and some were also master carpenters. Joseph Dimock was one such master carpenter who also owned and commanded the vessels he built. Some of the prominent owners were Joseph, Hosea, Edmund and Ralph Bulkley; Josiah, John, Samuel and Roger Williams; Justus, Jason and Frederick Robbins; and William, Nathan, Hezekiah, Samuel, Richard and Roderick Grimes. Many of those same owners and co-owners of vessels were also listed on the "Registry of Ships" as Master. All of these men living in or near the Old Town Yard were a close knit fraternity of its leading citizens prosperous enough to own ships. In Stiles' history of the area, Richard Grimes was listed as Master of the sloop *Eagle* but also as a co-owner with Joseph and Edward Bulkley. The Grimes, Bulkley, Williams, Griswold and Robbins families all played prominent roles during the crucial, early years of Stepney's development as a major port on the Connecticut River.

The Captain

Richard Grimes was born to the sea and from an early age, it was clear that his destiny was to command ships. In 1789, George Washington, as first President of the United States, took the oath of office in New York City. In 1790, the year of Washington's inauguration, Richard was born to Alexander Grimes and Mary Dunn. His generation would see the nation extend westward to the Pacific Ocean and it would be his destiny to be present in another struggle in 1836 when men in faraway Texas fought to live free.

Richard was the youngest of ten children and was named for his seafaring maternal grandfather, Captain Richard Dunn of Newport, Rhode Island. "Captain Dunn, having made a fortune in the slave trade, came to Stepney to spend his last days." Whether or not the slave trade was carried out from the wharves of this seaport, the good people of Stepney were no less enterprising than other New Englanders as the first slaves brought into the colonies were landed at nearby Boston. There was also a slave trade carried on between Rocky Hill and other ports. So many men in Rocky Hill owned slaves that a gallery was built in "the church." Robert Colburn also wrote that nearly all the land on the river had for more than a century been in the possession of one family which had never sold a parcel. The Captain's maternal grandmother inherited a large part of Stepney's waterfront which she owned until 1792. Grimes owners refused to sell any part of their waterfront property. ". . . The stubborn refusal of the Grimes family to part with any part of their property until after 1825, kept Stepney from being the place of importance that it would have been had a more liberal policy of expansion been followed . . . had they not been so obstinate about selling such important land for commercial development, Hartford may have had a rival in this now obscure town."

When the Captain was born the very essence of Stepney had been building and outfitting the vessels to fight the British and even though the War had been concluded six years earlier, post war activities now dominated the commerce and livelihood of all New England. It was an exciting time to be alive and the new country's prosperity caused the Old Town Yard to expand to include eight or nine ship-related stores. The proprietors of those businesses were often owners too of the vessels being built in the adjoining yard.

In this environment along the busy waterfront, young Richard Grimes was educated in the lore of the sea with a healthy dose of hero worship for the seamen whose lives at sea seemed so adventurous. Richard attended a school that taught navigation and other seafaring skills and of the seven sons of Alexander and Mary Grimes, five of them, Hezekiah, Nathan, Samuel, William and Richard would choose to follow the sea. Roderick, four years older than Richard, participated as a merchant on the Old Town Yard landing. William, who was eight years older than Richard and who was said to be Richard's favorite brother, was lost at sea on board a vessel that was to have been commanded by Richard. Some matter made it expedient for William to take his place or Richard would have been in command of the vessel which failed to return. How the ship was lost or the fate of its crew was never learned and not knowing how his brother William died, darkened Richard's life for many years. Richard's brother William was listed in the New England Registry of Ships as Master and part owner of the *Hornet*, a 73-ton brigantine commissioned in 1811.

When Richard felt he had suffered enough under school masters, he stowed away aboard a merchant schooner determined to make going to sea a success and judging by the rapid rise of his rank and fortune, at age 21 he sailed back into port the Captain of his own ship.

When ships returned to their home ports after months or years at sea, it was an occasion for show. In her 1901 memoir the Captain's daughter wrote about the dress for such occasions:

> *"How well the writer remembers hearing from an old citizen of Hartford a description of the garb of Captain Grimes when the narrator, then a boy, and native of Rocky Hill, like all the boys far and near, rushing to greet incoming ships, would go to the river to meet the brig* Marshall, *Captain Dick commander. Said he, 'how my eyes would stand out when Captain Dick appeared in the full glory of blue coat and brass buttons, a shirt frill four inches wide, and full enough to fill the entire 'waistcoat' front.' I tell you those ladies in those days could sew, and Captain Dick's wife could pleat ruffles. With black velvet knee breeches, buckles at the knees, silk stockings to meet 'em and patent leather pumps, buckles on them too, well, I just thought that . . . being Captain of a ship was the greatest thing on earth."*

Achieving Captaincy by his 21st birthday, was no small accomplishment for Richard considering the station from which he started and the things a young lad at sea was required to learn. Those were the days of cat-o-nine-tails and belaying pins as forms of "moral suasion"; days when sailors had no rights, and officers and seamen alike were bound to respect and obey the rule of autocratic Captains in sole command of their ships. The merchant service recruited from the slums of all nations and cooks being less than the least of the crew were not likely to offer a word of encouragement to a cook's helper or a homesick cabin boy. The Captain never reminisced about those early days at sea as perhaps the hardships imposed upon him were too unpleasant to recall.

In the prime of his life, the Captain carried on a large business in passenger traffic and freight and was a master of navigation at a time when voyages across the oceans of the world required the accounting for ocean currents, tides, wind patterns, and no small knowledge of Atlantic weather. The Captain circumnavigated the earth at least three times and affirmed that he entered every known port on the globe and some where no ship but his own had ever ventured. An East Hartford captain of note, said of him: *"Captain Richard Grimes was one of the best captains who ever crossed the Atlantic, exceeded in seamanship by none, equaled by few, and an example to all for his morality."*

Captain Richard Grimes—Owner, Master, and Commander of several sailing ships engaged in a West Indies and European trade. The Captain participated in the Texas war for independence and settled permanently on Matagorda Bay in 1837.

The Captain was described as being of medium height and very strong and several events have survived to describe his character. According to a statement by a deck hand who claimed to have been present, the Captain once struck a man so hard for insubordination that the sailor went flying overboard whereupon the Captain went over the side to his rescue. The same sailor then went on to add that this last dollar could be had by any shipmate in trouble or need. During a Yellow Fever epidemic in the West Indies the Captain went to the hospital where his crew were lying ill and helped nurse each of them through the disease without losing a man. When cholera was carried into a family by a visiting child, many people died and the Captain dug graves for three of the children who died after everyone else had fled the scene. While attending the sick and burying the dead, threats were hurled at him for the danger that he might cause to himself or as a carrier to others. His reply was, "I don't deserve to live if I can neglect others in such a strait."

In 1824, at age 34, the Captain married Charlotte Bradford, a daughter of William and Elizabeth Sears Bradford. In 1783 her father had built a home for his family in Rocky Hill which became a landmark property known always as "Bradford Hill." On a high promontory above the Connecticut River, it provided a welcome base and refuge for members of the family for almost two hundred years.

In the 1820's, ocean-going traders to the West Indies began to learn of the new colony being developed in the Mexican Territory west of New Orleans and the new port of Matagorda in the heart of the Stephen F. Austin Colony. The Captain began to sail and trade in these Mexican Texas waters.

Sailing ships built for trade were brigs and schooners, were rigged fore and aft with mains and overlapping jibs for easy handling with a minimum crew. Ships built in the early 1800's were judged by the amount of cargo they could carry. Size, beauty, sentimental qualifications or any one good feature alone counts for nothing against the economic and natural law of survival of the fittest. For the Atlantic coast and short, quick voyages to the West Indies, schooners and brigs were the ships of choice and for tonnage moved, these ships had the best design for rapid turnover and valuation; in short, they were very profitable.

During the War of 1812 and throughout the Napoleonic Wars, schooners carried the bulk of cargoes shipped in American bottoms because of their speed and ability to out-distance cruisers. Hull designs of the schooners and brigs were much the same and the two types differed principally in their choice of rigging. The advantage of schooners and brigs over square-riggers rested in smaller crews, greater handiness and surety working in narrow channels or in confined waters. They were also preferred over all others by slavers, pirates and privateers since they were dependent on speed to avoid capture. Nothing is more conducive to the attainment of speed in sailing vessels than to have the owner's property, and perhaps freedom, dependent upon this particular quality. Over the course of the Captain's maritime career the list of ships owned or registered to him were the sloop *Eagle*; the schooner *Marshall*; the brig *Roland*; the brig *Marshall*, the schooner *Viper*, the brig *Driver*; the schooner *Henry*; the brig *Coral*; and the schooner *Sarah Ann Jane*. The Captain's connection with all of these ships was as owner or as Master and Commander. One of the last vessels built in the Old Town shipyard was the *Marshall* for Roderick and Richard Grimes. In two of these ships, the *Driver* and the *Henry*, the Captain conducted several years of trading down the eastern seaboard, in the West Indies and around the Gulf of Mexico. Both the brig *Driver* and the schooner *Henry* were of the draft and burthen ideal for the Gulf of Mexico ports on Galveston Bay and Matagorda Bay.

Newspapers in port cities print Maritime Shipping News for vessels arriving and clearing their harbors. Maritime notices published in various port newspapers recorded the Captain's arrivals and clearings from 1830 to 1842 at New York, Baltimore, Barbados, Norfolk, Charleston, Savannah, Mobile, Trinidad, New Orleans, Bermuda, Mexico, Philadelphia, Providence, West Indies, Galveston, Indianola and Matagorda. In 1830 the Captain, in command of *Driver*, cleared New York Harbor bound for Mexico. In 1831 *Driver* cleared Port of Spain, Trinidad and arrived in Boston from Bermuda bound for Wethersfield on the Connecticut River. In 1833 Hartford printed shipping news of the arrival of *Driver*, with Grimes in command with a cargo of rum and sugar from the West Indies. Later that year Grimes cleared Charleston bound for Philadelphia with a cargo of Sea Island cotton and lumber. In October *Driver* was reported by a vessel off Charleston, as eight days out of the Connecticut River bound for Savannah and in December *Driver* cleared Savannah bound for Barbados with a cargo of lumber, staves and onions. In March of 1834 *Driver* cleared Philadelphia for Santa Domingo. In December *Driver* was bound for Bar-

bados and in the same month arrived in Mobile Bay from
Havana. In March of 1835 *Driver* cleared the harbor in Tam-
pico, Mexico and in July arrived back in New York Harbor.
The Captain was constantly at sea and under sail from New
York in the North to as far south as Tampico, Mexico with
many calls at the port of Matagorda in Mexican Texas.

Mexican Texas

In 1821, the final year of Spanish rule, the government
granted a man from Connecticut named Moses Austin
the right to bring colonists to Mexican Texas. He did not
live to exercise those rights but his son Stephen F. Austin
would. During the most active years of the Captain's life at
sea, word of Austin's colony in Texas spread throughout
the United States as sailing ships brought settlers down
and took news back about opportunities for cheap land
and fortunes to be made. The way to this new land was
on brigs and schooners out of New England yards built to
carry trade goods out from the East Coast and return with
goods from the West Indies. Those ships now brought down
the settlers. Cargo ships calling at the port of New Orleans and West Indian traders were transporting passengers
from all of the New England states and the Carolinas to
Austin's colony in Mexican Texas. Captains and their crews
came to trade at the new port of Matagorda and to profit
from supplying the needs of the settlers there.

The Spaniards had invited the colonization of Texas
with the idea that the Anglo settlements would act as a buf-
fer between the Mexican population and the savage, horse
mounted Comanches that held sway over the lands around
the early Spanish missions and the unsafe settlements
of northern Mexico. Under Mexico's new government, the
agreement with Austin stated that his colonizers would be
allowed to settle these lands with the proviso that they remain ten leagues away from the coast. Austin was granted
an exception by being allowed to locate a coastal site for a
fort and in his search, his surveyors selected and Austin
approved a town-site and named it Matagorda. The first
fifty-two families put ashore there were from New York and
Connecticut. One of Austin's surveyors, Elias Wightman,
made a hasty return to New York for his wife and more

settlers and they came back to Matagorda on a ship called *Little Zoe*. In 1827 Austin got permission to settle an additional 300 families inland and carefully selected colonists who were unique in the fact that they were quite literate and only three out of the 300 lacked an education.

Austin selected for himself a large tract on the bluff where the Rio Colorado curved into Matagorda Bay and parceled the remaining bay front into lots. In 1829 a town council was elected, in 1830 the town was incorporated and by 1832 it had fourteen hundred residents with another two hundred and fifty living inland along the creeks and rivers. The port of Matagorda became the point of entry for immigrants selecting land for planting and a landing for goods moving in and products going out. Under Austin's grant, settlers could acquire land for only one-half a Spanish Real or about six cents an acre so weighing the danger from Indians against the allure of large land holdings made it worth the risk.

The colony expanded peacefully with the quality of life steadily improving but a new risk was developing in the form of landlord trouble from the distant interior. Mexicans, suffering long under the elitist Spaniards, were now wary of the new and culturally different Anglos. They also were becoming paranoid by the fact that the United States had casually offered to buy Texas which made them certain there was a plan in Washington to take Texas from them.

As the Anglo settlements grew, the Mexicans began to take note of the settlers' propensity to ignore the laws under which they had been allowed to come into the colony. The Mexican Constitution written in 1824 was the law that governed the colony. It was written by a Catholic priest and provided that Catholicism would be the only tolerated religion. What made it onerous to Anglos was not the Catholic faith requirement but the fact that no provision was made for trial by jury as the colonists were coming from a system which provided this very important safeguard to liberty. Nevertheless, Austin's settlers considered the Constitution of 1824 as providing the terms of their entry and the laws governing their lives. Every colonist had sworn to become Roman Catholic but it was pragmatically understood by both settlers and Mexican officials, many of whom were Freemasons, that this law was to be ignored.

In 1828, when Mexican officials from the distant interior finally decided to come and have a look at what was happening, they were astounded at the progress the settlers were making changing the land, improving life and making the colony less dependent on the Mexican government. They were alarmed at the number of Anglos pouring in since the original idea was to allow just a few Anglos in to control the terrifying incursions of Comanche Indians. It now appeared that the Anglos were bringing in a threat to their national sovereignty.

The Mexicans came away from their inspection intent on finding a way to stem the incoming tide of Anglos and relying on some rather vague language in Article 7 of their Constitution, the Mexican Congress quickly passed a law in 1830 designed to prohibit further immigration. In presenting the new law to the Congress, the Secretary of State, Lucas Alaman, their most eloquent orator and a leading statesman, set forth the Mexican complaint as follows:

"If we now examine the present condition of Texas, brought about by the policy which I have unveiled at length, we will find that the majority of the population is composed of natives of the United States of the North; that they occupy the frontier posts on the coast and the mouths of the rivers; that the number of Mexicans inhabiting that country is insignificant when compared to North Americans; that they come from all directions to settle upon the fertile lands, taking notice that most of them do so without previously complying with the requisites of our laws, or in violation of existing contracts. The Mexican population is, as it were, stationary; the number of slaves introduced by them, and whom they retain, without manumitting them, as they should do, in conformity with 2nd Article of the Law of 13th of July, 1824.

This numerical superiority, and the legal supremacy which they will acquire from the act declaring to be citizens all who have resided five years in the State (in consequence of which, nearly all those foreigners will become so next year). Their having rendered themselves masters of the best points, and their having had it in their power to execute their policy with impunity, and without having being compelled to fulfill the contracts entered into for their establishment, or refrained from locating themselves on the frontiers, and other parts from which they were excluded by laws and orders; and, above all, the unrestrained introduction of adventurers; all this has given them a preponderance in Texas, which now hardly belongs in fact to the Mexican confederacy since the orders of the Government are obeyed or not according to the choice of the Colonists; and, the moment seems to be near at hand when the territory will be taken from us and added to the United States of the North. Hence we find that, besides this territory having been occupied by Colonists who never ought to have been admitted into it, there is not one among them, in Texas, who is Catholic; and, this is a circumstance which has been attended to, in all the contracts which have been formed, as one of the leading articles. Another abuse which recommends itself to attention, is the introduction of slaves, and the number already there."

New settlers coming in to the area were oblivious to the effect their success was having on the alarmed politicians in faraway Mexico City. The result of the new law would now set the stage for real conflict as it provided for the military occupation of Texas, the power of those in charge to summarily take back lands already granted, prohibit more Anglo-American colonists coming into Texas and suspended all unfulfilled contracts with colonizers.

Alaman also persuaded the Congress to enact into law the right to collect badly needed revenue by placing tariffs on goods coming into the Texas ports after January of 1831. The effect of the new law added prohibitive costs to the sale of the colonists' goods and meant that very soon the landlord would be coming around to collect. In July orders went out to send troops by ship to Galveston, Matagorda and Anahuac to establish Fort Velasco at the mouth of the Brazos River and to station troops in Nacogdoches, Bexar and San Felipe de Austin. Trouble was coming.

The Fuse Lit at Anahuac

Ship captains arriving at Texas ports in 1831 were suddenly faced with new customs laws that would affect their pocketbooks. It was inevitable that a conflict with deadly and far-reaching consequences would follow.

At the center of the conflict was a Kentucky mercenary named Davis Bradburn who began issuing ultimatums and enforcing the new laws with a vengeance; the locals described him as a man of overbearing disposition. To make matters worse, the army had allowed convicts to enlist in its ranks and men with criminal pasts began to order around and arrest Anglo citizens. A tyrannical Bradburn began voiding new titles, taking away land already deeded and imposing new customs duties, all of which intensified the citizens' hatred of him. In charge of customs was another overbearing, European soldier of fortune named Fischer and together they enforced these new laws in such an oppressive and tyrannical way that the situation became unmanageable. To further inflame citizen outrage, Bradburn ordered the closing of all ports save the port of Galveston and threatened to jail any who would oppose his actions. At Anahuac, he prohibited the ships already in port from sailing unless and until their captains first paid outrageous duties.

It is likely that their actions were influenced by rumors from New Orleans that the colonists were waiting for a pretext to revolt and that toasts were being offered in New Orleans to the Independence of Texas. These acts would culminate in an incident in the spring of 1832 which many regard as the spark which ignited the war for Texas Independence. The incident involved two men who would later distinguish themselves in battle.

The trouble started when William M. Logan from Mississippi had three slaves taken away from him. When he demanded their return and presented evidence of his ownership, Bradburn advised Logan that owning slaves within the colony was illegal, that they were henceforth under the protection of the Mexican flag and would not be returned. Logan immediately turned to his friend, attorney William Barrett Travis, to represent him in recovering his confiscated human property.

When Travis came to present Logan's case, Bradburn, had already heard rumors that Travis was organizing men to oppose his unlawful transgressions. Travis was well known for his outspoken opposition to Mexican oppression and when he came to present Logan's complaint, Travis, along with his law partner Patrick Jack and five others, were summarily arrested, shackled and thrown into a make-shift, brick prison where they were guarded by abusive convicts. Logan was deemed to be a conspirator as well but managed to avoid arrest.

When Austin's colonists learned that Travis and others were to be denied access to a fair trial, men were sent to all parts of the colony to organize resistance to such tyranny. Their resistance escalated into open warfare when on June 26th a crew of colonists aboard the schooner *Brazoria* moved up the bay and opened fire on the Mexican fort at Anahuac. After bombarding the fort with lethal effect, an agreement was reached under which the colonists would lift their siege and the Mexicans would be allowed to leave. The Mexican commander of the outpost at Nacogdoches, getting word of these hostilities and fearing more uprisings, ordered that custody of Travis be handed over to civil authorities and summarily relieved Bradburn of his position. Once in the custody of the authorities at Liberty, Travis, his law partner, and the others were released.

In the engagement at Anahuac, thirty-five Mexicans were killed and fifteen were wounded. The colonists suffered seven killed with fourteen wounded. This hot, shooting incident, resulting in the killing of Mexicans by Texans and Texans by Mexicans, was the engagement that put both sides on the path to war. Mexican soldiers under the command of Col. Jose Antonio Mexia immediately started marching northward to the site of the rebellion and General Santa Anna, who was soon to be inaugurated as the next president of Mexico, made it known his intention to deal with the likes of Travis, Logan and other rebellious colonists who would dare to make war on the Mexicans.

Austin, fearing that the disturbance at Anahuac would put an end to his colony, rushed to intercept Mexia on his march up the coast and pleaded with him not to attack his settlers. Austin argued that the trouble was really a minor uprising against Bradburn and his tyrannical orderlies put there under former President Bustamante and that his colonists were in complete support of Santa Anna, his popular plan for a new government and to his succession of Bustamante as President.

Austin's argument finally persuaded Mexia of his support for the Mexican Constitution and the loyalty of his settlers to the new regime of Santa Anna; and, to express his sincerity, Austin entertained Col. Mexia lavishly at Brazoria with a ball in his honor. Afterwards, even though Mexia was still suspicious of the Anglos, he came away convinced that the actions at Anahuac were not a rebellion against the Mexican government but merely a disturbance caused by Bradburn and his superiors. Now assured that the province of Texas in Coahuila was secure, Mexia gathered the remaining Mexican troops from garrisons around the area and marched back to Mexico below the Rio Grande. Austin had narrowly averted disaster. Meanwhile in Mexico City, President Bustamante reached a bloodless compromise which paved the way for Santa Anna to become President in 1834. Austin's settlers would go on with their lives in peace for a while longer, unaware of the political intrigue in Mexico City and with no inkling that when the Mexican army returned in 1836, it would come with General Santa Anna in command. This time he would come with a vengeance and a determination to end the problem forever by annihilating each and every single Anglo soul west of the Sabine River.

When war came a horseback courier delivered to Logan a copy of Travis' appeal for relief at the Alamo which prompted Logan to immediately begin organizing a force to come to his aid; and, having already earned a reputation for his stand with Travis against Bradburn, men quickly answered Logan's call.

On March 6th three groups of volunteers from Beaumont and Liberty combined and elected Logan their Captain. Many of these men, including Logan, had participated in the siege at Bexar. One of the more experienced volunteers was Dr. Nicholas Lababie, a French-Canadian who served as Company Surgeon and described by Logan as having distinguished himself in his earlier resistance to Bradburn.

En route to San Felipe, Logan encountered a second express rider who brought the tragic news that Travis had been slaughtered at the Alamo and that Houston was retreating from Gonzales. Logan ordered a forced march to San Felipe to join Houston encountering en route scores of citizens fleeing Santa Anna. Logan marched into camp and reported to Houston on March 20th with 80 men. He would command his militia at San Jacinto and survive to enjoy the liberation of a Texas that would become a Republic free from Mexican rule.

Death to the Losers

The colonizers who came to Mexican Texas and concentrating on developing their personal share in the colony, were totally unaware of the bloody warfare going on far to the south and the fate of those losing in battle. What happened in "Real Mexico" or in the regions around Mexico City, was history muffled by more than a thousand miles of unpopulated territory with little information disseminated to the English speaking world. News of mass murder probably never reached the ears of the colonists. The British could start a revolution in New England by shooting a few colonials in Boston but the massacre of the entire losing side was unfathomable. Leaders might expect to be hanged for losing but wholesale slaughter was not the Anglo way and the new arrivals in Mexican Texas were hardly prepared for the clash of two completely different cultures.

Just eleven years before permission to colonize Texas was granted, the Mexican war for independence from Spain began when a mob of ragged, down-trodden Indians with machetes and three hundred years of smoldering hatred for their oppressors came screaming *"Death to Spaniards,"* burning every vestige of privileged property and killing almost everyone in the city of Guanajuato. This first uprising, led by a Catholic priest named Miguel Hidalgo, swelled into an unruly mob of thousands of peasants in a movement that came close to overrunning the heart of the government in Mexico City. When the uprising stalled, Hidalgo was captured and shot along with other conspirators and their severed heads were displayed and left to rot in a steel cage at Guanahauto. Failure meant death to the losers but the uprising that began on the 16th of September in 1810 marked the beginning of the Mexican Revolution and Miguel Hidalgo would be hailed as the father of Mexico. After Hidalgo, Jose Maria Morelos, another priest sympathetic to the suffering of the oppressed, continued the rebellion with a cadre of well-trained fighters and while they were more successful with an appealing plan for racial equality and land, thousands would perish and Morelos would face a firing squad.

During the struggle to rein in Morelos, Antonio Lopez de Santa Anna gained great recognition by demonstrating his own style of warfare by shooting hundreds of captured mercenaries, cutting the throats of liberals, beheading officers, shooting guerilla leaders and murdering hundreds of their followers. Later he would bring his eradication style of warfare to Mexican Texas.

When order was restored, the very men who had murdered, tortured and gelded Spanish officers were allowed to change sides and be rewarded with royal commissions from the king; and, while the royalists had won, the desire for freedom and separation survived. By 1820 Spain had begun to lose control of all of its colonies in the Western Hemisphere and on September 27, 1821, after 300 years and six weeks, Spain's rule over Mexico ended.

Finally independent, the Mexicans found their resources depleted, their best lands in the hands of the descendants of the elite and that the Spaniards leaving Mexico had taken more than half of the nation's liquid assets with them. Their successors, having suffered through caste and class discrimination and continuous revolutionary war from 1810 to 1821, now struggled to govern themselves with an empty treasury.

As the Spaniards left, the Royal Officer Corps was subverted with the promise of promotions and new commissions. Generals, who had been ruthlessly murdering liberal insurgents, now donned new uniforms and the skulls of the instigators; Hidalgo, Allende, Aldama and Martinez, were removed from their iron cage at Guanejuato and buried with military honors.

The Mexicans, in assessing their legacy, found that the red and yellow Spanish flag may have waved from Guatemala to San Francisco, but the territory which the new Mexican empire now claimed as its own was a territory existing only on maps. In reality it consisted of only a few sparsely settled island communities up the Rio Grande to Santa Fe and a foothold in faraway California. The space in between was the land claimed by various tribes of hostile Indians that the Spaniards had found uncontrollable.

In trying to find a way to govern themselves, the Mexicans were changing leaders with coup after bloody coup and killing the losers at the end of every chapter. Meanwhile, the Anglos were filling up the empty spaces from Tennessee to the mouth of the Mississippi. Napoleon's sale of Louisiana brought the border with the United States all the way to the Sabine River and, with Jefferson pushing exploration toward the Pacific, a moving force was happening on the continent faster than anyone had thought possible.

The task that lay ahead for Mexico was enormous and emerging from a colonial past to contend with the United States for dominion over a vast, untamed territory of hostile Indians would prove to be impossible. Mexico, free of Spain but having none of the advantages of the United States, struggled to find its identity and a form of government that would work for it. In the process, it divided itself politically between those who wanted to retain the old, traditional ways and those who wanted reform. Conservatives who wanted to continue the colonial way included the elites, wealthy landowners and the church with its properties while the liberal reformers, intent on ridding themselves of the image of being ignorant, inferior Indians and castes, demanded a new nation with a new identity completely apart from its former master.

General Santa Anna had come to prominence fighting in the coups going on in southern Mexico and in 1829, leading a corps of fighters to repel a weak attempt by the Spanish to return, he had become a national hero. In 1834 Santa Anna had another opportunity to demonstrate his merciless method of warfare by putting down a rebellion in Zacatecas, killing thousands and gaining enough recognition to become Mexico's next President.

While the new Mexican empire struggled to emerge from bloody revolution, Austin's colonists, oblivious to the violent happenings in the country they had made a bargain with, merrily settled into their new homeland. In their concentrated energies and efforts to transform the land, they could not have imagined that when Santa Anna came to Mexican Texas a massacre at Goliad and the annihilation of every man at the Alamo would be the order of the day and to the Mexicans, nothing out of the ordinary. Nor could the Mexicans have imagined that General Sam Houston with a vastly outnumbered army could defeat Santa Anna and lead his ragged troops to victory at San Jacinto and Texas independence.

In February of 1836, with the war for Texas independence underway, the Captain cleared the Port of New Orleans in command of the schooner *Henry* bound for Matagorda as the siege of the Alamo was about to begin. Ten days later the Alamo had fallen. On March 23rd, 1836, the Captain, in command of *Henry* again, cleared New Orleans bound for Matagorda with volunteers and gunpowder. The Captain's presence during the struggle can be traced to the promissory obligations for payment issued to him in 1836 by officers and agents of the emerging Republic. A form of receipt for goods left in store at Matagorda was issued to the Captain on March 25, 1837 and describes a cargo left for Houston's troops made up of flour, palm leaf hats, cigars and four kegs of gunpowder. Later, in March of 1837, the Captain is up the Brazos River at Columbia. On April 30th he is in New Orleans and, on June 1st, he is back in Texas caught up in the excitement of victory and assessing the opportunities to be had in the new Republic.

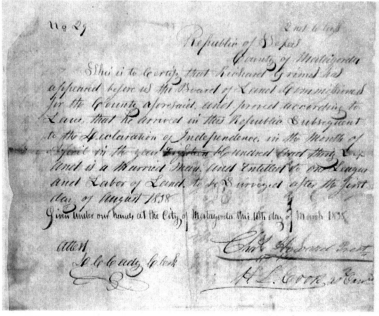

1838 1st Class Headright Certificate issued to Captain Grimes by the Republic of Texas for service during the war for Texas Independence.

Santa Anna's defeat at San Jacinto ended with his capture and Houston electing to protect him from men who wanted him killed in payment for the murders at Goliad and the Alamo. Houston's brilliant idea to protect Santa Anna and to extract from him a treaty of sorts would furnish the basis for Texas to claim territory north of the Rio Grande all the way to Santa Fe and beyond.

By the time Houston filed his official report to the new Texas Government on April 25th, the outcome at San Jacinto had become an international sensation. For Mexico however, the capture of Santa Anna, President and Commanding General of the Mexican Army, meant the nation's honor was at stake and in Mexico City, Jose Justo Corro, acting as interim President, and vowing revenge, issued a decree ending with:

> "... misfortune to the enemy of our country! The foreign will be vanquished and the domestic exemplarily punished if any such shall dare assist in this sacred war of the country, the criminal desires of the Texian rebels."

The following day Corro issued another decree ordering the Mexican flag to be flown at half-mast and a banner of black crepe attached to the flag which was not to be removed until President Santa Anna was released.

Meanwhile, the reaction of most Americans was euphoric. On the front page of the *New York Herald*, June 13, the editor wrote:

> *"We cannot refrain from calling up from the recesses of history, the great wars of former times, which changed the destiny of the nations and fixed the fate of empires. The Battle of Marathon controlled the fate of Greece and Persia—the Battle of Zama decided the career of Rome and Carthage—the Battle of Tours saved Europe from the Moorish dominion—the Battle of Hastings controlled the destiny of England and the Battle of San Jacinto will change the destiny and policy of nations on this continent . . . the victory of San Jacinto will send Europe into astonishment and the name of Houston will ring from one end of it to another."*

With the entire colony charged with the thrill of victory, the Captain turned the *Henry* north and charted a course for home on the Connecticut River. He meant to convince Charlotte to join him in a great, new adventure where there would be cheap land and profits for men with ships to supply the needs of the settlers streaming in. Back home in Connecticut, he could talk personally about Texas, the battles, his participation in the struggle for liberty, the victory and the formation of the new Republic, a subject now being talked about by all citizens of the United States.

At Matagorda, in the company of settlers from New England, the Captain learned of land to be easily acquired and land to be granted to men like himself who participated in the war by moving men, arms and gunpowder to the front. He was well informed that Austin's colony had within its boundaries the best of Texas real estate. Lands bordering the Brazos and Colorado Rivers and along the banks of Caney Creek held the most fertile lands on the entire coast. Virgin soils awaited planters bringing slaves and experience with sugar cane and their intimate knowledge of farming the South's most profitable crop, cotton. The Captain meant to acquire land too but he also knew that the plantations along the rivers and creeks needed transportation to Gulf ports for export.

Most of Austin's original three hundred were quite literate having been schooled in New England and many who came later were the well-educated, slave owning planters from the southern states. Almost all would apply for and acquire 4,428 acres of land, the maximum that Austin had the power to grant to one family, with the most desirable tracts being land bordering streams. By the time freedom was in hand, Austin's colonists and those who came later were already making great agricultural progress and with the growing demand for cotton and sugar from New Orleans, the east coast and foreign ports, they were prospering.

In 1837, Texas was very much on the mind of President Andrew Jackson who, with his final act as President, as the great friend of Sam Houston, had the pleasure of signing a bill giving official recognition of Texas as an Independent Republic. Jackson and Houston had long been of one mind that Texas should be brought into the Union and with the Spaniards gone and the Mexicans vanquished, there was a strong likelihood that Texas would become part of the United States. Acquiring land in the new Republic seemed a once-in-a-lifetime opportunity and as the Captain, growing older and tiring of long stretches at the helm of a sailing ship, began to think of owning land and trading from a home port in Texas which would provide a living for him and his family.

CHAPTER TWO

"Bound for Texas"

When the Captain left Texas for Connecticut he knew well the needs of the citizens on Matagorda Bay. In and out of the Bay many times during the war he knew just how much draft would allow a coasting vessel loaded with trade goods to clear the narrow channel at Pass Cavallo. The brig *Driver* had served him well in earlier days but *Henry* was slightly larger, fast, weatherly and tested. She fit the description of a West Indies trader and was listed as having a burthen of 120 tons, a measured deck of around 80 feet, two-masted and rigged to carry square top, fore sails on both masts.

When the Captain arrived back home in Rocky Hill he pled his case for a new beginning in Texas and after no small amount of advocacy convinced Charlotte to leave the comforts of Bradford Hill, and join him in making their new home on Matagorda Bay. He then began to choose carefully the cargo he would carry, and while preparing to sail, he got wind of a group of 26 vessels being organized to sail together for Texas via Havana and planned to cast off in time to join this flotilla of traders.

Square stern schooners like *Henry* were designed with cabins adequate for the comfort of the Captain and his family. Double-masted and rigged for extra sail, *Henry* was beautiful to look at and large enough to carry her costly cargo and crew safely through even the worst Caribbean tempest. She was Connecticut built and about to take them to the shores of far-away Texas where a far different life awaited them. They were not just passengers but the owners of their own transportation and a very valuable vessel it was.

In financial terms, this was perhaps the riskiest step the Captain had ever taken. With a small fortune tucked away from his years as a successful sea-going trader, the Captain had the enviable security most New Englanders lacked, but in recent years, an uneasy change had come into this mariner's way of life. Long, arduous months spent at sea over four decades had begun to take a toll on his well-being. Moreover, the energy and vitality of his Connecticut River home port town was declining. The shoals and sand bars that made Rocky Hill the preferred port on the river had been cleared away and traders from London and Europe were now bound for Hartford and bypassing Rocky Hill and the other small river ports along the way. Vibrant activity that once pervaded the docks was reduced to a dull pace. The town's shipyards no longer teemed with the frames of single-masted sloops and graceful schooners in various stages of construction as they had during the first quarter of the century.

Further aggravating the town's painful decline was the arrival of the steam ship, a new form of water transportation that would one day render the sailing vessel obsolete. Many veteran seamen, including the Captain, resisted its intrusion and would have no part in the change to steam. Others quit the sea altogether and took up other livelihoods and those endowed with a more adventurous spirit realized that their future in sailing ships lay elsewhere; it was to this latter group that the Captain belonged.

There can be no doubt that the Texans' victory over the Mexicans piqued the adventurous spirit of the Captain and led him to make the decision to uproot his family from their ancestral home to begin a new life in the faraway Republic. Over the course of several weeks he carefully laid out his plan and gathered his resources for the move. *Henry* would prove to be the most crucial resource for in a short time his very survival would come to depend on her. Those who had sailed under the Captain on *Driver* thought the vessel's name may have characterized him as he was square-jawed and stern-faced like his Scottish ancestors. He was, by all accounts, the embodiment of a complete mariner: methodical, disciplined and strong-willed and in every sense a Master and Commander. Now, after nearly forty years of sailing to every corner of the globe, this salty, seasoned, middle-aged mariner was charting an entirely different course.

Late October 1837, when the Captain with family and crew boarded *Henry* to begin the 2,400-mile journey, they weighed anchor just a few weeks before cold weather would begin to settle along the winding Connecticut River. They had packed up and stowed their essential possessions as the items first into the cargo hold of *Henry*, docked just a few hundred feet from their home on Bradford Hill. From Rocky Hill they set sail downstream for the forty-mile leg to Long Island Sound, then turned south and by the end of a single day's sailing, were within sight of the bustling wharves of New York City. Richard and Charlotte's 12-year-old son William Bradford would be left in the capable hands of his Aunt Fanny Bradford in Rocky Hill. She and Charlotte's family would see to young Bradford's education there and later in New York and Ohio. How heartbreaking it must have been to see his parents and baby sister sail away on such an adventure. It was an important decision for a father to make as the Captain had had little, if any, formal schooling after the age of ten. His son would have the advantages of a good formal education.

The Captain now set his mind on matters concerning the voyage ahead. Before clearing Rocky Hill, he had fulfilled his plan to sail out of New York, perhaps as the leader of several vessels whose owners shared a common interest in Texas. Like the Captain, they were merchant traders carrying cargo for trade first in Havana and to take on a cargo of much needed supplies for the new Republic. Whatever their mutual interest was, it is certain that they did meet, for within a few days *Henry* joined an assembly of twenty-six other sailing ships, a virtual flotilla bound for the new Republic.

Under way and commanding from *Henry's* quarterdeck with customary authority, the Captain would have taken a mental inventory of the conditions around him: precisely trimmed sails; wind direction; the formation of a few clouds to the west; and the rhythmic rising and falling of the endless waves just beyond the bow. As *Henry* plowed effortlessly southward through the deep blue Atlantic waters, his thoughts would have turned to the cargo she was carrying just a few feet below her main deck. Ever the enterprising trader, he would have filled her hold to capacity with a valuable payload of staples and other New England provisions in high demand and calculated to bring him a handsome profit. Also in the hold were the necessities Charlotte would need to add the comforts of home in a dwelling yet to be constructed; goods that would remain on board until the new home was ready for the move from ship to shore. A more precious treasure was two-and-a-half-year-old daughter Frances Charlotte, lying peacefully asleep in the cabin beneath the Captain's feet as the flotilla sailed southward on a course for Havana, a course the Captain had navigated many times before on voyages to the West Indies.

The Captain's official logs did not survive as by maritime custom a ship's official log remained a part of the vessel and when the vessel was sold sometime later the Captain's record of this voyage went with it. However, there are a few pages from a log kept by Albert Goodrich, a native of Rocky Hill, one of the Captain's crew and probably his First Mate. The Goodrich log recorded the departure from Rocky Hill on October 14, 1857 bound for Havana. A later entry recorded the departure from Havana bound for Matagorda on November 6th. After leaving Havana the Captain and crew settled into a comfortable northwestern course for the Gulf of Mexico. Cool, northern breezes would have become a thing of the past and now they would be under the influence of the sultry, sub-tropics and subjected to nature's more erratic whims.

Early into the leg to Mobile, the Captain out of the confines of his square-ended cabin would have observed seas running long with benevolent winds filling her sails and on a steady course for Mobile Bay; soon they would be face-to-face with the challenges of starting a new life. Suddenly, a pre-storm calm would have brought the entire fleet to an abrupt standstill with sails hanging lifeless at their masts. Even the least experienced seaman among them would have recognized the warning signs. Their pleasurable sailing conditions were about to come to an end.

A few hours later, the trouble would have begun with winds shifting to the southwest and with dark foreboding skies along the western horizon behind streaks of high, cirrus clouds and low rumbles of distant thunder, an ominous sight headed swiftly toward them.

The Captain, being well acquainted with sub-tropical weather patterns, would have instinctively known that severe, equinoctial storms could spring up suddenly in the Caribbean and the Gulf of Mexico. Since this storm was developing after the usual season for hurricanes, he might have concluded that they were coming up against a line of minor squalls with nothing to be alarmed about. Nonetheless, with the certainty of foul weather ahead he would have called for all hands on deck and ordered his crew to be prepared for whatever nature was about to deliver them. Orders would have been issued to get square sail off and to reef the main and over-lapping jib to reduce to manageable size the amount of canvas necessary to maintain way.

The Captain's will and fortitude would have been tested as never before as the leading squall was a harbinger of the nightmare that followed. According to his daughter's memoire, the Captain endured three days at the helm where he would have ordered his crew adjust sheets, halyards and rigging. He would have been unaware that he would keep the same unyielding grip on her wheel for the next three days as he stood confidently in the face of the storm and blind to the fact that he and *Henry* had just entered the path of a major hurricane.

Henry would have been pitching and rolling in heavy seas as the Captain sailed her close to the strong headwinds with sails furled and reefed. On the second day, *Henry* would have continued beating to windward in heavier seas with tall waves pounding at her bow and winds increased in velocity and rain pouring down in blinding sheets. The Captain recounted to his daughter that he had remained at the helm with his only relief coming from crewmen who dosed him with alternate swigs of coffee and whiskey to shake off the chill and help him stay awake.

Henry had taken the battering in stride but the Captain, watching her bow plunge repeatedly into the sea, with spray flying over her gunwales and drenching everything on deck, would have been deeply concerned about surviving in these worsening conditions with the eye of the storm barreling toward him.

As the weary mariner fought to keep *Henry* close to the wind, the fleet became so pulled apart by the howling gales and monstrous swells that all the other vessels completely disappeared from sight. With each of them now on their own, the Captain felt free to make a move that ultimately saved the lives of his family and crew.

The Captain had encountered many storms in his years and his experience gained from a lifetime at sea caused him to change course as he was now firmly convinced that if in fact it was a hurricane, it was only a matter of hours before they would be hit by its full force. Dawn of the third day would have found *Henry* quartering over calmer seas under full sail in abated winds and a thoroughly exhausted Captain but with his family safely out of the hurricane's path. With his sextant, the Captain would have determined his position while searching for companion vessels and sighting none. Among the grievous losses, the Captain soon discovered, were all of the other twenty-six vessels in his fleet and all passengers and their crews were lost to the sea. For the moment, though, he was concerned with only two matters: his family's future and whether his decision to leave Rocky Hill had been a wise one after all. As he ordered his crew to make ready to come about, he aligned *Henry's* compass to put her on a course to return to Havana. Shouting orders to come about, the Captain brought *Henry* around to the southeast and trimmed her sails for her new course.

The log of First Mate Goodrich recorded the return to Havana on November 9th. The return, after such a battering, was consistent with seeking a busy, safe, commercial harbor where repairs could be made to a vessel that had encountered a deadly storm. In Havana, any water damaged cargo could be off-loaded and sold, any shifted cargo could be re-aligned, shrouds and back stays could be tightened and adjusted and any needed repairs to the hull could be had. Havana was also a civilized port where the storm-weary travelers could regain their composure before moving on.

The Goodrich log records a lengthy layover of 19 days in Havana before proceeding on with new provisions for family and crew and most probably a fresh, new cargo to be traded at ports of call en route to Matagorda.

The Goodrich log records that the Captain did not clear Havana again until the 29th of November bound for New Orleans and arrived there on December 9th where they remained until the 30th of December. The log recorded that the Captain elected to sail from New Orleans to Mobile where they entered the harbor on January 6th and on the 23rd of January, 1838 the Captain, his family and crew finally cleared Mobile Bay bound at last for Matagorda in the new Republic of Texas.

The following is an excerpt from the log describing the cold, January weather on Matagorda Bay:

"Sailed from Mobile on the 23 of Jan 1838 for Matagorda
2 days to the Besleas Arrived at the Pernincerlar on the
30 of January within 5 miles of the Mouth of the Bay of
Matagorda their Lay to Anchor
at 4 oClock com up a Norther and Commenced for 3 Days
attended with Sum Rane and verry Cold the Coldest
Norther that Ever was none in Texas

the thermometer Stood at 20 the Deck and Riggon was
all Ice and it froze fish in the Bay
we Remained heir untill the 4 of February
took in a Pilot Past over the Bar in the Morning on the 5
and at 4 oClock Run a Ground one foot in the Mud

Took of a part of the Deck hook and Got off on the 7 of Feb
I Arrived at Matagorda within 8 Miles of the Town on the
10 of Feb Took a Boot and went to the town on the 11

Remained their untill 4 oClock and Returned Back to the
Vessel Started for Half Moon Point on the 12 of February
Which is 20 miles Below Matagorda
Situated on the West Side of the pernincesly Basin Nor
West of the Bay Arrived at Half Moon Point on the 12 of
Feb 1838 Went a Shore on the 13
a Norther Commenct at 4 (oClock on the 13 and contin-
ued until the 16 at 4 (oClock in the Morning of the 16 the
thermometer Stood at 15 it must of Stood at zero Be-
fore Morning on the 16) Our Riging was Covrd with Ice I
went on the shore at 4(oClock on the 16 we Started for
Matagorda again on the 17 at 3(oClock AM"

Joining the New Republic

W hen Captain Grimes finally reached Texas, he brought *Henry* through Pass Cavallo and into Matagorda Bay. After weeks at sea, the Captain eased *Henry* into its mooring at Indian Point, which later became the most westerly point of debarkation for thousands of German immigrants on their way west. Its name would be changed to Indianola but in 1838 it was a primitive town on a sandy strip of land with a flat, marshy plain and Powder Horn Bay behind it. At the time of his arrival the entire population of Matagorda County was only around 1,200. From Indian Point the Captain sailed across the Bay to the shallow Port of Matagorda to off load cargo brought for kindred New England settlers who eagerly awaited his return.

After the sale of his cargo, he began to build a home on a spit of land called Palacios Point. The site he chose was located about halfway between Indianola and Matagorda and came to be known as the "Point." It already had the beginnings of a port with a primitive wharf for a mooring, quick access to deep water and a loading dock for shallow draft vessels. Later, other ship captains built homes on the Point as it was ideally located for their trade in cattle, cotton, sugar and other products floated down the creeks and rivers to be loaded onto waiting ships. From that small port ships could quickly exit the Bay through Pass Cavallo and into the Gulf of Mexico.

Most of the Captain's neighbors and friends had come to Texas from the original colonial states of New York, Pennsylvania, Connecticut, Massachusetts, Maine, Virginia and the Carolinas. John Zipprian came with tradesmen from Weiler, Germany, and settled on Matagorda Peninsula. Elias Weightman came as a surveyor for Austin, Horace Yeamans and Emilin Savage came from New York in 1829 onboard the schooner *Little Zoe*. Albert Wadsworth came as a young sailor from North Carolina; John Rugeley came from South Carolina and settled on Caney Creek; John Partain came from North Carolina; Dan Braman from Massachusetts and George Burkhart came in 1838 from Philadelphia. Daniel Decrow, one of the original colonists in Austin's 300, came from Maine in 1824 and operated a sloop between Velasco and San Jacinto Bay. James Selkirk from New York and Samual Robbins from Virginia settled on the Colorado River and John Holt who came from Andover, Massachusetts chose Matagorda.

Austin's settlers were already proving the economic potential of the area between the lower Colorado River and Caney Creek, the colony's most desirable lands. The richest farmland in the colony included the twenty-six plantations along Caney Creek where some of the most successful cotton and sugar plantations were developed in the 45-year span between 1820 and 1865.

Caney Creek was described by Elias Weightman as:

"Before breaking the land for planting, the colonists would burn off the canebrake, a native bamboo, to enrich the soil. The Creek was sometime navigable for some distance upstream. Sugar production from the area was so successful that stately homes began to line the Creek's banks and part of its course became known as Plantation Row."

Success in farming these rich, bottom lands required more than one farmer using his own hands and experienced planters brought slaves knowing that a healthy slave could pay for himself in three years. A farmer was considered a "Planter" when he owned twenty or more slaves and a big enough operation to produce forty bales of cotton or forty hogsheads of sugar. Colonists coming in from the South wanted land for cotton that had never seen a plow and they brought along slaves to plant it and pick it; and so, along the banks of Caney Creek and the Colorado River there soon developed a "Planter Class." A true planter, freed from daily work by his slaves, was free to pursue his desires and could send his children away to be educated and he was wealthy enough to be influential. His wealth and success caused his neighbors to regard him with respect and deference and his family led the only true social life in the colony. Planters and slave holders from the southern states brought with them a plantation lifestyle and began to build impressive homes and produce large quantities of sugar and cotton. Meanwhile, the Captain was kept busy transporting their crops from the loading docks at Matagorda and the Point.

In 1841 the *Matagorda Gazette* described getting their products to market when it published the following:

"We already know of five planters from Alabama and elsewhere, who have purchased land in this county and will emigrate this season with an aggregate of 200 slaves. The cotton crop, which is expected to be raised this season on Caney and the Colorado is expected by well-informed and prudent judges at 5,000 bales; at least 150 per cent more than crop which is now on its way to market. The planters on lower Caney are boating their crops down to the mouth of that stream, hauling them 800 yards across the isthmus, and then transporting them in lighters, carrying from 50 to 80 bales each to the harbor of Matagorda."

The Palacios Point anchorage was described as:

"The western end of Matagorda County had perhaps better facilities to move their products to market by waterway. Wilson Creek, a tributary of the Trespalacios Creek, was navigable in the 1800's for several miles and Trespalacios was navigable five or six miles from the Bay to the port of Tidehaven."

In an article written in 1937 for the *Matagorda County Tribune* entitled "Century of Progress," Thompson Cyles, an old-time river boatman, recalled how cotton and cattle were shipped from Palacios Point:

"Previous to the Civil War a tremendous amount of cotton was raised in this section and the Trespalacios, Navidid and Guadalupe Rivers and Caney Creek, all of which empty into Matagorda Bay, were the routes by which most of this produce was brought to Matagorda Bay for loading onto coastwise and seagoing vessels for shipment to northern and foreign markets. During the years immediately preceding the Civil War, these rivers carried a large amount of traffic and were the main means of transportation for the heavier and bulkier merchandise, both imports and exports. Sailing vessels were used exclusively except for one steamboat built by Captain John Duncan . . . at this time Palacios Point had but a few houses (in one of which lived several ship captains including Grimes) and was mainly a loading point with, for that time, extensive wharfing and warehousing facilities for handling cotton."

Expansion by the planters brought growth to the Captain's freight and transport business. The fact that he was still much at sea is verified by a letter written on New Year's Eve in 1838 when Charlotte's sister Fanny Bradford wrote to another sister, Nancy Bradford Bulkley, that a ship captain arriving in port at Rocky Hill, reported that he had hailed the Captain and his crew at sea and learned that he was out of Havana bound for New Orleans. In her letter she writes: *"all well on board, I have been sending every day for a letter this long time but if they are cruising all over creation, I shan't expect to hear at any particular time."* The Captain was trading along the Gulf Coast to Havana and the West Indies, returning to Matagorda Bay with cargo and by 1840 the Grimes family were settling in.

In 1841 Charlotte wrote to her sisters in Connecticut about raising little Frances who was living a somewhat lonely but adventurous life as the only child at home and having little contact with other children. Her brother William Bradford, a decade older, was away at school in New York. Fannie was in serious need of civilization when these two 1841 letters were written from Texas by Charlotte to her sisters back in Connecticut:

"February 23/1841 Palacios, Texas

Sis is almost as large and handsome as her mother, and as wild as any mustang on the prairie. It will take a heap of prim to civilize her, I don't know which will have to untake the job, you, or Aunt Betsey. I think likely it will take you both to accomplish it."

"August 31 / 1841 Palacios, Texas

. . . the Capt is in New Orleans I shall look for him back in two or three weeks I expect it is sickly there. It is generally healthy in Texas as far as I hear.

The Indians have lately made us a visit. We have more fish and venison and crabs and green turtle than we can make use of when the Indians are here. we give them in return flour bread and corn. the turtle are very large and plenty.

I have no help except a man, and he is not of much account Our family, now consists of (as Sis says) I and Mother. Our domesticks are two dogs, two guinea hens, three ducks, a dozen or so hens, three horses, twelve mules and about fifty head of cattle. we have plenty of milk, and butter."

On the Edge of Comancheria

By 1840 the colonists around Matagorda Bay had little to fear from the coastal Carancahua Indians, although they had been a dangerous threat to the earliest settlers. During the Texas War for Independence the Carancahuas had rendered useful service to the Mexican cause by harassing the coastal settlers and in *Historic Matagorda County* they were described:

". . . they passed like birds of prey, silently and swiftly, in their canoes, along the shores of Matagorda Bay, always managing to elude pursuit . . . they swooped suddenly down upon these defenseless scattered homes, sparing neither age nor sex, subjecting every being to the general massacre. They were tall, between 6 and 7 feet, muscular, wearing deerskin breechcloths or nothing at all and smeared their bodies with a mixture of dirt and alligator or shark grease to ward off mosquitoes. In short, their

ferocious appearance and smell and their reputation as cannibals put fear and terror into everyone."

The settlers were keenly aware, however, of the presence of the much more dangerous Comanches on the fringes of the colony. In almost all of the history books written about the Comanche the 1840 battle of the Council House on the San Antonio Plaza has been told and re-told countless times. San Antonio had emerged as the oldest and most civilized spot in Texas and its Plaza had become a neutral zone where Anglos, Mexicans and Indians could meet and trade peacefully. The trouble started when a young captive girl named Matilda Lockhart was brought in by the Comanche to trade for goods. When the settlers saw that the end of her nose had been burned off with hot coals and that she bore signs of beatings and torture, they were outraged. When the Comanche chiefs entered the Council House to begin trading, they were told they would be prevented from leaving until all of their hostages were brought in to San Antonio. When the chiefs learned of that threatened restraint, the battle erupted and all of the chiefs, some of the squaws, and several of the settlers were killed. In the end, word of the killing of their chiefs resulted in the murder of the remaining hostages they held, and the uprising which followed resulted in the 1840 attacks on Victoria and Linnville. After attacking Victoria they then rode on to attack the small settlement of Linnville, only 20 miles from Palacios Point where a great band of mounted warriors attacked with the intent of murdering every settler. As they looted and burned Linnville, one settler escaped by jumping into a small boat and, pulling away from shore. From the safety of his small vessel, he was able to observe and describe their murderous rampage.

During this dangerous time an effort had been made to push civilized Texas westward by moving the seat of government to Austin, still quite a distance from the colony and deep into Comanche country. To the west of the new Capitol lay an unbroken wilderness which provided little consolation to the settlers as there was not a single human habitation between Austin and San Antonio. Primitive frontier life brought to the fore the clear difference between the life most of the settlers had known in civilized New England and life around Matagorda Bay in wild, frontier Texas.

The only dependable protection available to early settlers was from men willing to leave their farms to serve when needed as Rangers. One such band of Rangers tracked and intercepted the warriors that had massacred the citizens of Linnville and punished them severely in a skirmish south of Austin known as the Battle of Plum Creek. Well-armed mounted Rangers pursued and engaged in close combat with the mounted Comanches and fought Indians in their own, brutal, effective style. After each call to arms, they would disband and return to their respective settlements to care for their families and crops.

"In the 1840's and 1850's, neither the War Department or the U.S. Army had much understanding of the Plains Indian frontier. No state had ever come into the Union with more than half its territory unsettled and with at least 20,000 extremely warlike Amerinds living within its borders. And there were Indians of a type the Army had not fought before . . . Some two hundred Texans were killed by Indians or carried off into captivity in the year 1849 alone."

Whether protecting the planters or an isolated cattle ranch, the Rangers proved invaluable in the years both before and after Texas was annexed and they were critical in keeping the Comanches at bay and away from the settlements.

"In Texas between 1836 and 1860 an average of about 200 men, women and children were killed or carried off each year . . . Ranging companies dated from Austin's colony; they had been formed in 1823 and 1826. The term ranger was already old in Anglo-America; it referred to Indian fighters and the kind of men who carried war to the enemy, beyond the frontier . . . They were one of the most colorful, efficient and deadly band of partisans on the side of law and order the world had ever seen."

In 1842 Sam Houston, president for the second time, decided the Republic could no longer afford a standing army and when disbanded, it left only a few of the best companies of Rangers to defend against the roving bands of Comanches. John Coffee Hays, the first and best known leader of the Rangers, came to Texas from Nashville, Tennessee and, though only in his twenties, he became a legendary model for all future Rangers. Because of his father's close friendship with President Andrew Jackson, he became a close confidante of Sam Houston. As the most famous and successful leader of a Company of Rangers he was always referred to as Captain Jack Hays.

When Houston decided Texas was disbanding the army and decommissioning the Texas four-ship Navy, Hays asked Houston if he might equip his Rangers with the new Colt revolvers that had been ordered for the Navy. Manufactured by Colt in Patterson, New Jersey, they were to be used in hand-to-hand combat by sailors boarding enemy vessels. Houston agreed with Hays that the guns could be put to better use by allowing Hays to arm each of his Rangers with a pair of the new Patterson five-shot Colts and from that point on, the Comanches were no match for the pistol packing, dead shot Rangers. One Comanche chief, in awe of the effect of the revolvers, was said to have remarked: "*Captain Jack's gun shoot from all five fingers.*"

Mirabeau B. Lamar, second President of the Republic, had directed the Rangers to take the fight to the Comanches in their camps and on their hunting grounds. During his tenure, enough damage was inflicted on them by the Rangers to cause the Comanches to find easier targets deeper into northern Mexico. The constant pressure put on them by Captain Hays and his Rangers prompted them to make peace agreements with their Cheyenne, Sioux and Arapahoe enemies north of the Arkansas River. By making peace on the northern fringe of their hunting range and by avoiding the Rangers around San Antonio and to the east, the Comanches were now free to leave their women and children in camp during their long distance forays into northern Mexico.

To illustrate just how dangerous these Indians were, records kept by the Mexican government reflect that from 1840 until 1846 Comanche war parties struck Mexican settlements as far south as the State of San Luis Potosi. The plunder sought was primarily horses, captives and the things they had once traded for peacefully in San Antonio. Pre-adolescent children were particularly desirable prey as they were easily integrated into the tribe to do useful camp chores and, with their Spanish language, were used to scout out the richest Mexican targets. Texans soon learned that children taken as young captives and living a few years with the Comanches preferred the free, roaming life on the plains to the settlers' civilized ways.

To Comanche warriors, the ranches in Mexico meant easy plunder. The State of Durango with an estimated horse population of around 150,000 held attractive treasure and with the leadership of Mexico in turmoil, no protection was given to the northern ranchers. The Comanches faced little opposition and thousands of horses and mules were easily taken from Mexican haciendas.

". . . people on the plains needed a minimum of six horses per capita to lead a fully nomadic, equestrian lifestyle and as many as twelve each for comfort and security . . . established men used large herds to get what they valued most: social prestige and political power."

After the loss of Texas, sending a Mexican military force into Comancheria meant that the troops had to come from Santa Fe or march through territory defended by Anglos. With the central Mexican government in political chaos, their citizens were left virtually defenseless. Mexicans living in the northern states could in no way defend against hordes of murderous, mounted raiders that struck without warning and with hundreds of warriors in their war parties.

Statistics from the northern Mexican states for the period from 1831 to 1848 recorded more than 2,600 Mexicans killed and 1,000 abducted and the actual number was probably twice that. Thomas Falconer, an Englishman, writing about the central government's failure to protect its citizens, observed:

"This state of things may not last but it has been the consequence of an unsettled government, which has hitherto been compelled to concentrate its forces in the interior to sustain itself while its frontier has been commanded by savages."

Another observer wrote:

"Being torn to pieces by civil and central revolutions, which, succeeding each other in rapid succession, their finances were exhausted, their armies were wasting away in civil wars, their convulsions were so quick and terrible that they could not spare either men or money to defend the frontiers against hostile Indian tribes"

The annual, continuous raids left many of the ranches and haciendas completely deserted. Settlements were turned into ghost towns and the Mexicans constantly were risking their lives to protect their families. In one incident in the State of Durango in 1845, the mayor of San Juan Del Rio watched helplessly as Comanche raiders set about slaughtering 120 of his citizens. The Mexicans did not lack courage, only the resources and leadership to fight them. In the end, fear of the raids led to literal depopulation of northern Mexico.

Relief to northern Mexico was coming but for the heart and soul of political Mexico it would come as war with the United States. In 1836, a defeated, captive Santa Anna had signed conventions to end hostilities with the Texans and these signed papers became known as the *Treaties of Velasco*. Even though these conventions were immediately refuted by the Mexican Congress, in 1846 they provided President James K. Polk the excuse he needed to plunge the U.S. into a war that would forever change the geography of both nations. The loss of Mexican Texas had been a national humiliation and inflicted a bitter wound to Mexican pride, but what was about to come would bring radical, permanent change.

The citizens of northern Mexico had fled from the Comanche terror in such great numbers that when invasion from the North finally came, a single regiment of U.S. troops swept unopposed from Santa Fe to El Paso then south to Chihuahua City. A second force rolled in through a vacuum on the eastern flank to Monterrey. One American soldier wrote:

> *"The great fear among all classes of Mexicans was not the Americans but the extensive raids from warring bands of Indians from across the Rio Grande."*

Geo. Kendall, publisher of the New Orleans *Times Picayune* wrote:

> *"A large force of Comanche Indians are committing depredations and murdering the inhabitants with impunity . . . at Guerrero they have killed several of the principal citizens, among them one of the town council. In October of 1846 eight hundred and a thousand warriors crossed the river . . . attacking eastern Chihuahua and Durango . . . in the course of their campaign the raiders killed at least 100 people, captured dozens more, slaughtered animals, set fire to ranches and disrupted communications across the state."*

Torment of the beleaguered populace came in another form as Anglo soldiers and Texas Rangers with the army attacked Mexican citizens directly in retaliation for attacks from Mexican guerillas.

"Following Taylor's victory at Monterrey, Texas rangers stormed through the city and murdered scores of civilians, more than a hundred according to a disgusted American regular . . . A group of Texans rode into Little Rancho de San Francisco, bound all of the men they could find to posts, and calmly shot each one of them through the head . . . by mid 1847 the general requested that the War Department send no more volunteers from Texas, given that they had scarcely made one expedition without unwarrantably killing a Mexican . . . Northeastern Mexicans took to calling the volunteers 'Comanches of the North.'"

And so, for all the earlier glory earned protecting Texas settlers from savages and for all of their brave exploits, actions of some men from this rough group of Texans were questionable. Fear of barbarous Yankees and tales of atrocities committed by their volunteers spread. In the end war with the U.S. only complicated and aggravated struggles with wild Indians. Even as the U.S.—Mexican war continued, Comanche raids reached south to within a few miles of Mexico City.

"there are now known to be more than 400 unfortunates whom the Indians have killed in the countryside and at the watering places they have visited, committing a thousand iniquities and every class of cruelty as is their custom, sparing neither the decrepit nor children nor women."

A consequence of the end of Spanish rule was the exodus of skilled politicians and those needed to wisely govern; they had emigrated or been exiled. The wealthy had left behind agents to manage their haciendas, depleted mines and other income producing properties. Now dependent on foreign financial recourses, Mexico could not repay its debts. The turmoil continued and lacking the resources to defend its citizens, the war was soon over and U.S. domination all the way to the Pacific Ocean was a fact.

CHAPTER THREE

Delightful Matagorda

Lithograph of the Port of Matagorda circa 1856. The Colorado House Hotel is pictured left of center.

When Stephen F. Austin brought in the first colonists, his surveyors searched for and found what they believed would be the perfect site for their settlement and excitedly described as follows:

"We discovered to our admiration and surprise, one of the most beautiful situations for the building of a large, commodious and tasty commercial town that our utmost imagination could conceive—a large amphitheater, a semi-circular bluff of about six or eight feet above the high water mark of very dry, permanent soil, and ascending back to extensive and beautiful prairie, about 200 varas in diameter, making a very regular curve—resting one end on the Rio Colorado and the other on the bay, the margin of both being very straight and regular. In the front of the amphitheater is a rich,

low marsh prairie though not stagnant waters—The beauty of the whole and particularly the Colorado is past description."

Out of all of the counties comprising Austin's Colonial Grant, Matagorda County was the engine of the concession. The great wealth it produced and shipped from its ports on Matagorda Bay made it the linchpin of Austin's colony. Following quickly behind the earliest settlers from New England were the planters coming in from the southern states. The area was becoming southern in culture, making a major contribution to the economic development of the new colony and creating fortunes from cotton and sugar. Matagorda County was the beating heart of the Colony. Bountiful land grants and access to previously uncultivated soil made it desirable to southern planters coming in with know-how and slaves. Land was granted generously to veterans of the War for Independence and since many were neither farmers nor ranchers, most of the veteran land grants were transferred to permanent settlers.

The plantation economy exploded up the creeks and river bottoms until much of the coastal plain was in play. Planters cultivating lands in the county owned forty thousand slaves and made the land around Matagorda Bay different from rest of Texas in that it had a "Planter Class." The cotton and sugar produced had waiting markets in England, France and in the northern states with mills. The plantation system of the South produced more wealth than any of the areas farmed in New England. Rich merchants in the East could not be compared in grandeur to the planters with their vast estates and there was a noticeable trend of New Englanders moving south in search of opportunities.

Social conditions were described in *Historic Matagorda County* as:

"During the days of the Republic a great change took place. A wealthy class of planters moved into the county. Many of them built homes palatial in extent and appearance. It was not uncommon for planters to have second homes on Matagorda Peninsula or in the town of Matagorda. There was wealth and style in Matagorda County not excelled in any part of the Republic of Texas.

The planters and merchants had their carriages and drivers. Their sons were sent to Harvard or to the Uni-

*versity of Virginia and their daughters were educated
in seminaries in Virginia or the Carolinas."*

Samuel and Mary Maverick were early San Antonio
settlers who later authored books on early Texas. Included
in their books was their first-hand account of the famous
Council House fight with Comanche chiefs in the center of
San Antonio. Mary A. Maverick, who lived with her husband Samuel on Matagorda Peninsula from 1844 to 1847,
described the Port of Matagorda:

> *"At that time Matagorda had probably the most culti-
> vated society in the State. Matagorda then had good
> schools and several churches. Many well to do people
> who had plantations on the Caney and the Colorado,
> where the summers were quite unhealthful, had their
> summer residences there . . . "*

In the 1850's, James Hawkins built and operated one
of the largest sugar mills in the state on his Caney Creek
plantation. In antebellum Texas, as in the rest of the South,
cotton was king. In the spring, slaves were planting it and in
August they were picking and ginning it. Sugar cane was a
year-round activity for slaves with cutting and milling in the
fall. Slave labor was very much a part of the equation and
because of it the ranchers and planters were enjoying their
newfound wealth and status. In 1858 the *Matagorda Gazette*
summed up the lure of slavery in an editorial stating: *" . . . a
good field hand could easily pay for himself in three years . . .
that is if a planter is successful who has 20 hands at the end
of three years he will have 40; and in six years he will be rich."*
The Port of Matagorda was a bustling city teeming
with rich, young planters, shippers, merchants and everyone involved in exporting and importing the goods to keep
the plantations running. The Colorado House was a first-
class hotel surrounded by shops offering imported silks
and linens and the type of merchandise found in shops in
New York, Boston and New Orleans. A gay social life was
developing and with the demand for cotton and sugar at a
peak, the nearby plantations were thriving profit centers
and the area was fast becoming known as the sugar bowl
of Texas.
Social life in Matagorda was southern in style like that
of Natchez, Mississippi, with carriages, mansions and lots
of servants. The *Texas Forgotten Ports* author wrote: *"On*

July 13, 1837, one of the first of hundreds of slave ships tied up at Matagorda docks." Early records show that most of the slaves were the property of plantations owners along the banks of Caney Creek. Although Grimes was considered a cattleman and not a planter, the census of 1850 listed W.B. Grimes as the owner of 16 slaves.

Mary A. Maverick wrote of the planters on Matagorda Bay:

> *"The wealthy planters did not know the hardships of poverty, but on the contrary, lived in luxury. They were the most liberal and hospitable entertainers. They kept numerous, well trained servants. While the overseers superintended the slaves and worked on the plantations, the planters, with their families and friends, enjoyed a continued round of pleasure. They always kept open house and visitors were met at the gate and conducted to elegantly furnished rooms in those palatial homes and everything was bountifully provided for their comfort and convenience."*

Other accounts about the culture of plantation life tell of the hospitality of the planters who always kept their houses open for visitors. One owner kept a servant stationed on the roadside every evening to offer any belated traveler lodging for the night without charge. Fehrenbach wrote of the planter class:

> *"The planters, and generally the more affluent townspeople, possessed the usual cultures of all squirearchies, especially those of short tradition. They read imported books, sent their children away to school, conversed about public affairs, enjoyed relaxed, enormous meals; they hunted and rode. Hanging out in polite company was matched by furious activity in the saddle. . . . There were thousands of slaves who were treated like prize pets or even lesser members of the family, there were others who were bred callously for their increase and worked to death under a boiling sun generally considered too hot for white men to endure. But there is no question that on the better plantations slaves lived a better life, materially, than the poorer whites. In one important item, medical care, slaves fared much better than the people on the frontier. No planter could afford a sick slave and he could afford doctors."*

In Arda Talbot Allen's book about the life in early Matagorda she describes the times:

"Thus by 1846, when the Republic of Texas accepted the United States' most gracious invitation to become one of the states of the Union, Matagorda was one of the largest and more cultural towns in the Republic . . . many of the families were quite wealthy. They came with their slaves and with boatloads of furniture, linens and silver that had graced their homes in the older states. These people, unlike many of those who go to a new country, had generations of culture behind them. They brought their books, their music and their way of life.

The town had broad streets which with their tops of finely crushed oyster shells, shone white in the sun. The blocks were wide, and they were never occupied by more than three houses. Thus each house faced the bay so that the breeze might have a free sweep through the rooms. This allowed also for space for carriage house, stables, chicken house, smoke house, calf lot, garden and orchard . . . All of the houses had broad front galleries."

The hotel Colorado House is pictured as part of the street scene engraving of Matagorda that survives. Built in 1852, it featured mahogany, walnut and cherry furniture and was said to be one of the finest hotels in Texas. It had 14 guest rooms upstairs, each with its private dressing room and downstairs there were five great rooms. Colorado House was owned by Galen Hodges and was at the center of the plantation society. Guests from all walks of life came to stay and enjoy the good air from the Bay and one of these bay front houses, moved twenty miles inland, survives today. It is a beautiful, two-story structure owned and lived in by present-day rancher Helen Cates Neary and maintained the way it was over 150 years ago when built in old Matagorda on the Bay.

In further describing life in old Matagorda, Arda Talbot Allen wrote:

"Many of the ranchmen or planters had their homes in town so that their families might enjoy the privileges of the school and church as well as the social life. Many

of those who lived on the plantations brought their families down to the hotel or to board with some of the families who took boarders during the summer, when chills and fever were so prevalent on Old Caney and across the river. . . . Thus Matagorda came to bring her contribution to Texas not only through her good harbor and usefulness as a port but in her gayety, her culture and her tradition."

Allen wrote about the important role of the Episcopal Church in Matagorda under the guidance of its first pastor, Reverend Caleb S. Ives. The church was unique in that it was actually constructed in New York and shipped in sections to Matagorda where the cornerstone was laid on October 14, 1840. In her book about this she writes:

"Prior to the War between the States, the slaves frequently attended the church where their masters worshipped, and many of them might have been seen in the section of this church reserved for them. Some of the older ones continued to worship there until their deaths. In fact, old Aunt Hannah, in her snowy apron and cap, was an esteemed member of the congregation until well after the turn of the century. Mr. Ives organized a Sunday School for the slaves where, every Sunday afternoon, Mrs. Ives and one of the other ladies helped him as teachers. Bishop Gregg was thoroughly in accord with the inclusion of the Negroes in the church service, for he had spent most of his early life on a plantation in the Old South. He brought to Texas the mind and heart of the best type of old-time 'Master' and felt keenly the obligation of the church to care for the slave population. . . . There were many other noble women, but perhaps the woman who really kept the church alive in Matagorda was Mrs. Stephen H. Wright, the wife of the minister. With her husband she had conducted a girls' school in Alabama, and when she found the desperate need for a school in Matagorda, she opened one for both boys and girls. The advertisement of her school appears in the Matagorda Gazette, though her school had been in existence for several years at that time."

Included below are excerpts from the writings of Fannie Grimes about the port.

"Well here I am once more in the City. I do so love to be at the home I love so well. If there is any place in the world I'd like better to stay, 'tis here at dear Mrs. Hilliard's. She is so kind and goes on so finely . . . well, I'm going to enjoy what I've been yearning for for two nights, good rest. How much one has to be thankful for. Kind friends, health, every bodily comfort; and, above all others, fresh air, good water and a clean house. Ah! one ought not to whine one word of discontent and I'm sure I've no desire to tonight—my heart is thankfulness."

From 1850 to 1853 young Fannie's winters were spent in school in Matagorda boarding with Mrs. Hilliard, and she describes one of the new additions to the thriving port:

"Mrs. Hilliard is kind and cordial as ever. . . . Mr. Thompson took dinner with us by invitation from Mrs. Hilliard but was so late in coming that Mary and I started uptown to get Mrs. Hilliard for a promenade on the wharf, a new feature in town beauty. We had a delightful walk tho' we were rather tired, having been shopping and making calls a good part of the evening . . . Matagorda is a very flourishing seaport seen from the end of the wharf a mile long and the large, white, private residences, palatial in their appearance when compared to those in Texana and loom up against the sky in sweet contrast with the vineyards and shrubbery surrounding them."

On many occasions Maria Louise and Bradford were in Matagorda and staying at the Colorado House to attend services at the Episcopal Church. All of the Grimes' 13 children are listed in that church's birth records.

The Hurricane of 1854 did great damage to the port, but it quickly recovered and the hotel registry from the Colorado House in 1857 recorded guests from all the surrounding plantations and ranches, including Wm. B. Grimes, and guests from New York, Dallas, San Antonio, Louisville, Corpus Christi and other areas.

The grandeur in Matagorda and elsewhere in Texas, however, lasted less than a half a century. The Civil War brought an abrupt end to farming the rich plantations and the planters turned to raising stock. With the loss of their investments in human property, cotton and sugar plantations became grazing lands. Those who held title to large land holdings turned to serious cattle ranching and the end of one era led to another that was far more rambunctious and romantic. The era of the cattleman, the cowboy, and the cattle kings had begun. It was here, in the coastal rangelands of Texas where the cattle industry began and where William Bradford Grimes was already a cattleman with no need to make the transition.

Birth of a Kingdom

As delightful as life at the Port of Matagorda may have been, the citizens around her were experiencing growing pains. Santa Anna's second invasion came to Texas in the spring of 1842. After a show of force, Santa Anna retired to Mexico and sent General Adrian Woll back into Texas with an army of a thousand men. Woll quickly captured San Antonio, Refugio and Goliad and once again the panicked citizens evacuated to the east as Mexicans under Santa Anna's direction now had a well-earned reputation for murder. Santa Anna, however, having developed a healthy respect for Houston and his fighting Anglos, left General Woll to face the Texans. The new threat was met by General Edward Burleson and to assist Burleson in repelling the invasion, President Houston dispatched a group of Rangers to the fray. Captain Jack Hays came with 750 Rangers and Woll made an election to lead his army in retreat across the Rio Grande into undisputed and safe Mexican territory.

News of the campaign published in the maritime news tracked the Captain's arrival at the Port of New Orleans where, on October 16th, 1842, the *Times Picayne* reported that the schooner *Henry* was in from Lavaca Bay and that her commander, Captain Grimes, reported that Gen. Burleson had driven the Mexicans away from San Antonio and was awaiting reinforcements. On October 21st another article appeared in the Augusta, Georgia *Chronicle* picking up the same maritime news and printing that the schooner *Henry* had arrived in Savannah at a late hour from Linnville on Lavaca Bay and that its captain reported:

"Gen. Burleson, with 1,100 men, had driven the Mexicans from San Antonio without loss. The Mexicans

were fortifying themselves at the River Medina, 15 miles West of San Antonio. Gen. Burleson was within four miles of the Mexican camp awaiting the arrival of artillery and reinforcements. Long before this time a decisive engagement had taken place, and we deem it probable that not a single Mexican is to be found in Texas. We are informed that almost every able-bodied man in Western Texas has rallied in defense of the country, leaving the crops to the care of the women and children. It was reported that a detachment of Texians from Gonzales, in attempting to join the main body of the Texian Army, had met with severe loss and that about forty men were found dead upon the field."

Charlotte Grimes, isolated from her son Bradford and sisters Fanny, Nancy and Betsey, finally returned with young "Sis" to Rocky Hill in 1844, leaving the Captain alone at Palacios Point. It would be five long years later before the family would be reunited when Bradford came to Texas with his mother and her sister Fanny Bradford. Charlotte's decision to leave may have been influenced by Santa Anna's second invasion but it is more probable that she was motivated by the need to get wild, young Fannie into a real school.

The Captain arranged passage for Charlotte and Fannie on a ship bound for New York and when they arrived, Charlotte wrote back about her return and that in her long absence from New England *"Bradford has grown so and changed so I hardly recognized him."* In her letter she left a space for young Bradford to write a few lines to his father and he expressed his strong wish to come to Texas. Charlotte then closed with: *"I should not mind coming back so much if I could go easily as I came, if you thought it best for us, but I could not return without my children."*

Soon after his arrival in Texas, the Captain, like many of his New England neighbors, began to acquire land from veterans who had earned land certificates for their service. He purchased two such Certificates for Grants of 320 acres each issued by the Secretary of War in 1838. The Captain's participation in the War also entitled him to a Headright Certificate from the Republic under which he acquired a parcel of land containing 4,632 acres. Early maps from the General Land Office in Austin show the parcel granted to Richard Grimes bordered on the south bank of the Carancahua Creek just over into Jackson County. He wrote to

Charlotte that he had also acquired 1,000 acres of land on Coleta Creek, ten miles west of Victoria, 900 acres within a mile of the Colorado River and that he had recorded a deed for 371 acres more on the banks of the Trespalacios with more claims pending. In his letter he added a prediction that: *"this land may be worth a small fortune to our children for certain if we are annexed to the United States or if we get our independence acknowledged by Mexico."*

The Captain, then living alone, gave little thought to raising commercial herds of cattle and at his home on Palacios Point where only a few head were kept for meat and milk. Cotton and sugar were the primary interests of the planters and the Captain continued his shipping trade getting his neighbors' goods to distant markets and bringing in cargoes from Havana, New Orleans, Mobile and elsewhere.

Early in 1847 young Bradford, apprenticing as a merchant in Circleville, Ohio, wrote to his father about making plans for his future and how he badly wanted to join the family as he sees great promise on the Texas frontier. The Captain encouraged him to come and by November Bradford booked passage aboard a vessel that sailed down the Atlantic coast and into Galveston Harbor on December 7th, 1847. He had embarked on a life-changing new adventure and got his first glimpse of the Texas frontier.

The Grimes men were both in Texas now but there would be no real home there until joined by the rest of the family. Charlotte was in Rocky Hill with young Fannie but by 1848, and with Bradford now in Texas, she decided to return. They were joined by her sister Fanny Bradford, an independent minded Yankee spinster willing to leave the comforts of her New England home for the wilds of Texas. There she would lend emotional support to her sister Charlotte and financial support to her nephew Bradford.

In December Fanny Bradford, Charlotte and young Fannie arrived in New Orleans on the final leg of their riverboat journey from Connecticut. They were met in New Orleans by Bradford and together they sailed to Palacios Point on Matagorda Bay. Upon her arrival at the Point, Fanny reflects about her new surroundings:

"Texas Dec 19 1848

We arrived here last evening found the Capt well, we had a passage of a week from N. Orleans it is pleasant here, and all things look fine the flowers are in bloom, and we have our doors, and windows open, we can see the vessels off 3, or 4, miles in the bay, and there is one boat that is making for our place that the Capt thinks is going to Matagorda, so I have rummaged something together while the folks are at breakfast to just tell you that we have got here after a very pleasant passage of 6 weeks as for fear I shant have another chance yet, but they have sent sis for this famous letter so let them have it, I will tell you the ticlars next time"

In 1847 Bradford and the Captain have examined ideas on the future and have made a commitment to enter the business of cattle ranching as a serious and full-time enterprise. They began building their cow herd by branding to prove ownership and transporting marketable cattle by ship to supply the demands for beef in New Orleans.

Taking stock of his surroundings, young Bradford saw oceans of free range where thousands of unbranded cattle roamed and he imagined profits on the hoof. He had arrived in the embryonic years of the Texas cattle industry as one of the first ranchers and intended to prosper from it. Barbed wire had not been invented. Fences in Connecticut were made of stones piled one on top of another and timber was used for fuel and building houses. Down the Atlantic seaboard, men were splitting timbers with mauls to make rail fences. Here there was free, open range and fortunes on the hoof to be claimed by branding calves and rounding up fat animals to be shipped to market on cattle boats. The operation got an added benefit in 1851 when the Morgan Steamship Line was extended from New Orleans to points along the Texas coast.

Samuel and Mary Maverick were neighbors for a while when the Mavericks made a brief foray into the cattle business on the Matagorda peninsula. Mary recorded in her diary that in 1845 she and her husband Samuel were guests of Captain Grimes at his residence on the Point. On the land that they bought in the middle of the peninsula they built an eight-room frame home they called "Tiltona." Four hundred head of cattle came with the land and in 1847 when the Mavericks decided to return to San Antonio permanently, they left behind their free ranging, unbranded livestock that became fair game to anyone who found them wandering about. Thereafter, his name would be perpetuated in the vernacular of cattlemen forever as any unbranded stray was called a "maverick" and laying claim to unbranded cattle wandering free was called "mavericking"; in practice it became somewhat of an unwritten law.

In reality, all of the wild cattle in Texas were descendants of cattle brought to the New World in the 16th century for the Spanish missions and were considered abandoned. With the Captain's land purchases and young Bradford's financial backing from his Aunt Fanny, the partnership business began and Bradford started to gather and brand cattle from the surrounding free range land. Operating miles from Palacios Point on the Bay required the building of a second ranch house inland to work closer to greater concentrations of cattle. At the new headquarters on Trespalacios Creek Bradford added a strong set of working pens, organized branding crews, bought horses broken to ride and began breaking and making cow ponies out of the younger ones. From here in all directions lay miles of open prairie and with money to pay cowboys, Bradford became a true cattleman.

On this range, men found great, open spaces of prairie covered with lush grass, where wild cattle and buffalo grazed. Barbed wire fencing would not come until 1874 so early cattlemen lived by the rope and the branding iron. One of the earliest ranches was Bradford's WBG located among the settlers of Austin's colony where the cattle industry was dawning. The early cattle business came with some limitations as men venturing too far west were met with mounted Comanches ready and eager to kill any who would encroach upon their traditional hunting grounds. In this environment, without the need of taking title to the land, cattlemen adopted a set of rules that were all the law they had. One author writing about the times said:

"In this setting cowmen built their empire . . . they formulated rules governing the use of the range and they worked out customs which were, by their hierarchy, the equivalent of law. Within their code were regulations to which every cowman was committed . . . the Law of the Open Range. Few cowmen owned their ranges. Few individuals could finance the purchase and maintenance of immense amounts of acreage needed to support both summer and winter grazing. Few made any pretext of ownership or any practice of leasing. Free use of unoccupied government lands was the foundation of the range cattle industry. The Law of the Open Range was the unwritten rule of free access to grass and water . . . Newcomers were thereby forewarned not to stand in

*the cowman's route to the ranges, not to block his way
with towns and fields and—of all things—fences."*

By 1850, the two homesteads, separated by several miles, had the Captain working east and north from around Palacios Point and Bradford working all quadrants of the compass from what he called his Lower Rancho and his Upper Rancho. Working in tandem on two spheres of range they were furiously branding more and more cattle. At the Point, wharves and loading docks were added to accommodate ships that could carry live cattle to markets. The 1850 Matagorda County census listed the Captain with ten acres of improved land and nine hundred acres of unimproved land and Bradford, with one hundred and seventy five acres of improved land, five thousand acres of unimproved land, a hundred head of horses and fifty-five hundred head of cattle. The operation at the upper WBG ranch had become the well-known headquarters of a budding empire and Bradford was the largest rancher in Matagorda County. The Captain and Bradford together were gaining historic and lasting reputations. In a book published about the earliest Texas ranchers, *Cattle Kings of Texas,* the author devoted an entire chapter to "Grimes of the Trespalacios."

Original WBG Ranch home and Ranch store on the west bank of the
Trespalacios River.

In a short letter from Bradford in Matagorda, sent by boat to the Captain at the Point, he described some of the trials and hardships of herding and driving cattle as he writes of pursuing cattle lost in crossing the Colorado River. Communicating by mail sent on ships was painfully slow and in a note about trying to gather a scattered herd, Bradford added other news for the Captain that one of his fellow ship captains, Captain Duncan and his daughter, are expected to arrive in at the Port of Matagorda from New Orleans.

Life on the ranch in 1852 was being organized by Fanny Bradford who was by that time totally involved in the cattle venture, living on the WBG, managing operations around the headquarters and practicing medicine without a license. She had organized the help and the kitchen, feeding cow hands, supervising household slaves and field hands while the Captain, Charlotte and Fannie were living and working from Palacios Point. In July Aunt Fanny wrote back to her sister Nancy Bulkley and her doctor husband in Connecticut asking for medical advice from Dr. Bulkley. She adds that Bradford had just bought 28 horses, bringing the total to 48 and describes the weather as too hot for anyone to endure comfortably or safely:

". . . it is not sickly here as yet, . . . at least no epidemics, but some are complaining of chills and fever. One Dutchman has had it 3 or 4 times. He is green right from Germany 4 years ago and I have had to be his doctor. I gave him calomel and castor oil. I wish you would ask Dr. how much to give and how long between doses. . . . I have another Dutchman on hand. I gave a half a teaspoon of quinine as a dose and he never had another chill or fever after the first day. . . . We have been very well so far . . . I wish I had something new to tell you . . . its not like hearing from your old home as there is no news from there that wouldn't be interesting . . . I may never again see the old one . . . "

As fate would have it, Fanny would never again see her old home in Connecticut and would die on the WBG in 1862. In her letter seeking medical advice she wrote further:

"Folks and boats are up and down quite often now days and we are getting more folks than we want in these diggings; we won't have room for our cattle and

*horses and sheeps. Bradford has branded over 300
calves since January and the Captain 200. How many
more they will have can't say . . . they sell at $5 per
head if you want to sell general stock so their stock is
worth $3,000 more now than last year. . . .*

*the Captain appeared, got his breakfast down and,
with his branding gang, is going to drive cattle again.
They camp in our new house, get their breakfast and
come back here for dinner so we must be ready from
three o'clock in the afternoon until dark. It rained like
fury yesterday and they came home wet as rats and all
mud; today is better . . . we are as busy as bees."*

Another snapshot of life on the WBG in the winter of
1851 was in a letter from Aunt Fanny to her niece Fannie
who was in boarding school a short distance away in the
Port of Matagorda. She named various people coming, going and staying and talked about feeding whole gangs of
people in the new ranch house. Drovers had heard about
the new pens where cattle could be more easily branded
and sorted and Fanny describes some of their activities:

*"Monday morning we started fresh but about 11, up
came a horse at full gallop with Ward on his back to
let us know his troop were advancing and wanting to
know if we had a good pen. When he had seen the new
one, he wheeled about and was off as fast as he came
telling Bradford he would be back in 20 minutes and
wanting Bradford and all hands to be ready as soon as
they could eat their dinner. He was true to his time and
his gang and with Bradford we fed 10 . . . I don't think
there was one left on the premises in one hour."*

The WBG ranch house became more like an hotel with
the cattlemen coming through to take advantage of the new
pens and a chance for a good meal; she continued:

*"We're getting along much as when you were here
though not so much in a hurry since the beef men left.
After the drive, they came back and lodged in our hotel and left at daylight. Oh it was just the thing they
thought. Ward was much pleased with the accommodations, pens and all . . . I can see him now as he sat*

by the fire in the morning combing his hair and grinning and telling everyone how good he slept and how warm and what a first rate place we've got here."

In 1854, Bradford was shopping in Matagorda and redistributing necessities to the ranch operations along the river and sending correspondence to his family. Mail coming in by sailboat was important but the only way to get mail anywhere up and down the Trespalacios or around Matagorda Bay, was by sailboat. A short letter from Bradford to his sister at the Point is an example:

"Dear Sister

I met Mrs Hillard a few moments since,—she says her children have the measles,—and that if you have not had them, it would be unsafe for you to come up for 2 or 3 weeks to spend any time with her,—She says you spoke of going to Mrs Burkharts in which case there would be no risk,—Mrs H—says it is reported Miss Cap is to be married next week,—I have heard nothing said about it from anyone else,—

I will send by Ellick linen for two vests,—I would like one to be made like my old bard silk vest- the other to be made after I see you or Mother,—

you want any Mesquitoe Barring you can take as much as you want from the piece I send to the Rancho,—tell Father he can take 2 ropes from the piece I sent,—I sent you one Bhl Sugar & one Bhl Molasses,—I send one foot tub for Palacios,—If you could get Father to take up about ½ Bhl of Bermuda Soap & send by Ellick I would like it for the Lower Rancho,—you can take as many buckets as you want,—you can send by Ellick what things you may have for the Lower or upper Rancho,—

I shall expect to be at the Lower Rancho when Ellick gets there,—good bye,—

have heard nothing of the bags Demings friend was to send—If they come here Mr Hillard will pay the freight on them and send them to Palacios or to Fred C it is near 12 oclock and I will try to get home this ev'g or rather to the Lower place

As ever   Wm B. Grimes"

By now, the Captain, feeling his 65 years and intent on securing his own legacy, had decided Bradford needed no further additional help from him. The wise old Captain may have worried that Bradford was borrowing heavily and feared that his share of the cattle were at risk in Bradford's rapid expansion. He had decided that after his mortal exit, his daughter's interests should be protected from creditors. In a significant but brief way he provides for Fannie.

Palacios May 17th 1854

This is to certify that I have this Day Given, Assigned and Conveyed to Fannie C. Grimes all my Right, Title and Interest on and unto all my Cattle Marked two slits and Branded RG on the right shoulder

Richard Grimes

Signed in the presence of L Dobbin
Charlotte B Grimes

New buildings were being added for housing and feeding single men and a ranch store was built and added on next to the main ranch house on the WBG headquarters. In a letter in June, Bradford writes to his mother and sister about the need for more space, more help and about his livestock dealings:

"Bluff Rancho June 20th '54

. . . on adjoining the dining room, similar in shape to the present kitchen, but large enough for two rooms one of which to be used as a kitchen, the other room for the servants sleeping room,—the style of the building could be decided upon at any future time,—

learn from Mr Smith that Mr Fitzgerald has sent Hagar to Town to be sold or hired—

I shall go Town tomorrow to see Mr Fitzgerald, and Franks Father and his intended Father-in-Law If I hear

*of nothing better from Fitzgerald or anyone town I shall
probably sell my Sheep to the Smiths for Cattle,—If I
can get from Town in time I will call by Palacios I am
compelled to be either at my lower Rancho or at Palacios
on Monday next one week from today,—*

*I sent a Load of wood, two bags of Potatoes, the cast
wheels etc by Ellick he will probably be down this week*

from your affectionate Son & Brother   Wm B. Grimes

*I sold 50 of my Beeves and one of Fathers,—Mr KuyKen-
dall will be at Palacios next Monday or the Monday following to commence getting another drove*

Wm B. Grimes

A Rhode Island Hired Hand

Samuel Allen Robbins, a fellow ship captain and friend
of Richard Grimes, had settled on Matagorda Bay the
year before Texas independence with his son Fredrick
on a farm nearby. Among the Robbins clan were several
generations of Connecticut and Virginia ship owners and
commanders. Captain Archibald Robbins was a contempo-
rary of Captain Grimes and earlier ship commanders in the
Robbins line were Captains Joshua and Jason Robbins.

Samuel owned a small, seaworthy boat which he used
to carry provisions along the Texas coast and he and his
son Fred also owned a small herd of cattle. In 1848, Captain Robbins had just returned from a sailing trip to Corpus Christi when a band of renegades came aboard, murdered him in the pilot house, looted the boat, and threw his
body into the bay. Several days later, a search party, led by
Captain Grimes, found his body and took it ashore for burial. At the time of his murder, Samuel's other sons, Chester and Frank, were living in Petersburg, Virginia where
Chester was employed in a store run by a man named Abel
Head. A fellow worker and close friend of Chester's was
Head's young nephew, Abel Head Pierce.

Upon hearing the tragic news of his father's murder,
Chester immediately left Virginia to join his brother Fred

in Texas. Once in Texas, Chester became enamored with the life and opportunities there and after deciding to make it his permanent home, began to write back to his friend Abel Pierce in Virginia about the wonders of Texas and its abounding possibilities. He told long and thrilling stories of the new frontier and young Abel Pierce listened intently and dreamed of the exciting new land.

Abel was born the son of a blacksmith in Little Compton, Rhode Island, and at the tender age of 13, had been assigned to an unhappy apprenticeship with his uncle in Petersburg, Virginia. It was not much of a life for a young, ambitious boy and after five years of mercantile training and a serious quarrel with his uncle, Abel walked off from his job saying later that he had received too many doses of sanctuary. Prowling the docks in New York, he finally landed a job on a schooner bound for Texas which sailed June 29th, 1853, on Abel's 19th birthday. Four months later he walked ashore at Indianola on Matagorda Bay.

Young Pierce had a booming voice and a remarkable physique which attracted attention everywhere he went. When he arrived looking for work he already knew from Chester Robbins about Captain Grimes and sought him out. When they met, the Captain introduced his son Bradford who looked over the tall, young arrival from Rhode Island. Bradford, by that time was building a cattle enterprise and needing hard working cow hands, agreed to take Abel on. It was a decision that would forever change the lives of both men.

Under Bradford's tutelage, Pierce quickly learned to cowboy and became a top hand. His talents earned him more and more responsibility as a respected horse breaker, and a trusted branding crew boss. A warm relationship with the Grimes family followed and would extend for the life of the Captain and beyond. After the Civil War, a "falling out" between Bradford and Abel developed and the differing personalities and ambitions of these two men would lead to a potent rivalry in the years that followed.

Soon after Abel began employment on the WBG, Bradford recognized that in spite of his eastern breeding, Abel was "born to the business." In his book, *The Cattle Kings of Texas*, C. L. Douglas described young Abel's skills: *"No man in the country could throw a better rope at branding time. No man could turn an unruly bronc in quicker time. No man was better acquainted with the whims and instincts of the cow brute."*

Bradford's Aunt Fanny had clearly taken on the job of personally caring for affable Abel and reported about him and ranch business in general while Bradford was on his way to New Orleans. On the advice of Dr. Pilkington, the local physician, she had applied a cloth medicinal plaster to an infected sore on Abel's backside and gives a good-natured account of his recovery.

"Monday morning August 28th, 1854

'Spect you are near N Orleans by this time if nothing has caught you such as Yellow Jack or Cholera, hope you will dodge both, we are pretty much like we were when you left,

Abel is getting on smartly, he is hungry all the time, he wanted two of our large cups of coffe this morning, and all the venson we carried him, when Patience took him the last cup, he told her he could do better if his mouth was not so sore, she said, she don't want him do better, neither do I, if I have got to cook for him—

Abel had obviously developed a serious infection of some kind and the recommended plaster was not working and it had attracted ants. At this point, Aunt Fanny took matter into her own hands.

The day, and day after you left, he was so weak he could with difficulty raise himself on his elbow to drink his tea, and eat nothing, we all thought him weaker than before, and losing ground all the time, and addled at that, he could not get up at all, but he could make noise enough, he call'd Jake and got him down there, his room was full of Mexicans he said, and wanted Jake to drive them out and Jake said he look like if he sceart to death, he smelt worse and worse,

Dr wanted me to try this, that and another thing, but I thought I would practice on my own hook. I put a greasy salve on his back at night, and before morning he was raving. Martin said he olla, olla all night. I had to go down as soon as I was out of bed, O he was dying, he was crazy, his sore back would kill him sartin as the world, O dear do look at it, (he had on drawrs),

just turn'd over the top of his drawrs, and the way the
ants tramped and poured out it was in Texas fashion,
I don't wonder the fellow was crazy, he had twisted
and turn'd, to make it feel better, untill he had travell'd
his plaster all over his back, and drawn all the ants in
the room, in his bed, and what could not get into, and
round the sore, travell'd on after the plaster

I threw plaster, ants, and all, out the window, and
that's the last of I and the Dr's partnership but Abel
was so anxious I thought I must do something and I
wash'd off all the ants and cleans'd out the sore by
bathing it in tar water, and put a piece of clean white
paper, wet through, over it, the paper would stick, until
I took it off for the next dressing, in a few days it improved greatly, it is nearly fill'd up now, and he doesn't
complain of it at all, I commenced giving him 3 times
per day, the root bitters that all take here. I think they
gave him a start. Something has brought him up, as he
now gets up alone, sits up an hour at a time in a chair,
walks to the door, back to bed, when he pleases, sleeps
first rate he says, and will eat anything we give him,

Abel is improving, he dresses himself and comes up to
breakfast, some times before we are quite ready for him."

Having described Abel's delirium and her cure, Aunt
Fanny continued her letter with a general report on ranch
operations:

"[T]he Mexicans have their saddles, rigg'd, complete,
and are braiding whips, lariats, ropes, and rigging for
driving and branding, Mr Moore has not shown himself
this week yet but one of his slaves, Alfred was here
to day, he says they have been Mustanging. He and
Moore went with Wheeler and can't find his strays,

I sent Jake to the Middle Ranche yesterday, and your
letter also, Abel attempte'd to write two or three days
ago, but could not steady his hand sufficiently to make
it legible, if he could, I should have his name on the
note, he thinks he can write soon, and then shall have
him do it, I hope he will succeed for he wants me to
write to his Mother,

Saturday 9th   Moore is to commence driving next week, it is now fair pleasant weather, but has been much such weather as when you left untill the moon full'd, it looks like a chance for good weather for driving, we are looking for the Capt today, I sent to Cash's Creek for the brand to day.

Andrew wants you to get some good powder that doesn't smutty his gun so. Today he bought me the nicest whip I have seen, requesting me to hang it up straight till Misser Grimes comes home

Yesterday Andrew kill'd a fine deer, and Abel put almost a quarter of it out of sight for supper and then travelled down to bed. He was hobbling along up to breakfast quite as soon as he was wanted and this morning he can dress and come and go alone now and he makes the most of it. Abel has written his folks, and will send with this, and wants me to mention to have you get a box of hats, caps for your rifle. he sign'd the note yesterday. FB"

An often told story regarding Abel working for Grimes was that while breaking horses on the WBG, a lady called out from the ranch kitchen strongly suggesting that an expensive black slave named "Jake" should not be risking his life breaking horses and was supposed to have said, "*put Abel on the bad ones.*" This fits the character of Bradford's Aunt Fanny who, with some of her own money invested in the business, was enjoying her role as a manager on the upper ranch. Another version of the story was told by Don Worchester in "The Chisholm Trail" as follows:

". . . Pierce recalled that as a young man working for Grimes, he and a slave cowboy named Jake drew straws to see which of them got to ride an outlaw dun horse. Jake won, but the outlaw fell on him, leaving him stretched out unconscious on the ground. Grimes' aunt Fanny Bradford had been watching and concluded that Jake was dead. There's $1,500 gone, Bradford! Why didn't you let Abel ride that horse instead of Jake."

The slave Jacob was married to Patience, a household servant who lies buried in the Grimes family ceme-

tery on the Trespalacios along with Jake and other identified Grimes slaves. A reference to Patience and Jake was
entered in the 1852 minutes of the Trespalacios Baptist
Church, just upstream from the WBG ranch:

*"On Sabbath afternoon Sarah Anne Moore and Mary
Green came forward and were baptized and while at
the water side, Jake and Patience, a colored man and
his wife, presented themselves as candidates for bap-
tism and were baptized straight away."*

Bradford's building of his cattle kingdom was interrupted mid-stream by the two major events described in
the following two chapters.

CHAPTER FOUR

Hurricane

In late September of 1854 the weather along the Texas coast seemed calm and beautiful. Meanwhile, Bradford Grimes and Chester Robbins were traveling to New England in search of soul mates. Suddenly and without warning, a deadly storm struck the coast of Texas head on. The "Gale," as the family would refer to it afterwards, destroyed almost everything in its path and wreaked havoc on Matagorda Bay and the Grimes ranches.

Bradford's sister Fannie was left alone on Palacios Point while the Captain and her mother were sailing up the winding course of the Trespalacios River to its mooring at the Upper Ranch. Because of Bradford's trip to New England, the Captain intended to leave his wife Charlotte with her sister Fanny at the WBG. As the weather began to change, the old sea Captain, always familiar with the signs of imminent, stormy weather, sensed the need to return to the Point. Fannie, just 19, had been left alone with her dog "Doctor," her adopted stray cat "Puss" and her horse "Kitty Clover." It was her *"first experience in solitude."* Several years later while revisiting the Point, she penned her recollection of that terrifying experience to friends back in Connecticut. In the main, it is as follows:

"I think 'twas the 18ᵗʰ Sept, 1854—that with anxious eyes I scanned the horizon for my father's sail—as I closed the windows against the breeze which even then promised to become a blast. This was on Sabbath eve'g at 4.P.M. Father had been gone about about a week to the Ranche up Trespalacios, near where his remains now rest, he had taken Mother away and 'twas my first experience in solitude and it had become very irksome, beside the norther which had been blowing

all day and was a fair wind (the first since he left) for him to come home, was now increasing so much that I feared for his safety should he be out when 'twas at its height, and with the old glass which has borne him company through many a storm and calm I searched the northern bay for the well known bit of canvas that should herald his coming—my eyes were rewarded by the sight of the boat five or six miles away and with a sigh of relief I greeted my dog with the salutation 'well old Doctor, he'll be here before it blows a gale' and returned to my duties quite convinced that I'd nothing more to fear, yet I instinctively kept anxious watch of the boat and fastened the windows a little more securely and ran out of doors to tie up with extra care some pet plants of mothers for even then the wind was doing some damage among the more tender shrubs—And my unaccountable nervousness was much increased by the fact that 'Doctor' would not let me get a stone's throw away from him but persistently followed me indoors and out—upstairs and down with a piteous look in his almost humanly loving eyes—poor Doctor! . . . . Everything on that memorable Sabbath was peculiar—the air seemed a sort of haze of blueish tint sometimes hued with pink and wherever one moved about he seemed to be in a sort of vacuum immediately inclosed in a more rarified ether than the so to speak _outside_ air. A queer sensation this produced a sort of an asleep and awake existence in two states, quite an indescribable state of the atmosphere and an equally indefinable state of feeling seemed to pervade all nature animate and inanimate. Puss, usually shy and preferring outdoors to in, she was a stray that came to me, seemed anxious to keep near me—but Doctor was her mortal terror and not daring to face him when I could no longer shelter her in my arms for need of attending to household duties, she sought shelter in fathers room huddled tight between a trunk which stood under his bed and the mattress—there she meowed piteously whenever I approached—which was not very often after I had seen that everything was secure for my time was occupied with domestic cares.

Father had come in a very short time across the bay the storm was steadily but slowly increasing in violence yet I thought it only a hard norther and felt no fear. I think 'twas some time in the night rain commenced, the cold increased and Monday morning the yard looked very forlorn. A portion of the fence was down, smaller trees and many of the shrubs were uprooted and much of the time I spent out of doors with Doctor close by my side trying to right them. Father told me 'twas useless work but did not tell me any of his forebodings. Indeed, I think he only thought of the danger to shipping, as such a storm had never before visited Texas on land and I don't think he thought of what a hurricane could be on shore. By noon on Monday I had abandoned all idea of saving the shrubbery but yet had no thought of personal danger; not so Doctor. He fairly hindered my progress from room to room by jumping up on me and growling. His every demonstration seemed trying to tell me something. So troublesome did he become that at last I tied him up but whilst I remained in sight he contented himself with mild efforts to break away and whining . . . but when I left the room he seemed raving, giving such terrible howls as would make ones blood curdle and almost hanging himself in his efforts to get loose, which he did several times. At last, unable to hold out against his appeals, I gave him liberty to stay with me and that he did until fate separated us. Poor Doctor, I suspect that lonely hour or more out of doors added ten years to his two.

The wind had increased frightfully toward nightfall and the rain fell so densely that we could not see far. Just before nightfall, our nearest neighbor sought protection with us. Capt. Bridges and my father were old friends, and indeed we all esteemed the Captain highly but his wife and I had quarreled so that I had forbidden her in the house. Father so far sympathized with my animosity that he left me to say whether we should receive them or no. Truth compels me to say I'd not have been sorry to refuse Mrs. B. a kindness. I did hate her so cordially and for long after until I learned that her mind was wholly unbalanced. I *must* forgive a crazy person anything, but an unprovoked blow from a sane person, *never*.

Whilst we took our tea the front gallery was blown off and striking the kitchen broke in the windows. This created a momentary panic but with the damage temporarily repaired, we finished our meal and proceeded to investigate the extent of injuries. We found the shingles fast leaving the roof . . . the upper windows had to be barricaded. Capt. Bridges' house had settled into a shapeless mass not more than four or five feet high on the ground and whether the others were gone we could not see. We took bedding below stairs and huddled the children together on a sofa where they disposed themselves to rest as best they could. Just at dark the top of the chimney came tumbling into the kitchen with a noise and clatter worthy of a greater catastrophe. By the time 'twas impossible to keep lights the wind found so many ways of ingress so I lighted lanterns and hid my matches in the coffee mill as a sure place to keep them dry, for the rain speedily followed the wind into the house thro' broken windows and holes which flying timbers had made. A little time later as the parlour north door was burst in, Capt. B and Father sprung to catch it. By the exertion of all their united force they succeeded in holding it whilst I crept out the south door to get a plank to nail it . . . this after hurried consultation being decided to be the best plan. I got out easily and went the length of the kitchen without much difficulty, bracing myself to face wind and rain so I turned the corner of the house which was to my right and suddenly felt myself struck in the left side. Clutching whatever my hands could reach I found on feeling about that I'd been lifted from my feet and blown about ten feet against a fence post from which all the fencing had been blown off. Gathering my wits, I crawled for the board pile and securing a couple of planks which I dragged after me I wriggled back to the house which I couldn't see but knew as soon as I got in the lee of it on account of not feeling the force of the gale. 'Twas now I lost my dog, I had forbidden Mrs, B letting him out but he made so much ado she did, and whether he, like me, was blown off, I don't know but he wasn't on hand to go in with me and if he howled a death warning at the door, it could not have been heard. 'Twas only by screaming we made each other heard in the house and that only by placing mouth and ear in close proximity. I was out of doors, I presume not more than two minutes at the utmost but I was drenched thro' and thro', and after securing the door, took a lantern and went upstairs to find dry raiment. The parlour where all were congregated was the centre room in the house and still dry and well protected from the cold which was not *severe when not exposed to wind and rain. The upstairs desolation met my astonished gaze. The north side of the roof I think hadn't a shingle on it, the water was pouring in in torrents, not a bed was dry nor an article of clothing which had been in use, which proved a blessing to me. I was driven to reserved stores packed away and found nothing dry until I stirred down to mother's winter clothing. From this I selected the first that came to hand for I had grown timid being upstairs long and, for the first time, feared the total destruction of the house. Securing a quilted petticoat , an enormous sack made of serge and lined with domestic flannel, wadded two blankets and a quilt, I hurried downstairs. It seemed so much quieter, so warm and dry in the parlor that my fears subsided. Indeed, if Father had been with me I presume I would have felt none upstairs, for I was accustomed to kno'ing of his battling with and outriding storms so long that without much reasoning on the matter I didn't exactly think he could control the winds and the waves but thought he could and would manage them pretty well. That faith has not left me yet, nor centred in any other mortal and I never now treat wind and tide as heedlessly as I used to. When I sailed with him, fearlessly holding the helm myself, when as I've heard my Father say some sailors would have been nervous, I had no anxieties.I busied about things which demanded a little care in kitchen and parlour nd stopped only long enough to exchange my wet clothes for dry ones not waiting to put on my stockings, and when a leisure moment came, I curled upon the sofa with my feet under me to warm then when suddenly, with a mighty lurch and thud, the house came down off the supports with about three feet of fall. Mrs. B, who had long been clamorous that we should leave the house, now became frantically urgent. Father, to whom I had submitted the matter, thought best not and I refused to go but now that she became so clamorous I told her to go if she chose. I'd had enough of out doors and should stay in so long as Father did, he said wait for one more lurch and so we waited.*

The fall had ripped up the floors on one side inching them greatly . . . the furniture was moved and we again sought refuge in the kitchen as being the higher frame and likely to give more chance of escape in case the walls should fall in. In the melee, I'd no time to put on my stockings but kept my feet in the dry shoes (mother's) and huddled under the stairway close to the partition, we stood waiting for the next blast. The hurricane came in gusts, blowing a steady gale all the time and we would get an extra rush which seemed to be solid substance driving against all opposing matter like a battering ram. I judge it must have been about 10 p.m. when the house went off its supports and I was that time quite adept at reckoning time from long practice with my Father, either by appearance of the sun, the moon or even without any guide. It might have been a half hour, more or less, before the next gust struck us that thumped the devoted old shanty something as you've seen a card box drawer with vigorous jumps over the carpet when so little one's baby was taking a ride in a carriage without wheels. How far we traveled we couldn't judge then but next day's investigations proved that the house made a journey of twenty feet, stopping in a considerably lame condition just south of where 'twas built.

Father then yielded to the demand to leave it, though I think even then he was rather inclined to stick to the wreck . . . we got out the south door and I furnished Mrs. B with a bed quilt, took a blanket myself and gave one to the children. Outside, we stopped in the lee of the house to decide what to do. 'Twas arranged that Father and I, with one of Capt. B's children, should head the way with the two children in the middle and Capt. B and wife with their baby should bring up the rear. Thus formed, and planning on keeping huddled together, we started off guided by the wind at our backs, for Mrs. Ward's house, thinking of it as being so low as to be out of line of the gale. We had just started out when my blanket was torn off and the lantern which I had sheltered under was now without protection and the light was at once extinguished. We now were in _palpable_ darkness as we stood, not able to see each other, I felt something cold on my hand and closing my fingers about it, it proved to be Doctor's nose. I suppose the flash of my lantern as my blanket left me disclosed us to the faithful watcher. We made a few steps before we were beyond the lee of the house and the wind blew us all into a pile in the water. I lost my shoes, which slipped off easily, but I felt around until I found them. Gathered up, we started once more but without knowing much about our order, 'twas so pitchy dark nothing was visible, neither your hand before your face nor your neighbors head. By using the entire force of their lungs, Father and Capt. B could understand each other, accustomed as they had been as sea Captains to roar down the wind but 'twas useless for landsmen to try to see or hear.

The second time we started off again we found ourselves flying thro' the air or sprawling in the water. 'Twas difficult to tell which, for the rain fell not in drops but sheets of water. How we breathed I don't know for it seemed just like one continuous torrent pouring over us and the wind, as I said before, seemed a solid wall. However, we began to feel for ourselves and at last after many fruitless efforts to find anything, I clutched my Father's foot which I held on to until I had again fished up my shoes. I then began to feel about me to determine how many others I could find but Father and the child he held to were all that were there. He shouted with all his might but heard no answer and Capt. B told us the next day that he too had used all his strength to make us hear but without avail. Father, the child, the dog and I were all that remained of our company, so far as we knew until morning. We tried to travel on our knees, I taking child which was too much for Father and even in this mode of progression, we could not pursue and that fact saved our lives, for had we gone on as we were going, we would have gone straight into the bay. The wind, having veered two points to the east after dark was blowing us not toward Mrs. Ward's house as we supposed, but toward the bluff, over which hundreds of cattle and horses went to their destruction. Having tried everything we could do, we did nothing and in doing so, fared very well tho' 'twas but a poor bed on an ant mound cross which we lay in as compact a mass as we could. Father, on the windward side, I in the middle with Debbie inside my thick skirt and mammoth sack, and the Doctor on my feet. 'Tho there was water under and water over us and the wind, rain and hail beating us into the ground, I think I must have slept and dreamed. If I did not, my mind certainly wandered for I can remember even now the strange vagaries which flitted thro' my mind.

I was as well protected as I could have been under the circumstances except that I had no bonnet nor any stockings on, but as Father was clad only in summer vestment, I ought to have thought of something more for him. I did not think while lying in the prairie anything about our apparel, I only realized that the exposure was terrific and had no thought whether it could have been better provided against so I had no tormentings of conscience of not being more thoughtful at the time. I did not think of any relief, It simply seemed impossible we should any of us live thro' the night unless 'twere Doctor and I fancied he would bring someone to give us a Christian burial tho' we should die as the beast dieth. That, and the thought of waiting for my summons after Father had gone were the hardest of all to bear and, as usual, that which I suffered so much in anticipation of, I was never called to meet. I often put my hand in Father's face to see if he still breathed and tried again and again to make Doctor lie close to him but in vain as the moment I relaxed my hold of him, back he crept onto my feet.

Father thought 'twas about 3 a.m. when the storm had so far abated that we could stand and could see too a sort of greyness flash thro' the blackness when in an occasional flash of lightening, we were shown the outline of each other's forms. Once again we made an effort to reach shelter and this time we got along very well . . . holding tight to each other. Once my foot went down into a deep hole and I fell. Going over the same ground the next day I saw 'it was a post hole I had fallen into and near it was the basin from which a cistern had been taken up. The hole was deep enough and large enough to have drowned us all three had not providence guided our steps to one side. We were brought however safely to a chapperal mott on the bay where, on a shell ridge, we found shelter from the wind and where, here out of the water, we huddled together as the best thing we could for we could not tell where we were and 'twas still pitch dark save the grey streaks the lightening made. With the rain still pouring down and bitterly cold it seemed, we remained in our nook having a good nap until day break when we started off once more. The wind had fallen so that 'twas now not very difficult to walk. The rain was still falling heavily though not in torrents and as dawn revealed our house was still standing and we were not more than half a mile from it . . . we really thought ourselves well off and started cheerfully for home.

The water was over a foot deep all the way. Debbie was an <u>uncommonly</u> heavy child and how I accomplished that half mile back after the night's exposure is still a mystery, but we always accomplish what we must do and that I did whilst the excitement lasted, not knowing that I was over tasked. On our way we saw a tree which had been torn from the chapperal and hurled into the prairie and judging from the time it took us to reach it, very near where we had made our bed in the night . . . another narrow escape.

Reaching the house we found it barely standing, the side walls had been wrenched from the ends leaving a two or three feet space at the bottom. The floors were halfway to the ceiling on one side and fastened on their original timbers the other side, but the preservation of furniture was marvelous in all the rearing, splitting and turning over. I think there was nothing in the house broken except the crockery and one chair.

Leaving Debbie who, for the first time was taken out of her sheltered nest in an outhouse, I crawled into one corner of the house, crept over the teetering floor and up the trembling stairs and such a scene met my vision. The north windows were blown in and clear across the room wedged into the south wall in a perfect hash of bedding furniture and wearing apparel. A glass candle shade which had stood in the southeast corner of my bedroom on a stand held its own unbroken crystal upright on the north side of the room . . . how it got off the stand and with a head wind and reached the other side of the room, I don't pretend to explain. The 'why' of any of that night's doings is beyond my ken. I only narrate as accurately as I can after sixteen years of what I saw and felt.

Securing a bottle of wine, I cautiously made my way downstairs again, stopping in the dining room to find the pantry carried away and the flour barrel half full of flour, broken crockery and debris generally. From the shelves above I found a half barrel of crackers uninjured as they were covered with a pewter platter so as to keep that in place. I took some out with my bottle of wine, but it seemed long before I could find a piece of anything large enough to drink from. At last, in the kitchen, I dug from the wreck a tin cup which would hold, notwithstanding the gale which had given triangles to its rotundity and armed with my refreshments, I joined the party in the outhouse. My dog followed me and Father went part way. Debbie asked for some milk after she tasted the wine, but docilely drank a little when bidden to. She was perfectly quiet all the time, giving no trouble and making no demonstrations until she saw her father who came in quest of us after we had been home perhaps half an hour. He had found himself nearer Mrs. Ward's in the morning and gone there with his family. The baby was dead . . . when it died no one knew but it was most likely the first time when we were blown down. The children had suffered considerably, as we all had, but Debbie looked so bright and rosy cheeked as tho' just taken from her comfortable crib and her father's eyes filled with tears as he received his favorite child alive and well."

The destruction of the town of Matagorda put a halt to Fannie's formal education for the time being. Her friend and schoolmate, Jane W. wrote to her about the devastation and suffering caused by the hurricane.

"Ducro- Brazoria County Nov 24th 1854

Dear Fannie

Your kind and welcome letter came safely to hand by the mail of last Tuesday and it is with much pleasure that I hasten to answer it but fearing I cannot interest you as much as I was interested in your very entertaining and well written Epistle, However you must make all the allowances imaginable,

I left the ruins of Matagorda some time since and was delighted to get away once more though I disliked the idea of leaving my friends yet there is very little inducement for a person to be at such a place now where all is confusion and noise, it would be very little pleasure to you to visit Matagorda now you cannot conceive or imagine what a change there is in the Town even in the people I never have seen such times Fannie nor do I ever wish to again

I thought of you often during the storm and wondered
if you were exposed as we were to the dangers of the
mighty tempest which I since heard that you were."

One tragedy of the storm was the loss of the side-wheeler steamboat the *Kate Ward* which went down with all hands. Captain William Ward and his wife lived at Palacios Point in a home nearby and in 1857 Fannie was visiting the home of Captain Ward's widow and wrote about the aftermath of its sinking:

"Right here I have an example of trials borne of real not
imaginary griefs, of loss, of real survival and not the
ideal happiness one imagines when tragedy mingles
with ones experience in a life in this world. My hostess
(Mrs. Ward) has been a wife and mother; now she is
neither. No relatives now in the world to depend on or
care for her . . . Oh! in how exaggerated a form came
this last and greatest trial. The cold, crashing waves
cast the mangled bodies of William Ward and his broth-
er, beloved as well as tho' of kindred blood, upon the
desolate beach and left them there for strangers' hands.
Left coffinless from the glaring sun and the fury of wild
beasts. After days of agonizing suspense, a friend with
cold and heartless word, broke the news to that lone,
frail woman as gently as might be. For her the earth
held naught but trouble, for days we tho't she could not
rally. We tho't she would find relief where she so longed
to, in the final <u>resting</u> place of all, but we were mistak-
en. Months and now years have passed and still she
suffers on. Three times has our planet journeyed around
the real source of light and she is with us still, but it can-
not be <u>much longer</u>. Her great griefs are with her still."

Shopping for Brides and Slaves

In the summer just before the storm, Bradford was putting the WBG brand on every animal within the reach of his crews. Life was good but he lacked the companionship of a wife and family of his own and in August he and Chester Robbins began a trip North to Hartford, Connecticut where they planned to find wives. The Captain knew well that the master of the ranch needed a mistress and that if his son was successful in finding a bride, the Captain's job was done.

Bradford and Chester travelled as far as Mobile Bay, Alabama, where he wrote back to his sister Fannie about the journey:

"Providence permitting we shall stop there about four hours when we take the steamer up the Alabama to Montgomery. we are now on the Steamer Florida one of the finest Steamers I am told in the South,—we have had a very pleasant trip since we left N. Orleans,—I have wished ever since I came on board of this Boat that you were here to enjoy the trip with me, although I do not think Chester has enjoyed it as much I have done, from very sea sick, and perhaps that would have been your fate, . . . we have been on the water all the time since we left home,— for fear of the Yellow fever in Galveston we did not go ashore. I sent up for Mr Iurnge to come to the Boat—he said there were about five or six cases of Fever a day on Saturday & Sunday—there are but few cases in New Orleans except at the Hospitals, it is confined almost exclusively to the lower classes,—I am in hopes that I shall find time and means to go and take you all around early next summer before the sickness commences, nearly everyone has gone to bed so I will close for tonight—

Mobile Friday morning Sept 2ⁿᵈ

We did not find a boat yesterday as we had anticipated . . . we start at 4 oclock tomorrow for Montgomery,— This is a very pretty little City about the size of Hartford there are quite a number of fine Public & private buildings the city is very regularly laid out in squares and fronts Mobile Bay,—Negroes are very high here,—I was offered a girl about 15 yrs old at $775—for good cook I was asked $1,200 there are very few Negroes in market at present,—with Love to all I am your affectionate brother   *Wm B. Grimes"*

On September 2ⁿᵈ, Bradford wrote to Fanny Bradford, now in charge in his absence and gave her the particulars about their steamboat trip up the Alabama River from Mobile. He reported on his quest for slaves and about their intent to board a railroad passenger car once he and Chester reach Montgomery:

"We left Mobile Friday 8 o'clock p.m. I wrote to Father and Sister, both of which letters will go by the steamer that leaves N. Orleans tomorrow. . Negroes I find very high at every place I stop. Boys from 11 yrs to 16 yrs old are worth $700 to $1200—women are mostly from $800 to $1200; the above are Negroes that are warrented.

Mr. Foster told me in Galveston that he should sent for my beeves about 10th of September . . . he was very kind while I was in Galveston—the yellow fever was raging there so I did not go up in town.

Tuesday morning we arrived in Montgomery at last . . . this is a very pleasant place—we shall leave here on the cars at 8 o'clock . . . We shall be in Petersburg in about two days where I shall probably spend a few days . . . Tell all folks that I hope they are all getting on well and I want to find them so when I return. With love to all I am ever yours, Wm. B. Grimes"

Finally in New England, Bradford wrote back to Fannie about the progress he and Chester are making in their search for brides:

Rocky Hill, Oct. 13th 1854

". . . Chester came here at my request to see the girls of Rocky Hill. He seems to have taken a fancy to Carrie's sister Chloe—whether he will be able to persuade her to go to Texas I am at present unable to say. Carrie has this moment called here to invite me to take tea at her house this evening with Mr. Denning, Chester and sister—they are to leave for Hartford this evening on their way to Virginia (after tea). I presume Chester will ascertain this afternoon what his prospects are with Miss Chloe, and whether he will have any inducement to come to R.H. again before he goes to Texas—as for matrimonial affairs I think I am no nearer making a selection from all the pleasant acquaintances that I have met since I left than when I first came. I see a great many good girls that I presume would make good wives, but whether one of

*them will ever make it at that capacity for me, at present
seems very doubtful. I think if I were to stop in Conn't for
six months I might make an attempt to persuade someone to become a sister of yours and in doing so, I should
have the feelings of my friends (at home) at heart in the
matter I hope, as well as my own—from my feelings on
the subject. At present I think my choice is as likely to be
for one you have never heard of as any other way. . . ."*

A November letter from Bradford to his mother and
Fanny speaks about finally finding his "true love"; he cannot have learned about the storm by this date and writes:

Rocky Hill, Nov. 1st 1854

Dear Mothers,

*". . . I should start immediately for home, but as you are
aware before this, I have made an acquaintance from
whom I regret to be separated from and whose future
happiness I wish to live for. I am afraid you will think I
have [been] too hasty on deciding upon so important a
step without a longer acquaintance of the person who
is to be my partner through this rough world, but I think
I studied her traits of character well, as well as those of
her family. I think I am certain that I was not governed
by beauty on forming my first impressions, as since
I have left home I have made the acquaintance of a
number of ladies, several of whom the world would call
handsomer than the one I now think is best suited to
my tastes that I have ever seen. At least she is the only
person that I ever saw that I really wished to marry. In
making my selection I endeavored to have your feelings
in view as well as my own, as I expect one or both of
you will always live with me, and next to feeling prepared for another world I wish to have a family in this.*

*. . . my intended bride is Maria Louise Robbins, the
eldest daughter of Philoman Robbins of Hartford. Mrs.
Robbins was a Strickland from Glastonbury. Maria is
seventeen years old and her mother thinks she is at
least two years too young to get married but has giv-
en her consent to let her go next fall. Maria is not of a
robust constitution but rather delicate. She is in looks*

and size and in fact in every respect very like Louise Robbins was before she was married.

I feel certain that you will all like Maria Louise when you know her. I brought her down to see Aunt Nancy, Aunt Betsy and Doct and they seemed very well pleased with my choice—and Louise was much pleased with them. If nothing happens to prevent I shall come for her next summer and take her to live with us in Texas. She now thinks she is giving up a great deal to leave a pleasant home and kind friends—of the latter she has a great many—she is one of those good little creatures that everyone loves because she loves everybody and has a kind word for everyone she meets.

I shall probably wait until Chester is married, which will be in about two weeks from this before we start for home. . . ."

Both Maria and Chester had seafaring relatives who were contemporaries of the Captain. Her mother's father was Master of the Stepney Shipyard and there were numerous other interconnections between the Grimes and Robbins families.

Late in November Bradford was returning home and wrote to his fiancée in Hartford about the slave family he bought when traveling North in September. The slave Jerry, his pregnant wife Iris and their children have been staying in Virginia and now will accompany Bradford to the ranch where the couple will remain a part of the extended Grimes household for many years.

"When I arrived in Petersburg I found my Negros doing as well as I could expect the woman being in rather delicate health at present, her husband thought it best for her to keep house for him, while he went to work at his trade, he had made one Dollar and a half per day since he left his old Master but when I came to settle with the man for whom he had been to work I found that Jerry has taken nearly all he made to live on,— but I was satisfied to find them safe and well,—Jerry and his wife both seemed glad to see me,—they said they were tired of being so unsettled they wanted to get to a permanent home,—

They all seemed to enjoy themselves, ever since they left their old home, Iris the woman has suffered from the fatigue of traveling more than her children, but she was in fine spirits when we arrived this morning and I think by tomorrow she will feel as well as usual"

In a letter to Maria Louise dated December 7th and mailed from Powder Horn Bay at Indianola, Texas. He does everything he can to keep his newly acquired property from dying as a good slave in good health are worth a lot in Texas.

"My time since I left N. York has been as I anticipated constantly occupied in trying to get my people and luggage home safe & well,—

The woman Iris was in delicate health when I started from V'a and the children being young I had to be looking after them at every change of cars, Boats etc to try and guard against exposure & sickness,—they all kept well untill I arrived at N. Orleans,—there the oldest child sufered a great deal from a cold which from exposure on the Gulf made it quite sick but by proper nursing & medical treatment she has nearly recovered,—the Man Jerry was taken with the Cholera while crossing from N. Orleans to Galveston caused by exposure and change of water, climate etc but most particularly from want of judgment and care of himself on its first stages,—he did not let me know what his real situation was, untill I had nearly reached the place,—as soon as I arrived here and after giving him a good dose of Laudnum & Camphor I called a Physician to see him who pronounced it a verry serious case of what is here termed River Cholera,— which by the by is verry diferent from Asiatic Cholera,— we had great dificulty in keeping up a proper circulation of blood & for two days the Doct thought it verry uncertain whether he would live or die, during which time he required my constant attention, and the night of the change for the better the Doct staid with me untill after two o'clock, and when towards morning I became satisfied he was much easier, I called his wife to watch him and went to bed and slept better than I have since I left H'tf'd untill 11 O.Clock, since which he has been gradually gaining strength, and I think tomorrow he will be well enough to cross the Bay to Palacios"

By now, Aunt Fanny's letter about the storm has reached Bradford and in her letter she gives her own account of the ordeal she and her sister Charlotte suffered during the blow at the WBG:

Texas, Sept. 25ʳᵈ 1854

". . . The wind commenced blowing lightly from Northeast at 10 (morning). It increased gradually through the day and night, with occasionally showers of rain. Sabbath it blew hard, in gusts, at sunset it increased in violence with less pause between the gusts and by nine evening, I was well convinced it was no common storm. I trimm'd my lamp and prepar'd to watch until a change of some sort should take place. Hoping (faintly) it would be for the better. Charlotte went to bed, and to sleep. I let her sleep until 11, when I woke her and got her up and she dressed herself. She lay down again with her clothes on, but not to sleep. I told her we must be ready to leave any minute, but could not make her believe it for some time. She could not hear the wind as I did or she would have felt more as I did. The storm kept roaring on, louder and more terrific, until between 1 and 2, when it exceeded anything and everything, I ever heard or thought of, or thought wind could do. It was a sissing whistling sound combined with one long continued awful roar which lasted till near dawn of day. We staid in the house till past two. I should have left much sooner but could not get Charlotte to go. She thought we could not reach the kitchen, I thought it doubtful but was determin'd to try. We went out and remained under the gallery some minutes in the vain hope of a light lull, but was soon convinced it was useless.

I started first, and after making three attempts succeeded in reaching the south kitchen window where I staid till Charlotte got there also. Patience open'd the window, put out a chair and took us in where we staid until daylight. When we looked out we hardly knew the place—every tree and fence was flat on the yard, a part of all the fences down around the field, cowpen, potato patch and sheep pasture. Water full halfway to the top of the hill and broader in the gully than 2 rivers. The live oaks twisted off and large limbs deposited in every part of the yard. Still the wind was so much louder that we heard nothing of the crush. Our house moved about 2 inches on the blocks and Wheeler and John Moore said the gallery posts were all that saved it. Wheelers house blew down early in the night and his wife and children and John Moore's wife and children were out in the prairie all night, blacks also. Kitchen went first and French Irishman's house went all down and left his wife and child to the mercy of the storm, until morning, she could not stand before it at all, and had to crawl into the bushes on her hands and knees. They started for our house at day break and Wheeler, J. Moore and all hands got into boat and came down in front of the house to land and before we could get a comfortable fire and breakfast. We had 25 to breakfast, all hungry as bears and wet as drowned rats just as they had soaked in the prairie bog holes all night, afraid to move for fear of losing each other—all they could do was to hold on for they could neither see nor hear. . . .

More than three months had passed since the hurricane that came roaring over Matagorda Bay and Bradford is about to see the aftermath for the first time. His plans for the future, his family, livestock and workforce all await his arrival and he continues a letter he started to write on the 7th of December :

"I have seen a number of my acquaintances here who have been at my place and at Palacios, they give verry gloomy accounts indeed, but nothing worse than what I heard from home while in H'tf'd, they tell me my Fathers place is a total wreck and that he and his family are at my upper Rancho which is not injured to any extent, but that the house at the lower Rancho had the roof blown off first, and then the whole body of the house was turned completely over, the top being underneath but as long as we are alive, we can allways find something to be thankfull for. I hear of many who have lost everything nearly that they had in the world,—

I have a great deal to be thankfull for in not loosing my Negroe man Jerry,—the Steamer that came over two days after we did brought one corps here and left one at Galveston both from the same disease that Jerry had, one was a white man the other a slave.

If I had not suffered so great a pecuniary loss, I should certainly spend verry little time in Texas this winter, but return immediately to H'tf'd to attend my <u>business affairs</u> in that vicinity, you are aware that my motto is business before pleasure, and you are aware also that my affairs were in a verry pressing condition in that vicinity nearly all the time I was North"

December 18th, after Bradford has seen the situation first hand, he summarizes the damages and tries to give Maria Louise hope for the future.

"I have found the reality from the effects of the great Storm here, is worse if possible than I had immagined it could possibly be,— you can form no Idea of the change in the appearance of the country wherever there was any buildings or timber,—my losses are verry heavy and I expect I shall be compeled to use a great deal of economy for a year or two to come

My Negroes have all entirely recovered and I have set them all at work and every thing is going on as well as I could wish,—Aunt Fannie got along with the assistance of my overseer as well with my business affairs as I could have done myself,— when I got to my Ranche I found Mother & Sister there, and my Negroe woman Patience cooking supper, just before day Mother was called out to the kitchen to see the cook, and before breakfast they brought me word that I had a fine girl added to our list of servants so you see they are all making preparations to have their new mistress provided for when she gets settled in her Texas home—"

A year away from his wedding to Maria Louise, a lovelorn Bradford sends a Christmas letter filled with love but mixed with poignant realities.

"Matagorda Dec 24, 1854

The ev'g after I wrote you last, I attended a little party in Matagorda,—I met a number of my old acquaintances some of whom you have heard me speak of,—the meeting was to me entirely unexpected and from that fact made *much more pleasant—we had some fine music on the piano, but <u>the piece</u>, of all the pieces that could have been played, to suit to me at that time, was sung & played,—I was conversing at the commencing of the piece with an interesting young Lady, but as soon as the words struck my ear, you can easily suppose that I could think of nothing else, when I tell you that the piece was none other than my favorite at least for this winter "would I were with thee" I was so completely carried away, with the words, and associations connected with them, that I could not keep away from the Piano, it seemed as if it was some consolation to be near the words & music if I could not be with thee,—the dancing commenced soon after and in a short time I was in better spirits than I have been since I left Htf'd,—we danced untill about 12 Oclock everyone seemed to enjoy themselves very much—*

I had no idea that I could enjoy society at all this winter even if there should be any parties given in this vicinity,—there are but three or four houses in Town that are in condition at present to receive company,—You will never know what Matagorda was like from what it will be when you do see it, at least for many years—you can never realize the changes that have taken place in this vicinity since I left here to go North"

Chester and Chloe Robbins were married in Hartford and returned to a temporary dwelling where they resided while replacing the one destroyed. Fanny Bradford writes back to her sisters in Connecticut about the rebuilding efforts of Chester and Fred Robbins and compares their industrious Yankee ways to those of lazy native born Texans. In her letter of December 28th 1854 she writes:

"I did not think that Chesters business was to get married, but it appeared so and made quick work of it too, they have been bothering Fred for years, about getting married, but Chester has stole a march upon him, in good earnest,

they are all blown down flat everything but hen house, and Fred has been sleeping in that, while Chester is off getting a wife, but he wont mind that, he wants a lady there badly, a feminine as he calls them, he made us a visit, and staid over night, I gave him a dish of

*preserved peaches, O he did like such things, but they
had nothing to make them at his house, I think they
will all be pleas'd to see Chloe, and try to make home
pleasant for her, there never lived 2 better, pleasanter,
more obliging, men than Fred and Chester, and they
will all help her*

*. . . few girls get as good husbands as Chloe has got,
Fred and Chester are well off as to property, Fred has
got built up again partly, if not wholly, they are industrious, and take good care of things, they have not lost their
Yankee habits yet, a native born Texan, with one half or
one quarter of their property would lie in the sun all winter and the shade all summer, only when they happen'd
to get dry or hungry, the first, happens offten to some of
them, but there is no danger of F and Chester."*

The new Robbins home, when finally completed, would
be called "Tadmor" and was one of the more celebrated, antebellum homes of the region due to its unique, octagonal
shape designed by noted architect Orson Squires Fowler.
Remains of the great house are visible today with its octagonal outline crumbling to dust. Its biblical namesake was
taken from Kings 9: 17-18, "And Solomon built Gezer and
Bethhoron . . . and Tadmor in the wilderness . . ."
  The correspondence that follows is between young Maria Louise in Hartford and Bradford Grimes back in Texas.
Maria is at the center of the abolition movement and she
has some trepidation about moving to a land where people
are owned as private property. Bradford writes to calm her
fears and tries to minimize the fact that families are living
without freedom.

Matagorda Jany 16ᵗʰ 1855

My own ever Dear Maria

*You kind sweet letter of the 2ⁿᵈ inst is rec'd this evg'.
I had business I wished to attend to & in not hearing
from the parties I had business with, I should have
been quite out of humour this evg' had I not rec'd your
kind favor to cheer me up you allways have some interesting news from Hartford & R. Hill—*

You speak of the case of our little Black responsibilities giving you a great deal of anxiety,—I think after you have had a little experience in slavery you will have a different opinion of Slaves & the Institution than you now have,—you ask the names of our serv'ts the first family I owned consists of Jacob & Patience Eliza the oldest is six years, Minerva four years,—& the new comes I do not know what her name is to be,—I wish you had sent her your choice of a name,—The family I purchased last summer consists of Jerry & Iris Charlotte the oldest child is five years. Jane the youngest at present is about three years,—I had intended Iris as a servant for Mother at Palacios—but Mother has not been well since the storm & she does not wish to go back to live at Palacios—but wishes me to bring the main part of the House at Palacios up to my Upper Rancho and keep all my servants together at present until I can afford to make different arrangements,—she says you & I can have the large house & she, Aunt Fanny & Sister will live in the old one that is now on the place—

with a kiss from your affectionate (would be)husband,— now I think that sounds first rate,—as ever yours

William B—

To Philomen P. Robbins, his prospective father-in-law, Bradford wrote frankly about his situation and prospects.

Matagorda Jany 16th /55

Mr P. F. Robbins

Dear Sir,

Your favor of Decr 28th was duly received & your Note forwarded in my last letter to Maria, dated the 13th inst. . . .

I had thought before I left Hartford that I had heard as bad accounts of my losses, as the reality would justify, but since I have returned and seen the effect of that terrible gale in all its bearings & heard the accounts from all quarters of the County, I feel satisfied that no one but myself could know the full extent of loss of property that I shall sustain, directly & indirectly from the best information I can get,

I lost from five to seven hundred head of Cattle & Father about two hundred,—among the number were a large lot of Beeves that would have been sold this last fall and next spring, the loss of the Beeves will cut off our resources for the present year verry materially,— the dwelling at my lower Rancho was blown completely upside down & smashed to pieces by its own weight, most of the fences shared the same fate,— at my upper place I lost comparatively nothing,— Fathers house was not blown to the ground but was so rocked and moved from the foundation that it has to be put up new,—I think I shall take the main Building at Fathers place, and bring it up to my upper place, by doing which I shall be able to get this place in good order and have plenty of house room here for both families untill I can make different arrangements

. . . The planters have suffered verry heavily in this County by the late Gale, the most of them will not make more than one third of a crop, this fact of itself has a great tendency to make money verry scarce here the comeing year,—owing to the loss being so general, all through the County no one has the conscience . . . many of my friends that were liveing in fine style in Matagorda from the rent of their Houses, are now compeled to take boarders & go into any kind of business that they can make profitable,

I have as well as my Fathers family, lived so long in this new country, that we can accommodate oneself to circumstances no matter of what nature they may be,— yet none of us can ever forget what we have undergone in getting accustomed to this kind of life,—

when we came here we knew nothing about the Institution of Slavery, and as a matter of course we labored under a disadvantage in every thing we undertook,— we flatter ourselves that with six years experience, we are now pretty well posted up both as to pleasures & difficulties in this section,—Every member of my Fathers family, as well as my Aunt in particular, wish me to make such arrangements for the present & future as will be most conducive to my happiness with Maria- from my knowledge of Maria's character I feel satisfied that she will be contented to conform to circumstances not as extravagant as they might be, for the sake of our future prosperity,—With my best Respect to Mrs Rob- bins & family I am my Dear Sir your humble servt

Verry Respectfully,

WmB.Grimes

Excerpts from one of Bradford's many letters written in 1855 contain his plans and dreams for the future with his fiancée Maria Louise.

Palacios   Feby 2nd   1855

My own ever Dear Louise

It seems an age since I have written or received a letter from you although the real time that has elapsed is but two or three short weeks,—in which time I have been constantly on the move—

I feel that you have every confidence in me & that my whole end & aim this winter is to so arrange my busi- ness, that you may be contented & comfortably situat- ed in your Texas home, & that I shall be able to carry it on with such sucess that we can afford to go North after a few years, if at that time we should think best, you are aware that my residence in Texas at present is not altogether from a preference for the State, its South- ern Institutions, its Climate or the occupation I have, but from a combination of circumstances, together with the fact, that it is for my interest and since I have had your consent to share my Joys & Sorrows, I feel that it is for our Interest instead of mine,—

I expect however that I shall leave home about the same time that I did last year which was about the middle of August, as it will not be safe to pass through New Or- leans probably after that time untill frost comes again & as you are to have your way, I will only suggest that our marriage may take place in October & that we start for our Southern home in November,—

I have had my hands at work at the upper Rancho making fences, ploughing the field, planting Irish potatoes, bedding Sweet Potatoes for Slips to set our—planting a part of the Garden vegetables—setting out fruit trees &c, &c. our English peas are comeing up & about five acres of corn has been planted now about a week,—the balance is to be planted as soon as the ground is in order after a rain,—

I came down here yesterday to take Fathers House to pieces & carry up to the upper Rancho, I shall leave him one small building, besides the shed room he put up after the Gale,—As soon as I put his little House here in repairs & put him up a strong Stock Pen I shall let the hands take the Lumber to the Rancho by water in a large flat boat I brought down for the purpose & I shall go to Matagorda on my way home for my letters from you,—

You know that every thing in a Slave State is managed diferently from what you have been accustomed to,—I may be mistaken in my opinion but I feel certain that Aunt Fanny & Mother will use every effort in their power as well as Sister to make it pleasant for you & have you pleasantly situated,—

You know I never write except at night & generally after the folks have gone to bed,—The Clock is now crowing for midnight

With a kiss & a hope that we dream of each other, I will say good night

Your ever Loving William

Late in the spring of 1855 Bradford is firmly back in charge of his ranching operations and again writing about business and he is quite engaged in the preparations for bringing his bride back to Texas in the fall.

Trespalacios Aprl 10ᵗʰ/55

Mr P. F. Robbins

Dr Sir

Your kind favor of 12th Feby was duly rec'd.

I think I told you last fall, that the most busy season, in my business, was from April to August, that is in collecting stock,—I have been trying to put my buildings & pens in order, for this spring's work

I do not intend to put up the house here in which we are to live, untill I have looked over all my stock range once, which will require about two months time—. . . . we had a great deal of cold weather last month, several frosts that injured the crops verry seriously, in this vicinity, some of the planters that made short crops of Cotton last season & during the heavy rains of last fall lost most of their seed first & almost impossible to get seed for replanting,—my little crop of corn has been cut down by the frost but is now up again & nearly plowed over once & is looking verry well—

I came here from the lower Ranche a few days since to look through the Cattle a little, previous to commencing opperations in the other prairie where the most of my Stock range,—the first two days I found Ninety eight Cows with young calfs—the next day I got about a dozen more making something over one hundred in three days & when I came home the last day I found a fine little Cow driver 'that is to be', Providence permitting, that the woman I bought last summer, found while I was looking for the cows—

You request my opinion in regard to what Maria will find convenient as to furniture in her new home—. . . In regard to the Piano I presume it would be a great relief to the monotonous life she would have here as well as afford the balance of our family a great deal of pleasure—. . . . Whatever you think would add to her comfort & happiness, that you can get for her without interfering with your business affairs will be sufficient,—

I think Beef Cattle will be higher this year than at any time since I have been in Texas,—the weather thus far this month has been verry fine & Cattle are in a fine way to do well this spring, as it will in all probability be dry, or at least not to much rain,—I shall drive among the Cattle in this prairie five or six days in all before I go to the Lower Ranche & from present appearances shall get about 150 head of calfs to brand which is about the same as I generally get in this prairie, in the same time, at this season,—so that it is not impossible but that I have nearly or quite as many Cattle now as I had last year at this time,—I had expected at that time to have branded 1,000 calfs last year, but owing to the Gale, I think, I did brand only 843—

I expect, you have had enough of Stock raising for the present with my respects to Mrs R. & all your family I am as ever your sincere friend

WmB.Grimes

Spring following the devastating September 1854 hurricane was a time of frantic rebuilding and preparation. Aunt Fanny Bradford tells her sister Nancy in Rocky Hill about just some of the work in her May 5th 1855 letter. And of course Bradford and his sister Fannie will both be headed to Connecticut soon for his upcoming wedding to Maria Louise Robbins.

"I spect B, and Sis, will show themselves that way this summer if nothing happens between now and when they get ready to start, I don't know when that will be, but I think as early as practicable, Bradford has one house, another partly finish'd, when he gets home he will begin the third and last, I expect, I shall be glad, and so will he when they are all finish'd he has had a mighty deal to do since he came home, but he sticks to it, from sunrise to sundown, and sometimes is up at half past three eats breakfast by candle light, and is off by daylight, It is a great job, and a long one, to repair, what the wind destroyed, in a few hours he would have had easy times this Spring, but for that,"

"Mr Ingles had been with us three weeks, he came just as all hands, (and horses) were ready for starting

orders, and like everybody else, he was ready to join
party, I thought one day would cure him, and give him
time and a good chance to make up his mind, to clear
out for good, from Texas but instead of one day, he was
gone a whole week, and came home saturday evening,
as bright, and pleasant as ever, we asked him how he
liked Texas life, 'O first rate, he never did anything in
his life, he liked so well'. he shall certainly stay here he
says, I have not seen him for a week they are at the middle and lower Ranchos, he may change his tune when
he comes again to night, I should think they would all be
tired to death, on horseback most of the time for three
weeks, and when one horse tires change him for a fresh
one, that _perhaps_ will pitch you over his head before you
can get seated, but it dont all frighten him, neither does
it tire him much he says he appears to be the one to get
along any where, all the folks, cattle drivers, mexiccans,
niggers, and white folks, all that have seen him, like him,
Bradford was much pleas'd to see him and they appear
to enjoy themselves, and get on first rate together"

the trees begin to look like themselves again, and I
hope houses, and fences will in an other year, but it is
some work to build a fence seven or eight feet high, of
pitch pine plank, with heavy cedar posts set three feet
in ground, around a pen of four acres, strong enough to
hold three, four, five or more thousand head of cattle,
and that is one of the jobs, that I hope is done by this
time, some of our neighbors were so discouraged that
they made up their minds to leave, others did leave,
but they have come back and the rest have concluded
to stay, while others are coming."

CHAPTER FIVE

Rebuild and Carry On

In 1855 Bradford was juggling his cattle operation and his financial future to accommodate his upcoming impending nuptials. He decided to drive a cattle herd directly to the market in New Orleans, a risky strategy, but one that allowed him to bypass the buyers in Matagorda and Indianola who had been able to undercut the market because of the 1854 disaster. His plan was to reach New Orleans, sell his cattle and travel to Hartford for his marriage to Maria Louise.

Abel Pierce's responsibilities were increased until he had become Bradford's boss drover, responsible for getting herds to the Point and loaded aboard boats bound for markets. In preparation for an overland cattle drive to New Orleans in 1855, Bradford wrote to Maria Louise's father, Philemon Robbins, and made reference to Abel's responsibilities:

"Matagorda July 28th 1855

I am now about starting my Beeves & from what I can learn this last Gent has been under the same influence as the first—& the probability is that I shall have to take charge of my Beeves myself.

By branding the most of the calves before I leave I should feel satisfied to leave the balance of my fall work with Mr Peirce, a young man from Rhode Island who has been with me about twelve months"

Now on the trail which will end in Connecticut, Bradford writes back to his promised bride about his progress in getting his herd to New Orleans.

"Brazos River Aug 31ˢᵗ '55

Dearest M. Louise

I have a few moments to spend with you again,—nothing is difficult or unpleasant for me to perform when I think that every day brings me twelve or fifteen miles nearer my Dearest Louise—

the weather has been verry bad ever since I commenced collecting my Beeves & still continues,—what would you think Louise to see me traveling along the road tomorrow before a drove of Cattle at the rate of fifteen miles a day through rain & mud,—I expect you would exclaim at once, I have seen enough of Texas Life, if that is a specimen,—I am in hopes however that when I get settled with one of the best of wifes to make a pleasant home— that I shall not take many such trips as this again,—

I crossed the Brazos to day with fine success—tomorrow I expect to cross Buffalo Bayou fifteen miles above Houston—the last of next week I expect to cross the Trinity River from there I shall be about three to four weeks in geting to New Orleans,—so that by reference to the map you can form a tolerable Idea as to my whereabouts,—from day light untill Ten o-clock p.m. at present, I am constantly employed,—

it is now about two o-clock a.m. yes while writing the last line the clock has tolled the silent hour—tonight is the first time I have heard a clock strike since left home ten days since, such however is the fact,—in crossing the River & comeing through the Timber today my Cash containing provisions, Camp equipage, &c has been detained from some unknown cause & the consequence is I am to have the pleasure of eating & sleeping in a house to night & more than all to have the pleasure of saying to my Dearest Louise that I am on the way at last. Providence permitting to receive that hand & heart I have so long wished for & am soon to possess—

Please remember me to Father Mother & family—with one sweet immaginary kiss from my own affianced—I will say good night,—from your affectionate

Would I were with you BG"

Continuing on the drive, Bradford crossed over Buffalo Bayou north of Houston and and wrote back to his mother:

"East Liberty Sept. 7, 1855

Dear Mother,

We are safe over the Trinity River. We have lost only one beef except what Brincklow took back since we started. I think we will hear of that when Able goes to Brincklows. We left Thomas on the Buffalo Bayou 15 miles above Houston. He expected to go back to the Tres-Palacios as soon as he gets well—I told him I had nothing for him to do there before cow driving this fall— that if Able wanted him & he was to come there at that time. Unless you have something for him to do more than I know of, I would not be willing to allow him wages.

I discharged Silvio, the Mexican I hired just as we left home. The next day after we crossed Buffalo Bayou I exchanged him for one I met on the road that is thus far an excellent hand who knows the route to the Mississippi. I do not want Able to hire Silvio if he should come there for work.

Everyone that sees our beeves says that they are as fine a drove as they have seen this year. They all think we shall get into market in a very good time. I hired a young man on the Buffalo Bayou to take Thomas' place. He was going to do stands & everything at the start but he has had to herd the cattle part of three nights & he has seen enough already. Tomorrow he goes back home. I am very well pleased with his going. I expect to get two more hands at Beaumont on the Neches River. We left seven beeves with Lewis Havermacher in Buffalo Bayou that were lame. He is to sell them and deposit the money at Hutchins. I expect to be at the Mississippi River in about 18 to 20 days from this time.

Tell all the folks how d'ye. Tell Able the little fat heifer is looking as fine as ever. Good night it has been raining all the time. I think now it has cleared off for the night. I will now take a nap. My watch at the herd commences at 12 o'clock & lasts until day tomorrow.

*I expect to make an early start and make a long days
drive. You will please write me at New Orleans to the
care of Smith & Bro. 79 Canal Street. I shall probably
not leave there before the 10ᵗʰ of Oct. I shall not be in
the city probably more than 2 or 3 days. As ever your
son,   Wm. B.G."*

Aunt Fanny wrote about operations in general in a
letter that Bradford received when he reached his Hartford
destination.

"Oct, 7 1855

Dear B,

*The Capt went for letters and return'd without one from
you, but we got one from Sis, last evening, he is going
again so you see I am trying to be in time, although it is
an unfavorable time to write, the folks came home from
lower Ranche, last evening, brought part of Sam Patch's
family, the youngerly portion of which they are branding
this morning, don't know how many, this noon they start
for Green Mott, to meet Kuykendalls company, when
they all leave for Turtle Bay, where they camp tonight,
and drive up, and round, and get home Friday night.*

*The weather has been very pleasant, and is, at pres-
ent, I have been to Palacios with the Capt and brought
up good half, and more, of the furniture, the glasses,
sofa, tables, chairs, stove, dittos and sundries, innumerable, besides oysters, and shells, enough to load
the boat three times Capt said, but I kept Patience toting, down, and handing, and he kept stowing, (and telling me, I need not think of carrying half I had got there
now,) untill he got it all in, about noon we started, and
got up to our landing before 9, all snug tied our boat up
to the skiff on the bricks and went home, now he says
he will go with me again for the rest, as soon as he has
finish'd attending to your business"*

A September 1855 letter found Charlotte Grimes at
the Ranch in Texas writing to her daughter Fannie just
then arriving in Connecticut. Both of her children, Bradford
driving cattle to New Orleans and "Sis" in Hartford having

her teeth fixed, plan to meet in Hartford for the marriage of Maria Louise and Bradford. Excerpts from her letter reflect the daily lives of the people on the creek.

"Monday Sept 3-55

Dear Sissy

Yesterday was Sunday, As a matter of course, I must get the news, As good luck seems to predominate just now, It sent me your two letters, one from Gorda & one from New Orleans, also account of your arrival in the newspaper, so you see everything, according to Texas rules comes in heaps.

. . . the Capt hasn't been home since lectionday, he helped two days, when his horse threw him and hurt him a little, so they left him at Palacios, to get well.

. . . Abel has got up a few more calves for B,—which makes 924 branded for B he will probably get one or two hundred more this year. the drove near 300 beeves, over 200 from his and the Capts stock (mostly B—) he says he will have 150 more to sell this fall.

. . . Iris says tell Miss Fannie, Henry sits alone on the floor—he has got to be a very good boy, almost as good as Mary, she can raise herself up in the middle of the room without taking hold of anything, she is full of her monkey shines.

Abel and all hands were picking corn yesterday, they pick'd and got in 160 bush Abel thinks they could get it all in- in three or four days if it ever comes fair weather again I hope to get a letter from you—when Abel comes back

Give love to all the folks especially to aunt B and N and Maria

Your affectionate Mother"

Hiring hands and breaking horses were clearly Abel's business as breaking and gentling a horse to ride was a special talent that few men possessed. Mexicans seemed particularly good at the art of taming wild horses. Abel had found a good one and Fanny Bradford marvels at the Mexican's skill in traveling with his wife and all their worldly possessions on a movable household.

"Octbr 4th 1855

Dear B,

. . . Abel has got a Mexican on trial, Thomas saw him at Haddens, I think he call'd it, and the Mexican asked him for a place. I told him, he might come and see. that was Friday, next Sunday morning he was here baggage, wife, 2 horses, and everything sufficient for housekeeping, none but a Mexican could have begun to put the one half of what he had on a horse, I was somewhat taken aback for certain, but they all said you had been trying to get a man and his wife to stay with you they all thought that you must have one to break your horses, you told Abel, if a Mexican came along that would ride the yellow dun and the Iron gray, to put them on, but not to let Jake ride them at all, that you wanted them gentled for Spring driving and so on . . . and as soon as I told him he might try him, every thing was ready in 15 minutes.

. . . he doesn't know so much about stock, but horses he knows all about, he had them up Monday, . . . caught "yellow dun", and tied him after he had broke 2, or 3, ropes he put on a saddle, and rode him 3 times first day a short time at once, and he says he will be gentle in 3 days, he made the least fuss and noise I ever saw riding a wild horse, he doesn't care what it is in shape of a horse he can ride it, and that is all he professes to know,

. . . he wants $12, a month, 2 lb. coffee, 2 of sugar, 2 peck corn, week, and he will stay one two or three month, and see if you keep him, if you will he stay long as you want him, he wants to get a home for himself and wife where he can stay, they never ask for anything more, . . . all I know about them is they are neat, and still, and mind their own business, he says he is poor, all he has got is his horses and horse trumpery,

we are through with our work in the field, house to finish, horses to gentle, stock to get up and brand is all we have on hand for the rest of the fall, Kuykendall is gone with his last beeves for Foster, and will be ready to begin for himself in about 2 weeks if nothing happens,

we are all well, Jake has had to take medicine a day or two, and Jerry laid up one day, they were half way sick, but are not, and Iris was partly laid up with 2 boils, but has got well, Tom was sick with one slight chill, but he took some blue moss, and got along without the next, and is well as ever.

I believe that is all the business I can think of and it is clearing, so good by,

FB"

In the fall the long awaited wedding was finally a reality. After over six months of travel and romantic longing, Bradford gives us only the barest facts as he heads back to Texas; he was ever a man of business.

"Hartford Decr 19th / 55

Dear Aunt

The important event we have been so long anticipating is at last over the ceremony as you will see by the cards, came off at the Episcopal Church last evening in the presence of an audience of about 2000 persons,—Tomorrow we start for New York we shall spend an evening in N.Y. & leave the following morning for Baltimore, where we shall spend a few days with Louise' Uncle.

We shall probably be at home about the 10th to the 15th of Jany,—I shall send my goods from New York about the 20th inst—to the care of Messrs Baldridge Sparks & Cg Powder Horn,— I hope Mr Lunn & Able will have completed the work laid out for them on the House & that Jerry has finished the work I spoke of in my last

I presume you are progressing as much as is possible under the circumstances,—

I have sent with my goods one parlor Stove & one dining room dt,—I have 16 feet of pipe for each Stove—so that it can be put up through the floor into the chimney up stairs,—I have shiped with my Goods Maria's furniture for our Room besides a Book case & Piano for the Parlor,—I shall also send one Bbl Potatoes & one Bbl Apples—shall probably be at Powder Horn in time to settle for the freight,—I think it will be necessary to have quite a large Boat to get our goods home, without letting them get wet by rains or saltwater,—my Goods are to go by the way of Galveston & Steamer from there to Powder Horn—

Enclosed I send you a sample of the cards, we sent out about 300 hundred invitations I also send Able an invitation to welcome us home,—remember us to him & all the folks,—I send you this evening's times paper containing a notice of a certain marriage in this city last evening

*Your affectionate Son
Wm B. Grimes"*

William Bradford Grimes, Founder of the WBG, and his wife Maria Louise Robbins Grimes of Hartford, Connecticut.

Fannie remained in Connecticut after the wedding and is enjoying the sophisticated social, cultural and spiritual stimulus she had done without in Texas. She will spend almost two years away from Texas, expanding her horizons and intellectual talents. In this rare letter from her father, she hears news from Matagorda Bay of her horse "Kitty Clover," his horse "Parrot," dying livestock from the drought and what her brother and Pierce are doing. The Captain writes phonetically and his letter has been edited for clarity:

"Powder Horn April the 15   1856

Dear Frances

I came down here today with Garnet in Mrs Ward's Skip Boat & will return to night I write you to let you & all there know that our & other Cattle have stop dying and appear to do well. The grass is good and there are a good many calves in the prairie. Bradford has commenced driving the West side of the Trespalacios and will commence the East side of the Trespalacios next week. There are a good many calves

Kitty is in fine order and retains all her quick and good action but it is by my taking good care of her & old Parrot. I have rode one or the other every day all this winter & spring Bradford & Pierce said if they could not live without care they had better let them die and Bradford has lost at least half of his horses. But Bradford left all in charge with Pierce & what I said was no don't. So they had to gather horses they will see that survive.

I have got the last hides I hope this year as well. The cattle look well and appear to do well. I will inclose you a ten Dollar Bill on South Carolina as I can get no other it will be at a discount at the North of ½ or a percent I got this for my hides and many other thing for the Ranch & my self

Mr Foster is buying beef cattle and he has been to see Bradford but has not bought his beeves as he is paying but $12 dollars. When we sell our beeves we will send you some money enough to bring all back to Texas all in a hurry give my compliments to all

Your Affectionate Father
Rich Grimes"

Maria Louise and Bradford had much to accomplish and as they settled into their first year of marriage their first son Bradford Robbins was born on October 26th, 1856. Sadly the baby died soon thereafter but a second son, given the same name, would be born in September of the following year and would grow to manhood in the rich tradition of a cattleman.

CHAPTER SIX

Fannie's Diaries

F annie remained in Connecticut after her brother's wedding in December. With her dental ordeals behind her she enjoyed the sophisticated social, cultural and spiritual stimulus she had done without and would spend almost two years away from Texas, expanding her horizons and intellectual talents. Fannie was in Hartford much of the time or in New Britain with her Bulkley cousins at the "State Normal School." The plan was to return to Texas in the summer or fall but in the end she spent the entire winter in Connecticut. She began her diary upon her return in May shortly after her 22nd birthday. Ahead are portions of Fannie's diaries from 1857 through 1861 capturing life on an early Texas ranch before the Civil War.

At the headquarters, Bradford added a ranch store, an employee mess hall, cook shack and single men's quarters in a separate building off of the main house kitchen. Fannie was becoming a skillful seamstress like her mother and the women of the Grimes household, made clothing and flat goods for the store. Fine dresses of the latest fashions were a necessity in Matagorda social life and Fannie was a popular addition to all the balls and parties and, as Bradford's sister, she was an attraction wherever she went. Much of her leisure time was spent riding horseback, visiting friends up and down the "Creek" and spreading her independent wings.

Away from the society and pleasantries of Matagorda, Fannie's 1857 diary describes disease, drought, illness and injuries caused by the hard and dangerous ranch work that made death omnipresent and survival itself a part of everyday life. She writes about the families living near the WBG Ranch. Within the circle of social contacts were the families of Wards, Kuykendalls, Rowells, Demings, Wheelers,

Lunns, Moores, Duffys, Partains, Laceys, Downers, Dawdys and Robbins. Fannie recorded travel, church meetings, social gatherings, her friendship with Abel Pierce, and the birth of her nephew, Bradford R. Grimes.

Her first entry describes a trip with the Captain on horseback to the family's original, storm-damaged home on the Point. They were still able to operate from time to time in what was left. The original dwelling was constructed when the family first arrived in 1838 and was where they lived until wreckage from the storm forced them to move permanently to higher ground on the banks of the Trespalacios River.

"May 19ᵗʰ, Palacios, Tuesday

Time has rolled on and at 22 years and one day of age I find myself once more on the desolate shell beach I've so long called my "home". After a day of what, to anyone but I, would have been called perilous adventures, I arrived to find that in preparing our provisions I had omitted a very necessary article, meat, which occasioned some little disturbance; but, soon all was right and I prepared myself for the first night in my camp home. This morning starting from home, we rode six miles to Downer's. There crossing, we changed horses, I riding one which never had a lady on it before; and, putting the pack on Kittie in order to favor her all I could, we arrived at the bayou and dismounted again. Father took the pack on his shoulder and I on Kittie, mounted on top of the pack saddle, made our way over the bayou. Father then went back again for my saddle; so much for Texas traveling."

"May 20ᵗʰ, Palacios, Wednesday

A busy day, sweeping down cobwebs burning mice eaten books and papers, washing dishes, and cooking. Father went fishing but got nothing but some oysters which we dined upon dressed out in various ways. In the evening rode over to Captain Ward's place where we spent some little time, rode home again and passed a second night"

When this was written Texas was in the grip of the severe drought of 1856 which accounts for the dry, scorched conditions she describes.

"This is a most abominable place I am sure and I'm thankful that so much good resulted from the disastrous hurricane of '54 as the blowing of my self off from here never to return as long as I can get shelter elsewhere. The river is silent enough but it's a paradise to this, a vast barren desert of prairie, scorched and dry, no vestige of life save of cattle nightly penned, and those almost eaten up by the flies, a sweet delightful situation for a fun loving damsel. Well, I have existed seven years here."

Later that month Fannie relates traveling on horseback with her good friend Mary Rowell who was also single and living with her tyrannical father on a ranch a few miles away on the Colorado River. Mary was urging Fannie to push on to her house or *"Pa will be so mad if we don't get home."*

"May 29th, Palacios, Friday

. . . Whilst I went over home after a package, the horses stampeded and left us all standing. I rode my horse some 3 miles after them but to no purpose as the Colorado horses took to the bayou. Mr. Gannett managed to head them off about 4 miles up and brought them home. After looking until 5 o'clock for the runaways, we started at Mary Rowell's urgent request to get on to the Colorado. But, we were unwise and I knew it at the time . . . the night overtook us, and I finally persuaded them to turn back to Palacios Point. Mrs. Ward received us pleasantly and said she was glad to have us come again and was very cordial. How different from how others would have responded at such a difficult time in a different land. I plan, if ever I have a house to call my own, to make all welcome from the meanest to the greatest of God's creatures."

The next morning Fannie and Mary were anxious to get started. The girls knew the horses that ran off would return rider-less to their home corrals on the Rowell ranch and Mary didn't know what to expect from her irascible father.

"May 30th

After an early breakfast, we started out on horseback with Mr. Gannett along with us. We had a rain shower to refresh us a few moments after, and on we came slowly. Part way I rode my old paint horse, Kittie, but she appeared too tired to be carrying me. When we got half way, Bill Rowell met us with two of those horses that ran away yesterday. Wearily, we dragged on through another rain shower ere we got here on the Colorado; the rain was quite heavy. When we got here, the Colonel was mad and felt it necessary to blame everything and everybody because the horses got away; he made himself generally disagreeable and everyone uncomfortable . . . . We would have gone on this evening and I'm very sorry we could not; but, the Colonel would not let Mary go, and the horses were badly rode down. Mr. Herndon agreed to furnish us horses but the Colonel would have none but his own."

"June 11th, Matagorda Bay

In preparing myself for the jaunt from home to Matagorda, I find that my horse was not in a condition to ride and I tried to get Bill Nye's horse but 'twas no go and Fred didn't see fit to volunteer one of his. When we got up to Colonel Rowell's place, Mary was going to let me have one of his, but it had a sore back. We then decided to take the buggy and start off in that, and did. We got about four miles and found one wheel almost off and another the next thing to it, so we returned and gave up for the night. . . . Mr. Gannett came back this morning with a horse for me named Naro. The Colonel went to town yesterday or we might likely have got a horse from him but now, thanks to Mr. Gannett, we are within ten miles of the City of Palacios."

Fannie had learned from someone that her favorite horse, "Kitty" lay dead in the shore waters of the Colorado River. Now without her usual means of traveling and socializing she laments the fact that she must now find a new mount.

"How I did wish yesterday, as I rode along to the Colonel's from our ranch, that I had someone at home to depend on. Lonely indeed it seemed as I bemoaned the

loss of my favorite horse, Kitty. Well, if she died, I cannot help it. Maybe I will also find some kind friends to help me to find a horse."

June 30th, Palacios Point (loss of her favorite horse)

". . . I have this morning selected the coolest spot I can find which is still unpleasantly warm and now proceed to chronicle what I have fancied might be defined—the Death of my only Horse, my darling "Kittie Clover". I did not see her die so that I hardly realize she's dead; but, I know beyond a doubt that she now lies in the Colorado. She has been a faithful beast for 5 long years and much hard work has she done; too much by far for her years and strength and for this reason I can part with her better. I know she will be beaten and savagely used no more; and, altho' I'm on foot now, I am almost glad for her sake. How well she loved me. I most regret now that I did not treat her better and yet my conscience does not tell me but I did the best was in my power for her. It was not all I wished to be sure, but she's beyond the reach of hard treatment or malice now. . . . Her poor little legs won't ache with running after cows any more. No more will she act fearful where there is no danger nor will I be in agony at her harmless antics; and, I shall be at peace as regards 'My Horse'."

It was evident to Fannie that her favorite horse had been used by the cowhands in rounding up and driving cattle and, in her opinion badly mistreated.

"I've seen, ever since that last cow drive she took without having been fed, that she was not long for me to ride; but, I had hoped she'd die at Home. However, as she's now beyond my reach, I'll be content to let her remain so, whereas had my wishes been granted there would have been another fuss about the hide, or something else, which no one should have had for anything short of a case of Life and Death. This depriving me of the means of leaving Home may be as a punishment for being so much absent from there; but, I don't think so and therefore and I'll not take it as such. Most likely, as has been the case some kind friends will be found who will think my company worth the time and trouble

necessary to obtain it and will help me find a mount. And so adieu to the subject, and to "Kittie Clover" as she'll never answer to my call again so she'll never feel the spur or whip, nor struggle over weary miles, and I'll never be put at farther away ever on her account."

"July 20th, Rio Trespalacios

I have several horses which are gentle enough for me to ride but rather too wild for most ladies. I am very fortunate in having been extended the opportunity to change horses; and, for the most part, it has been pretty easy going but, of course, none of them can equal Kittie. I will never find one that will."

In August Fannie writes about a trip to Texana, one of the early settlements to the west on the Navidad River. She is traveling in a buggie with her brother Bradford on a horse buying expedition:

"Supper over, we once more started for Mr. Davenport's plantation on the Lavaca River about seven miles distant. We had a most delightful ride by moonlight; only the cracks from the drought made it rather dangerous traveling. I feel pretty tired having traveled a full forty miles today and not very well either. Such horrid roads as we have in Texas or rather no roads at all, for when we do get on to a beaten path, with this dry weather 'tis very good traveling but 'tis most of the way over prairie ground without even a trail."

In September Fannie is back on the Colorado River with her friend Mary Rowell and departing from the Rowell ranch for the WBG. She is riding on a horse named Dacron and describes herself as an accomplished horsewoman.

"September 19th, Rio Colorado

We left Col. Rowells soon after sunrise, mounted our Nags which were not in the best humour and were not long in making the five miles which separate Messrs. Robbins and Brother, but I tho't good friend "Dacron" would trot me to a Jellie; how I do hate to ride a trotting horse but I'll get used to it sometime for I've not the slight-

est idea of giving up horseback exercise. I've got a name now thro'out the country where I'm known and many places where personally I'm a stranger, for being a 'good rider', 'an excellent horse woman', and I intend to keep it. I didn't think when I first commenced riding that I'd ever excel. My highest aim then was to ride so well that I'd not be an object of ridicule, and, so far I've exceeded my mark as to be a pattern. Good! I don't intend to lose ground if practice will improve, nor do I intend to be so much elated by a little praise as to glory in my achievement; but if the time shall come, when others than those who have already remarked shall say I'm the 'best rider for a lady they ever saw.' Aye, I think I can equal some."

Again in September in the city of Matagorda:

". . . I had previously a delightful ride on the Parson's horse, got up by daylight and started by sunrise with Mrs. Hillard. We had a little gallop of two or three miles and an appetite for breakfast, notwithstanding an unintentional attempt of mine to knock my brains out against the eaves of a food trough roof, which gave me a black eye and some little inconvenience, to say nothing of the vast amount of loss to my personal beauty in the retirement behind a bandage of one of these 'hazel eyes'. How excruciating, but I survived it all."

"September 24th

Yesterday morning Chloe, Frank and myself started in a bracing north wind from our present location, bidding adieu to the kind friends we 'left behind us'. We sped on our way rejoicing in the morning air and the freshness of our nags and presently we were at Col. Rowells. A light fire graced the Hearth very forcibly reminding us of the Winter which is close at hand. Miss Mary and Miss Susan Stanly who was visiting her were both slightly troubled with cold as was the Colonel and all our party."

It can be surmised from this entry that the Colonel was a heavy drinker as she described him as ill-tempered and hard on Mary. When Fannie relates that the Colonel had "been to town," she obviously means that he had been into the spirits.

"The Colonel 'had been to town' which would have been enough to confine him to his room without the change in the atmosphere. Alas! that those few words should have so deep a meaning, how many hearts have ached at their sound. A short stay during which I collected my scattered wardrobe which by the kindness of friends among the servants (I find them wherever I go) made ready for my coming, and we were once more on the road. Time and space were soon annihilated and we stood on the banks of our narrow, turbid stream, which, in moments of dignity, we term 'river' and at other times hail as 'creek'. A little time to cross and exchange news with our neighbor and we tracked our well known way thro' the rough tangled pathway of 'Bottom' which hinders our sight of our fellow mortals or at least the 'Dens' in which they exist. 3 o'clock found us comfortably ensconced in the Parlour and a few moments later we were veritable examples of the fact that 'man earning his bread by the sweat of his brow' (or his horse either) has a relish for it having dispatched the comforts necessary to the 'inner man'."

Throughout the summer and fall, Fannie wrote periodically of the dry conditions as they were enduring the severe drought that began in 1856.

*"June 11*th

What a great country this Texas is. Here on the beach in the shade of a little scrub tree, I may record my thoughts about as much as I like about Texas; but, as I don't like too much, I will write in shorthand."

Also in June:

"Oh! I reckon I will do for Texas, being in the boiling heat on the beach, was not altogether agreeable so I stretched my riding skirt on the surveyor's stake and some bushes. I then lay down on the shells under the shade of my riding skirt and presently in dreams. I was with Thee. How good the cistern water did taste when I got here and does yet; but an all day's ride of 20 miles is what makes it taste so fine . . . I'm going to improve my many hours on this Robinson Crusoe retreat where we are

afraid to stay much longer less the horses starve. There is no grass here nor any signs of vegetation more than there would be in Winter; as we have such a drought as does not often visit, even in our variable climate. We may well petition a merciful providence to here make remembrance of our parched earth. For surely, unless rain comes soon, we will have no need of the comet to burn us; Sol can do his work. Another week has passed and few pass in one's lifetime less free from care. I move peacefully and this dull, lonesome place affords me for a short time, negative pleasure as I enjoy myself from the very fact there is nothing to disturb."

July, from her makeshift camp on Palacios Point

"I want to be home again for a while. Summer is certainly here now with its full power and the rains being so few, I fear our crops will be miserable. Starvation has threatened the upper counties of our state for some months; and, should the drought continue, I fear their suffering must be great."

July from Rio Trespalacios

"'Tis the night of another Sabbath, a clear, beautiful day after two days of most refreshing and reviving rain; and, one on which we need to be unusually thankful for the abundant blessings bestowed."

October:

"Didn't it rain canine and feline quadrupeds. . ."

Fannie recalls that over the past three years many of her friends have died and been buried in this small church yard, another reminder of the high rates of mortality in this frontier community.

"June 6th, Trespalacios River

Once more in my life on the Sabbath day I've frequented the House of God. On the Last Sabbath I was here how different the scene as 'twas winter but our genial clime made all the natives appear in their summer garb and

*I, with light heart and lighter head, wended my way
reverently to the House set apart for prayer & praise.
Friends long loved, walked kindly by my side. Alas!
where are they now I ask of the simple board with
painted letters; which, in our rockless country, marks
their resting place, the last, the only resting place of
earth's toil worn children and the saddened hearts of
friends who now walk alone. There only are found the
records of 'the loved, the lost', those who have trodden
before us 'the path thro' the valley of the dark shad-
ow of Death'; who perhaps have lighted us on by their
cheerful obedience of the dread summons. Ah! how
many in those three years since I have walked here in
'the courts of the Lord' have gone to receive the reward
of their Faith . . ."*

Death and illness in the brief six-month period of her
diary included the plight of the Robbins family. Chloe and
Chester are still residing with their infant children in a camp-
like structure and "Tadmor" is still under construction.

"June 7, Colorado River

*Ah! me . . . the last 2 days have passed wearily. Poor
Chloe has such a hard time resting neither night or day.
If I should fall ill, I don't believe I could remain there a
week as all the discomforts so easily accumulated in
Texas are about her house. No servant, Dorcas having gone to her reward, with two twin babies and the
help of only one little ebony. fleas, mosquitoes, gnats,
a close and crowded room, how does she live? I cannot
see and I do not know that I ought to stay there when
'tis attended with such vast discomfort to me. Greater
by far I presume, than for her. I'm afraid I'm selfish, . .
. One thing is certain, I'll never voluntarily place myself
where circumstances can so situate me; no indeed! I
won't. Trials the like to beset me would drive me crazy
as patience and fortitude would be attributes unknown
to all who should come in contact with me. Aye! full and
well I know that much of myself, and I'll endeavor to let
well enough alone."*

Fannie referred to slaves as "darkies" or "ebonies" and
wrote that she would often read aloud to them, encourag-

ing them to attend Sunday school and church services and may or may not have had much patience with them.

"June 16ᵗʰ, Colorado River (Robbins home)

. . . I am thankful enough for one thing and that is, that I'm not Chloe. Heaven defend us! If I thought my future could be like her present, I do believe I'd be tempted to put an end to me. I've taken the young ebony under my especial charge for the nights and 'such nights'; she's going to have plenty of them. Well there is nothing so bad but it might be worse."

"June 28ᵗʰ, Palacios Point

. . . Chloe is sick I hear and perhaps will need my services. The little ebony which has caused her so much trouble is dead, which I think is quite a Godsend; at least I'd call it such I think. She has still as much care and trouble as I'd want, and some more. Oh, the day is so warm, I don't feel like sewing. I believe as I've nothing but fancy work to do, I'll read."

Back at Palacios Point in late June, and alone, Fannie is confronted with the sudden illness of her neighbor, the widow Ward. Captain Grimes and Captain Ward, long-time friends and neighbors and fellow ship captains had much in common. Captain Ward's widow is now living in a house that survived the storm near the partially restored Grimes home.

"June 28ᵗʰ, Palacios Point, at the widow Ward's home and last night, as I watched her suffering the most excruciating pain. I thought that she, who had watched the last breath come and go in so many dear hearts, was about to die in the arms of one but a short time since a stranger. Alone I watched her sufferings and, inexperienced as I am, I could do little to alleviate them. The two negroes, one of them an imbecile and worse than useless and the other, a mere child, could offer no assistance. It was a fearful hour in which, not knowing what to do, I supported her thro' two fits and then she fainted. How in that moment I wished for the skill of a doctor or help from the all powerful."

The Captain is off in his brig trading across the Bay at Indianola, Matagorda or elsewhere in the area and Fannie had been left alone and not prepared for the situation she encountered.

"I only asked for strength and guidance. I trembled as I thought that I, who had never seen the dread messenger at his work, must witness it anew, dependant on no one, but depended on by all. Truly then I felt the need of aid and my mind wandered to those who could give it but none were within reach for near 20 miles. No human being exists save those beneath this roof, but I was spared all further trial except the fear of her passage."

In all of Matagorda County there were only eight doctors, most of whom were at Matagorda or further to the East. Dr. Pilkington was the closest and he was miles away with no one to send for him. After Mrs. Ward survives and the Captain returns from his trading, Fannie finds more trouble back at the WBG in the form of injury to one of the hands.

"July 4ᵗʰ, Rio Trespalacios

When I got home last night, I don't know if I had anything to celebrate the Fourth . . . quite great doings have transpired since left home . . . I find poor Jake stretched out as his horse hurt him some two weeks ago and since then he's not been able to get about. His injury is probably due to the fact that the poor fellow does not measure up to the others who have the skill of riding all manner of horses."

Jake and Patience appear with several others in an early photo of the WBG ranch house. When Patience died in September of 1869, she was laid to rest in the Grimes family cemetery and her marble marker bears the inscription, *"Faithful Servant to the Grimes Family for 22 Years."* In his book *Shanghai Pierce, A Fair Likeness*, Chris Emmett's story refers to this same Jake as the slave severely injured trying to break a horse.

Settlers were constantly on the lookout for rattlesnakes, scorpions and other dangerous creatures. Fannie records a dangerous encounter in her bedroom:

"August 7th, Rio Trespalacios

*I feel I ought to chronicle the fact that I have today es-
pecial cause for gratitude in that I have been preserved
from immediate danger. This morning when I arose, I
found secreted in my clothes a centipede and only acci-
dentally or providentially, as the case should be stated,
dislodged it. Had it remained thus, a bite must have
been the consequence so far as I can see, and for the
poison of the centipede there is no known remedy. I am
not fit to die; and, while Mother lives, I'm needed here
and am sufficiently thankful that my unprofitable life
is spared a while longer. I am thankful that I live and
possess health, that I'm able to contribute, tho' slightly,
to Mother's comfort; and, that in some small degree, I
may return the debt I owe her. The care bestowed on
me in childhood may be in some slight degree repaid,
slight indeed tho' it is. Well I'll do my endeavors."*

In September, Fannie wrote again about the dangerous job of breaking and riding wild horses when she recorded an accident so serious it could take the life of one of
the ranch hands.

"September, Rio Trespalacios

*This morning Peter came home to tell us that Charly, the
Mexican, had been thrown and dragged some distance,
very much injuring him. Brother has gone down in the
buggie after him as he is down river at Johnson's timber
. . . Charly has got home now and there is quite a consultation going on as to the probability of mortification. Poor
fellow, he has friends somewhere I suppose, but if he
dies now, 'twill be in a strange land and stranger hands
will perform the last sad offices. All we can do now is to
soothe his pain as best we may and save his life, if possible. I have been preparing a room for him this evening."*

In late August, as Fannie is returning with her brother
on the buggie trip to Texana. Bradford had been shopping
for horses on ranches on the Navidad River. This was an
area where immigrants from Germany were arriving con-
tinuously and moving inland to Victoria, New Braunfels
and Fredricksburg. They were trailing a horse Bradford

had purchased and returned home to find more illness. With this entry she makes reference to Abel Pierce.

"September 2nd, Rio Trespalacios:

. . . I find on getting home that there is lots of trouble in this world that doesn't arise from inconvenience of traveling. Half of the darkies are grumbling and Mrs. Lunn is sick with chills and fever; and, Abel too, who I thought was well, has been across this week but I haven't heard since Monday how he is. The poor fellow must have a hard time with no one to take care of him, but Aunt Viny—wish he was here to be cured up again."

September found Fannie writing about the latest tragedy, the death of Chloe's twins, Mary and Chetty. Since Chester Robbins is related to Bradford's wife Maria Louise, they are family.

"September 4th, Rio Trespalacios

There is a land of pure delight
Where saints immortal reign
Eternal day excludes the night
And pleasures banish pain"

. . . the pure and innocent, the eviless infants are <u>sure</u> of that 'pure delight', and one of Chloe's has gone to its overpowering 'pleasures'. 'Little Mary,' has gone to him who saith 'suffer little children to come unto me and forbid them not.' Since Monday last she has been an angel and behind her is left the aching heart, the sinful soul, which would fain call her back, to sin and sorrow, to the trials & temptations which so finely encompass every child of earth."

Death, taking so many of her acquaintances, was ever on Fannie's mind and in just this short span she recorded the loss of so many, so often.

"Death seems to have put in his sickle and is reaping among those who are dear to me. 'Tis but lately that his strokes have affected me; but now lately, Death has taken a kind uncle, a dear schoolmate and the little one to

whom I had become so attached. Ah! I may well be thank-ful he comes no nearer, and do I deserve such kindness?"

With this entry Chloe had now lost the second of her twins, bringing the total loss of all three of her infant children.

"September 5ᵗʰ, Rio Trespalacios

Peter tells us that Chloe has been doubly bereaved. Lit-tle Chetty has followed his sisters to their glorious home and the childless girl is alone. She has been the Moth-er of three children, but is nearly two years younger than I. How much I pity her . . . Truly, 'misfortune never comes singly'. When will the news of trouble cease? I'm getting quite fidgety over it."

"September 14ᵗʰ, Rio Colorado

I came down Saturday, it was very cool and pleasant traveling. It being cloudy all the time, rained hard I be-lieve on all sides of us, but no one overtook us, arrived here about 3 o'clock. After dinner and a watermelon,, Mary and I rode down to see Chloe, but she and Chester seemed so lonely it would make one's heart ache to wit-ness their sufferings, here is <u>distress</u>, real and unmis-takable, and I fear they have <u>no</u> consolation for it . . ."

"September 17ᵗʰ, Rio Trespalacios

Tuesday we, that is Mary and I, drove down to Chloe's directly after breakfast and assisted her some little on a quilt. I intend to go again tomorrow. We had a good time down at Chloe's. It seemed by common consent agreed to lay aside all unpleasant thoughts and enjoy all there was to enjoy which is the only way ever to find pleasure here below, but I must not indulge in a hom-ily of sober reflections as I feel strongly inclined to do, must go and dress for dinner. Col Thorpe is expected up to dinner and 'twill never do for me to present my di-shevelled locks at the dinner table, tho' he being a man of impeccable taste I doubt very much whether he could tell before the discussion of that meal whether I had a head much less one with hair on it; so mote it be. What a delightfull breeze, how much to be thankful for."

Fannie's views of the local gentry make it obvious that she would prefer to remain single rather than settle for the overconfident, uneducated and immoral men she has found around her. Her high standards and her brother's position as the largest cattleman in the community limited the suitors she could take seriously. It appears that was the view her mother shared with regard to many of their unpolished neighbors. Fannie records some of her observations with respect of those in attendance at Sunday church services.

The Rev. Robert Paine Thompson was, in 1857, a circuit riding Methodist Minister, and was traveling through the county. Portions of the Reverend's diary reprinted in *Historic Matagorda County, Vol. 1*, mention his being at the Grimes Ranch on October 25th. He was only 25 years old at the time. Fannie makes numerous references to the young minister and was obviously influenced by his presence. There was no Methodist Church nearby and most of the locals attended services at the Baptist Church at Deming's bridge where the Rev. Thompson arrived on May 31st, 1857. When he comes to preach at Deming's Bridge, his request to use the sanctuary of the church was rejected by the new Baptist Minister, Mr. Hanie:

"We arrived at the house of worship at 11.00 to find everything in a state of anarchy and confusion. Mr. Hanie, the new Baptist Minister, in order to kick up the mess, refused to permit the rites of the Methodist church to be performed in the exclusive sanctuary, so, in the afternoon, amid the bans of his former congregation the Baptists, Mr. Thompson with his colleague, Mr. Foote, retired to a large Live Oak close by and there gave the best sermon I've listened to in some time; how well he looked when, as in simple dignity, he stepped forward to appoint a meeting elsewhere and make his new but pointed remarks. How much I felt like throwing my hat around my head and giving three times three when someone near the door cried "Hurrah" at the close of his very brief address; so much more eloquent than a long labored speech, it was just what best suited his hearers."

"June 1st, Rio Trespalacios

Contrary to expectations our meeting continued today. The disturbance, in some measure, abated tho' the Reverend Mr. Hanie still refuses the Methodists a showing;

but, he might as well keep quiet, for if he makes much trouble his congregation will either turn him out or leave themselves as they do not like his proceedings at all. Mr. Thompson, without an effort, carries the day. How much I do like Mr. Foote; he preached for us yesterday in our natural sanctuary of leafy green, and fixed the attention of his hearers decidedly."

In early June, the dust-up between the Methodists and the Baptists was subsiding and Rev. Thompson was a guest in the Grimes home. The ranch was a frequent refuge for travelers, many of whom were doing business selling cattle, or with whom the Captain was trading for goods to be shipped to New Orleans markets. Also, the practice of providing lodging and shelter was an early Texas tradition.

"June 2nd, Rio Trespalacios

I saw lots of folks at church whom I haven't seen in some time and some I don't care five cents if I never see; among them was Mrs. Deming who is rather frigid to me, of late. Bob and Henry were there too and made themselves quite agreeable, as do all the gallants of the day, always. Ah me! How overcoming to be the 'biggest Toad in the Puddle', to be the only half educated, half civilized young or otherwise unmarried, lady in the crowd."

"June 30th, Rio Trespalacios

How I do admire a native which delights in having bad news to relate and can scarcely wait for a chance to tell it. I always fancy it would be fine living with such and presume they could always find something with which to annoy those around them."

Most of the earliest immigrants to Austin's colony had come from the New England states, but a great many that followed were from the Old South and southern in their culture. Immigrants from Georgia and Mississippi transferred easily to the plantation life in Texas and along with them came the Louisiana sugar planters. A large contingent came from Tennessee and at one social gathering, Fannie recorded her impressions of a man coming from Tennessee looking for land.

"July 5ᵗʰ, Rio Trespalacios

Miss Fannie Lacey had a sort of an attendant in the person of Mr Brown from Tennessee who is looking thro' Texas for a location. I was not introduced to him which pleases me considerably as I've more acquaintance of his stamp than I want. Bob and Henry Hasbrook were there and made themselves very agreeable, of course, as well as Ed Deming, his wife and old Dr Pilkington, together with some few others some of whom please me and some of whom I particularly dislike . . . well, so goes the world . . . I put on the same face to all, and sometimes I enjoy their company and some times I'm amused to think how I ridicule them."

"July 21ˢᵗ, Rio Trespalacios

I'm very plebian in all my notions, as might be expected of one whose only cultivation is drawn from nature around, and whose only guide to gentility is one given by nature's God. 'As ye would that men should do to you, do ye even so to them.' This little rule always applied when my too cross nature does not hinder and is the only gauge I have of etiquette . . . Well, there is no accounting for the innate vulgarity of some folks. Nor their <u>disinterested kindnesses</u> either."

Fannie's mother Charlotte had always emphasized the importance of maintaining a certain station in life which meant not associating with the lower rung and keeping one's distance from the ill-mannered or the ill-bred and an even greater distance from uncouth riff-raff.

"August 7ᵗʰ, Rio Trespalacios

I must have charity for them too; the poor, illiterate, but good so far as they know how to be. Of course any one with knowledge of the world and of books must extend a mighty influence."

Opinions about the locals extended to itinerant preachers and she has decided that not all of them were well intentioned.

"I hope it may be for good but I fear that the result of last Saturday and Sundays sermons will not be all I could wish. Mr. Hanie is very canny in his remarks. He reads well the characters of those with whom he has to deal, and he will slowly but surely undermine the friendliness existing in our neighborhood. I would not like to believe all the evil I hear of him and yet my own heart never yet played me false; and, from the first moment I saw him, it turned from him; however, I will not judge him . . . he may be mistaken, but sincere."

The WBG home was open to most and due to the Captain's continuous trading there were an ever increasing number of guests. The homestead seemed to have been at the crossroads of travel from both directions. Indianola, directly across the Bay from Palacios Point, now had hotels, stores, warehouses and merchandise of every kind brought in to serve its growing seaport population. In addition to its long wharfs, a new rail line to Victoria was bringing more commerce. As a consequence both the Captain and Bradford were constantly trading at the port and inviting people of all stripes to the ranch.

"August 19ᵗʰ, Rio Trespalacios

I must treat every one that comes to the House well. I find not many whose company affords one much pleasure and the common pebble has become a gem. What a wonder worker is education and how mistaken a notion for those without it to endeavor to find pleasure with those who are blessed or <u>cursed with</u> it; I find myself <u>unable to determine</u> which 'tis. Tonight, with those on our own level, affords the truest pleasure. To strive to rise higher in the social scale than our education has fitted us for, is to gratify pride at the sacrifice of every other feeling. To sink lower than our level is to endure a spirit ill at ease or to be on a continual strain to appear pleased when we're only bored; it makes ourselves and others genuinely uncomfortable."

Once again Fannie lamented the burden of having to feed and exchange pleasantries with strangers with whom she would not otherwise associate.

"We had company last night, and I felt sorry for them as, they were evidently far from comfortable. They were emphatically 'in the wrong box', and I cannot blame them if they do not like to come here, neither if they call me 'proud' because I do not visit them. Really 'tis very dry business, except I go with other and more agreeable company and my powers of entertainment are too limited to fit one for other than a certain, defined, sphere."

The following entry indicates Fannie has run afoul of some person or persons who have wounded her deeply and the thoughts related in her diary are unforgiving.

"October 1ˢᵗ, Rio Trespalacios

I did resolve that I'd be still more circumspect in the governance of my tongue and injure neither enemies nor friends by indiscreet or malicious speeches. Some time since I've laid the practice of repeating ill reports, aside, and of listening to them too in a great measure and now I'll try still to think or say no evil of my neighbors. I don't know that I can <u>Love</u> my enemy yet, tho' I know not why as there is in my heart <u>hatred</u> for any mortal here or gone before, tho' those have existed whom I hated with a most cordial abomination and those now exist whom I pray heaven I may never see again until I meet them when this mortal shall put on immortality and be freed from carnal passions."

Another October entry recounted the cooking, baking and life in general around a country kitchen and also made it seem she was somewhat smitten with young Reverend Thompson.

"October 28ᵗʰ, Rio Trespalacios

Brother went down to court Monday of last week, and the cattle drivers all went to Herndon's ranch so, of course, peace and quietness resumed their sway. I was right in the middle of baking Thursday morning, my sleeves above my elbows, dress richly brocaded with flour and grease, vibrating between the kitchen and the nursery (when I'm in my small consideration, I weigh near 100), when the cry was 'Mr. Thompson's coming'. I ran of course, but 'twas for the parlour door where I greeted the Parson as demurely as tho' I had on a collar and had just smoothed the wrinkles out of my new black silk apron and my hair. Fortune favored me and Auntie and sister (her Aunt Fanny and her sister-in-law, Maria Louise) were both able to grace the 'salon' with their presence. Time passed quickly and so did the baking, leaving the 'cake' pretty much 'all dough.'"

In the diary entry below, Fannie was once again confronted with the sudden death of her brother's business associate and neighbor. The Partains were early Austin colonists and held a large grant of land across the river and upstream. She mused dramatically on her certainty of the rewards in the life hereafter for the worthy:

"Sabbath morning Chloe and I set off alone, save the ebonies, for church at the river and were met by Mr. Thompson and Mrs. Lunn, with whom we rode up to church. On the road we met Abel, Mr. Green and some others who shocked us with the tidings of John Partain's death. Its been scarcely a week since he left us in perfect health . . . now his body lies cold and stiff beneath the valley sod . . . the husband, son, and brother, who but a few days since were with him in business, has gone to receive the 'crown of Glory' for I fully believe he will receive the reward of faith. God help the widowed mother who, in her grey haired loneliness, has listened twice to the dismal sound of the earth clods settling on the coffin lid beneath which lay the mortal remains which she had looked to as the support of her declining years."

It was obvious that Fannie and Abel are close friends when he appears in her diary in July, he has taken a job as foreman on another ranch.

"July 12th, Rio Trespalacios

Abel came over this morning and spent the day and went down to Sabbath school with me and has now gone to Cash's Creek, La me! I have not chronicled his departure from our family and his installment as the new Master of Ceremonies at the ranch of Major

Herndon in place of Wm. H. who resigned. But, such is the case nevertheless; and, for one year now, the gentleman is 'his own master' in a measure. . . . In Texas, Sunday is the favored day for trading, visiting and business, generally."

"August 7ʰ, Rio Trespalacios

Last Sunday I went up to Sabbath school. Abel went with me, and the Sabbath before that, but as I had many duties to perform, I was late."

"August 19ᵗʰ

Abel was over Wednesday, Thursday and Sunday. He went to Sabbath school and stopped all night with us. We have had company every day for the last two weeks."

The entries above made it clear that Abel Pierce was welcome at Grimes' ranch when she wrote "*he stopped all night with us.*" Abel had his own cattle now and is beginning to branch out on his own. Her reference to his being far from home reveals her concern and sympathy for this single, lonely young man with his only kin-folk living in far away Rhode Island.

"On August 30ᵗʰ

Abel brought my trunk over from his house where it has been for a week or so, having brought it over from Colonel Rowells, but the poor fellow was taken sick and stayed with us until this afternoon. I feel so sorry for him. Alone, so far from kindred and home in this God forsaken, heathen land, with no one to care if he lives or dies. 'Tis a hard case. Auntie doctored him and I hope he will soon be better. I had a long chat with Abel when he helped me across the creek and came home. Now here I am on the eve of departure for a little trip west where I don't know anyone. One thing I know, is that my mind ought not to be so much occupied with it tonight as I ought to be thinking of better things. As we pass the Sabbath, so we'll pass the week; am I entitled to a pleasant one?"

"September 4ᵗʰ

Mrs. Lunn is better and I am glad to be able to say I fear she is not well yet. From Abel, I don't hear anything. He might die by himself and no one would be the wiser, however, I hope he is better and if only he was here where I could, and would, gladly return some of his many kindnesses, but I can do nothing as it is."

"September 5ᵗʰ

No news yet from Abel. Well, no news is good news now-a-days. I will hear tomorrow, I reckon."

The following entry indicates that older brothers presume they have something to say about the courtship of their little sisters and now that Abel was no longer worked for Bradford but was constantly with his sister, big brother may not have approved of the relationship.

"September 7ᵗʰ

. . . yesterday, our uneasiness, relative to Abel, was entirely appeased by the appearance of the gentleman himself. He came over early in the morning and went to church with us. . . . I never thought to have lived to see myself the cause of so much excitement; however, it is very consoling to know that the fever is confined entirely to my own family. Tho' it is far from agreeable to have them so immensely concerned, it places me in a very ridiculous light before the world. If any of the gaping mouths and staring eyes became in the least acquainted with the case, they are very likely to do so when brother and Father are interested. Unfortunately, they are not given to venting all of their disapprobation on me, but needs let their annoyance be shown to the unoffending man, who presumes for the sake of whims of the moment, to favor me with his good company rather oftener than they think orthodox; and, not only to him but to all who may chance to be near, making me look as much like a fool as many a pair of pantaloons has done ere now by appearing to think that it is only necessary to say the word, Bah! It makes me sick as well as mad. How can such Solomon's be so simple?"

Bradford had again inserted himself into Fannie's private life by assuming he had the prerogative of passing judgment on any male friend who found her company enjoyable. He had obviously brought the Captain into the mix and she was not pleased.

"Well, it must be so, the old gentleman took the measles now but likely he passed the crisis when I got home from church and hadn't anything further to say. After all his fire he is very easily mollified. Ah, me! One half, if not more, of the trouble we have had has been the fruits of our own misconduct, but it is terribly hard to act rightly. Mother is in distress for fear I will act the Coquette. (I rather think I'll get a chance before I try it) and the others fear I'll trifle along until I'll never have a chance to get off their hands or some other species of brain fever has settled upon them. I'm quite a 'Leonne' for the second time since my return and I'd no idea I could create such a sensation in the family, unless I overturned an inkstand on brother's new coat, or broke the new clock face. Well I reckon the age of wonders is yet in embryo, and the next wonder, that which can arise no greater."

Her final words about the matter give credence to there being a fond friendship, but leave no doubt that any decision about the matter will be of her own doing and of none other.

"One will give some *foundations for all these sports and innumerable lectures, but there'll never be a super structure 'certain and sure' for that 'tis with me. I've marked my course, and intend to go thro' life on just the path I'm now in, one foot before the other. Pigeon toed right after my nose, until I step quietly into my grave, and some stranger writes 'F. B. Grimes' to mark the spot where I enrich Mother Earth, and yet not I. My efforts now not being for naught and where petty annoyances and weighty trials are unknown, where sorrow and sighing cometh not, I do trust I'll not be without those dear friends who are so unnecessarily solicitous about me now."*

"October 1ˢᵗ, 1857—Trespalacios

Sunday I started early in the morning for church but didn't find myself very early after all, for when I got

across the river I should have been the last one to start
had not Abel waited for me for a few moments, I think
I might be considered lucky though as I was in sight of
the crowd at the beginning and with them at the end.
In the evening a message arrived that Mr. Lunn was
in a dieing state . . . Abel and I got there among the
foremost. I had never seen death and when I looked
at Mr. Lunn's glassy eyes and set features I thought
the Grim visitor looked on them with me and had set
his seal on the motionless limbs. But, I was mistaken,
and a few simple remedies promptly applied partially
restored him."

"October 28th, 1857—Rio Trespalacios

Saturday morning, Mr. Lunn called and accompanied
us to church but Chloe excused herself. We had a very
pleasant class meeting, only a dozen present. As we
crossed the River we met Abel en route for 'our house'.
He seems like such a stranger as it has been a long
time since he has been here; it must be that he doesn't
get lonesome now that cow driving has commenced.
Lots of folks I knew came but some I didn't and don't
want to. We had such a nice ride."

Chris Emmett's book about Pierce deals in depth with
Bradford's objection to Abel's interest in Fannie and her
diary lends some support for that and a prediction of the
serious feud to come. Because Abel and Fannie were about
the same age and seen publicly together when attending
church and at other gatherings, there was plenty of fuel for
the fire. Fannie was determined that none would interfere
with their friendship.

In retrospect, had the romance been allowed to devel-
op without the intervention of Bradford and the Civil War, a
union of the two might have produced a happier outcome.
Fannie would have many close male friends in her lifetime,
some with whom she corresponded for decades. She would
marry one of her friends much later in life, though the marriage was childless and unhappy. When she died in Rocky
Hill, Connecticut in 1904 her will stated that she had not
lived with her husband for many years, believed him to be
living in another Connecticut town and that he was to take
nothing from her estate.

Fannie wrote below about the birth of her nephew, Bradford Robbins Grimes, whom the family would call first "Braddie" then "BR." He will figure prominently in this story with his extensive narrative of life on a cattle drive up the Chisholm Trail to Dodge City.

"October 1ˢᵗ, Rio Trespalacios

Well Mid day came and with it Patience and my nephew . . . at 12 o clock on Tuesday the 29ᵗʰ day of September in the year of our Lord, One thousand, Eight hundred and Fifty-seven, was born an heir to the venerable old gentleman in blue, and frontal buttons, a pretty little wee angel to be fitted for his maker, to be trained to do his masters will and meet in days to come the little brother who has preceded him in a holy, happy world beyond the sky where is no such suffering as I have witnessed recently. It hardly seems as tho' the little stranger belonged here, and yet our hearts yearn strangely towards it."

"The wail of feeble infancy has sounded within our dwelling, and it seems so strange to look on the tiny breathing bundle and think that within the fair casket 'tis a jewel of priceless babe and Soul to be "fitted for the skies". How <u>awful</u> the responsibility. It makes me tremble to look into the future and think what it may contain for our cherished little one, what it <u>must</u> contain if he be not "brought up in the nurture and admonition of the Lord, and who knows how difficult that may be of attainment. Sin dwells inherent in the human heart. He is pure <u>now</u>, but a few months of constant admonition and example will be necessary in order to withstand the sinful bias of his nature. Truly the human life is a mystery, from its commencement to its end. Our nameless little one is now sleeping the innocent sleep which comes only in childhood, and I will leave him now to his communications with the angels which guard the slumbers of the pure."

Thirteen years later, young "Braddie" and his younger sister traveled with Fannie to New York to be educated. He spent five years in school in New York until at 19 he was summoned by his father to leave New York college schooling behind to meet him in Kansas with a herd of cattle and be initiated into life on the trail.

Fall 1857 found Fannie living in Galveston, Texas with the Journey family. She had been encouraged by her mother and brother to *"mix in good society"* and speaks of sewing her clothes to fit in with her *"many associates."* Money was always tight and she appealed for additional funds for her fare home. Included along with her diaries are some of Fannie's correspondence and her friendships indicate a fondness for the city and her host family. She stayed in Galveston through the winter but in early April 1858, she received devastating news from home.

"April 7th, 1858

Dear Sis

I am just from the breakfast table, and have but a minute to write, we have a Dr here from Texana who will take this, one Bradford sent for, for the Capt, has been unwell, but we all thought him getting well again, he went out, and came in, and staid out as long as he pleas'd, came to dinner with us and eat like a well man, but in the evening he had a distress'd turn, which lasted say an hour, or half that time, it left him stupid, or was so from the effect of the medicine given, it has upset his mind, and left him <u>one side</u>, entirely helpless,

Dr says it was a stroke of Paralysis, he says he is in no immediate danger, but thinks he will never recover the use of his limbs, the Dr appears to be a very candid man, and pays good attention to his patients, I like what I have seen of him, and have more confidence in him, than most of them,   So Goodby   F.B."

The dreaded news of Captain Richard Grimes' death on April 11th was delivered to his daughter Fannie with three voices in a single letter. First her mother Charlotte, then sister in law Maria Louise and finally her brother Bradford delivered the sad news. The funeral and burial in the Grimes Cemetery had already taken place in her absence. Fannie adored her father and carried her grief for decades to come.

"April 17 1858

Dear Sis

Before this reaches you you will hear of your poor fathers death thro' bubs letter to Mr J—as I suppose he
wrote the particulars I will not repeat them, he has
now done with all the troubles, sorrows, sickness, and
pains of this weary world. If you could have seen him
in his coffin you'd have thought to judge by his looks he
had never known any—he look'd so good so calm and
happy so perfectly at rest. It seems as if the spirit must
be happy to leave the body looking so happy as his did,
his face bore the expression of perfect peace.

With love and respects to Mr J and family—I am, my
own dear Sis, as ever your affectionate Mother

Dear Sis Your letter to Auntie came last night, We all
thought that you would take that letter as a request to
come directly then, for we did not know but you would
like to see the Capt once more & as long as there was life
there was hope . . . he lived six days after like a dead
person merely breathing like a child perfectly unconscious seemingly, so if you had been here he would not
have known you. . . .I have no news & little to say—for
although I know I'm wrong & God loves cheerfulness in
Christians, it seems a task to live,—I expect I'm so selfish
to think too much of my own troubles—Well I'll say no
more but with much love I always hope to be a sister—

Her brother Bradford wrote:

Dear Sister we are now without our Father at least in
this world & although he made no profession of doing
Gods will I cannot but think he in his mercy will deal
lightly with his faults & that he is now at rest forever,—& I sincerely trust he is happy—

I am as ever your affectionate Brother Wm BG

The Captain's death in his 68th year brought an end
to a dynamic chapter of the Grimes family history under
the guidance of this venerable old sea Captain. Among his

possessions at the time of his death was a gold watch in a small blue serge bag made for him by his mother. The Captain's holdings were willed to his wife and Fannie, as he must have felt that Bradford was well established in the cattle business and the owner of the WBG Ranch. Bradford would keep detailed accounts of his management of the Captain's estate for many years thereafter.

After the Captain's death and just prior to the outbreak of hostilities, his widowed wife Charlotte returned to Connecticut with her daughter Fannie, leaving her favorite sister Fanny on the WBG with Bradford, Maria Louise and their growing family. Charlotte never returned to Texas and died in 1887 in the Bradford Home in Rocky Hill. During the Civil War in 1862, Aunt Fanny died on the ranch and a marble headstone marks her final resting place in the Grimes cemetery on the Trespalacios River. Her niece Fannie's last will decreed that part of her estate be spent in moving her dear Aunt Fanny's remains from Texas back to Rocky Hill, a gesture of her love and fondness for the aunt who was so dear and generous while she was growing up on the WBG. The removal was never done and Fanny Bradford remains at rest in the Grimes cemetery in Texas.

In February 1858, just prior to the Captain's death, Abel Pierce wrote to Fannie in Galveston from the Herndon ranch where he is now ranch manager and refers to Fannie as his best friend. She is 23 and he is 24; and being frequently in each other's company, and from the tone of his letter, one might infer that a romance was developing. However, in a hint towards the future, Abel refers below to *"our other Miss Fannie"* Lacey whom he does in fact marry in 1866. His letter is quoted here in its entirety.

"Willsons Creek February 21ˢᵗ/58

Dear Friend,

I take my best pen in hand to write you a few lines to let you know that Shangha is still living and has not forgot his best friends yet and to let you know how things are going on on the Trespalacios & Willsons Creek and in the range in general.

I was over to your house today everything was going on pretty well Jacob & Patience were gone to Dr Pilkintons to see sister Palina Jerry & Iris were at home cooking and taking care of the children The first thing Iris wanted to know was who I came to see now you was gone I told her I came to see her & she burst out in one of her big laughs and I went on to the house there I found the rest of the Folks all reading the news as the Captain had been to Freds a day or too since & got the mail &c they were all well and in good spirits except young Mrs Grimes She seemed to be rather lonesome as she did not expect Bradford in some time your mother looks very well as well as I have seen her for a long time they are all busy as bees ploughing & Planting,

I have not seen our other Miss Fanny since you left Miss Bradford said today she was sick with some kind of a breaking out which had been through the whole Family Miss Jane I saw at church last Sunday and the last I seen of her she was standing by the horse block waiting for her horse brother Wheeler did not seem to be quite as attentive as usual and I saw Mr & Mrs Robt. Pardon and it looked odd sure to see such a little girl married,

Cousin Fred came up and brought our new Preacher Mr. Philpots I did not get a knock down to him but think him a pretty smart man and very pleasant, he gave us two very good sermons and gave notice that he would preach here the second Sabbath in every month, but some of the big headed Baptist thought he was to well educated to preach up her that they could not understand him, and some allowed he denied his Faith, I told them I did not think so but they stick to it that he did I think that if these Trespalacios Baptist get to Heaven that they will be always quarreling about their religion but I am very doubtfull whether they will all get there or not,

Dr Robbins was up here Two weeks ago and he took down those two letters you left for me to take I went over to your house with the Dr. & Patience gave me the letters and I thought it a good chance so I sent them along

Since I got back this evening it has come out a cracking Norther and I am afraid it will be pretty cold in the morning I have been planting corn the last few days and I want to Finish tomorrow if it is not to cold,

I have got my cow pen done all but the gates and a good pen it is to and I built it to suit myself the Captain came by here going to Freds and I was working on the pen and the first word he had to say was that looks like something

Charly Herndon, Bill's brother is here, the one that went out west with him he says bill will be in in two or three days and from what I can learn from him he is not going to stay long, and if he has got the big Head as bad as when he was here before I do not care how soon he goes, the sooner the better, I am going to try and get along without having a fight if possible & I guess I can make it out, however I will let you know how we make it some these days if you don't break my head from writing this letter

Neighbor Ben & His Wife get along about as usual she gives him the devil once in a while. John Moore has been doing a binge business in the spiritual sassing line telling everything by the table and for a while you could not here anything else in the neighborhood, I told every body I heard speaking about it I thought it was the Spirit of the devil

Well it is ten oclock I guess and I must stop pretty soon I am going to back this letter so Fred will not know who wrote it if possible for if he does he will carry me high I have no doubt,

I don't want you to forget your promise for you know leap year comes year after next and I am waiting very patiently for them two years to fool around. I have kicked my chair over backwards once and fell over backwards once and I suppose that must be two years any how   So good night

I Remain Yours
A.H.Pierce"

This letter supports the diary reference that Abel was not working exclusively for Grimes and the visit from the Captain is a further indication he is building a pen for his own livestock. In it, for the first time, Abel is now referring to himself as "Shanghai." In Emmett's book about Pierce he wrote that someone had observed his long legs, pants stuffed in tall boots and spurs with large rowels sticking out behind his boot heels and remarked that he looked like a Shanghai rooster. Apparently he liked the appellation and the nickname stuck.

The decade of the 1850s was drawing to a close. War, hardship and more change would mark the next decade but in her diary of the winter of 1858-59, Fannie gives us a few more glimpses of this formative and energetic period. As we see, Abel "Shanghai" Pierce is still an integral part of "Creek life" and the Grimes operation.

"Thursday *Rio de Tres Palacios* *Dec 9th/58*

I did not know so many days had elapsed since last I penned the "stirring events" of our Creek life, but as we cannot "run round to the store" whenever we want any thing not contained in our little "assortment".

Last week Thursday we had three or four men here to dine, who did'nt kno' enough to leave if we did want'em to tis very convenient to have the house right next the store where folks can belatedly stop for their meals and it sometimes happens that tis pleasant for us too, but last week some of our guests happened to be repugnant to my fancy,

Brother started for Powder Horn to collect a second drove of Beeves & Mr Kuykendall met him there and tendered the pleasant information of a disaster to his boat and the subsequent non-shipment of his beeves which I presume they are herded there still as Abel went down over land the same day & has not yet returned,

Abel & the Mexicans must have suffered intensely camping out all this time, and Brother may be wind bound which even if he have a shelter will be almost as hard on him as he is so anxious to get his business on. I've been doing what I could by keeping open store and cutting negro clothing all the time tho' more fit for bed than elsewhere."

"Sunday   *Rio de Tres Palacios*   *Dec 19ᵗʰ/58*

Brother & Abel both arrived last Sunday from thier perilous & troublous trip. Rain, sleet, hard riding a stampede & failure of shipment forms a synopsis of thier
annoyances. 69 cattle are now roaming at large owner-
less in the vicinity of Chocolate unless Abel who started
a drove last Friday has fallen in with them,

Friday there were some six or eight cow drivers here to
diner. We sent for Chloe to come up & spend the Holidays with us dont kno' but but the water will prevent
her coming, no doubt twill this morning Mr Kuykendall
started a herd Beeves to PH.

'Tis work all day Sunday now, but thank Heaven I can
find time for rest & devotion I have spent my hour with
the negros & as usual reaped the benefit in peace full
feelings, true I do get a few Fleas & my humble hearers
try my patience somewhat but withal I deem it a priv-
ilege to be able to teach them some little, and this one
instance of effort for good has its visible good results in
a temporal point of view at least"

"Sunday   *Rio de Tres Palacios*   *Dec 26ᵗʰ/58*

Christmas came & went with the labor, annoyance,
pleasant anticipations & disappointment usually attendant upon festive occasions We had invited a troop
among whom were a few whose company we prized.
After a week of intense labor both in the Store and the
house the eventfull morning dawned, but the clouds &
rain permitted us mundane bipeds only light enough to
render darkness visible.

Brother came home Christmas eve quite unexpectedly,
we had prepared ourselves to be compelled to pass the
Christmas without him, he left in the morning with Jake
& Joe (who poor fellows have gone to P.H. where they
may or may not find Christmas times) to go as far Ed's
from where the herd started, after a while the Lacey girls
& Mrs McCrosky came up two at a time, Lucy & Kitty in
the kitchen completed our dining party rain without &
"quiet" within we passed an evening of unusual effort

to enjoy ourselves The Misses L. deeming it always advisable to speak only when they've something to say, and being in the same position as the most of us young ladies at the present day seldom found in that fix. Brother was the only gentleman in the group and he is naturally taciturn.

Heaven defend us from the next dinner party with the like material, eight of us women and only one protector I'm sure I've seen enough of Trespalacios Society unadulterated, uncultivated tho' I may be far from one of natures nobles, I can appreciate refinement & politeness in others,. I hope the Ladies enjoyed themselves but I'm afraid they did not Our dinner was so late that they did not get off untill dark, and there being only two horses Fanny & Nannie preferred taking it on foot, thro rain & water to waiting for their return, a glorious tramp they must have had"

"Friday   Rio de Tres Palacios   Dec 31ᵗʰ/58

For the last time my pen traces 1858: tis the eve of the new Year, but seems so little like it, I verily believe I had forgotten it.

Wednesday Abel & the hands started for another Herd to be back no one knows when. Brother has gone to day to meet them, and I'm standing guard in his absence. I've no fears of any one running away with me on this "happy new year" eve

Upon my word! The clock movement heralds the advent of the New Year. I had thought it at least an hour distant, thus time gains with rapid strides upon us and brings long before we are prepared for it each changing scene & varied duty, there's no time now for contemplation of the errors of past & good resolves of the improvement of the future year,

The clock has warned of the present existence of a new division of time . . . almost a year since I was left Fatherless. One little year ago he sat in my room above & I trimmed his hair as he thought better than anyone else could do it, and we conversed of that separation *we little thought would be final lightly on the same spot where mortal remains have reposed, a little year & the hallowed spot where all we have of him is laid, is almost forgotten visited scarcely at all by any save the child beloved so well in Life, and even I spend only a small portion of the Sabbath there"*

Fannie's observations of blacks from other ranches who have come to trade at the ranch store gives rise to her opinion of slavery in the midst of a continuous onslaught of abolitionist fever.

"Sunday   Rio de Tres Palacios   Jan 2ⁿᵈ/ 59

We have had an influx of visitors in the 'basement story', Mr Hasbrook's servant, Mr Demings, Mr McSparran's, and the Dimock's ebony muscular servants. Ah! indeed, 'twas a spectacle for abolitionists to behold to see them mount & file off as the Sun drew near the horizon. A slave well kept is happier far than his master, such is my belief after eleven years among them, notwithstanding I'm a native New Englander & my predilections are for freedom,

And then she writes further of the Mexicans who have become part of the Grimes cowboy force. They have come to work for the Gringo now that the war between the U.S. and Mexico has left northern Mexico without much opportunity. Mexicans have a reputation among Texans of being dangerous.

I dont expect to be present at five o clock when Brother and the two Mexicans start Beef driving. We have now four Mexicans at our board what would our Yankee friends think if they could see their swarthy skins and glittering eyes? They may be a treacherous people but I like those we have very much and wish we might ever secure more of them instead of white labor. One month more and these scenes of turmoil will be over for a time as Beef driving time will be at an end."

"Wednesday   Rio de Tres Palacios   Jan 12ᵗʰ 59

I'm just in from the kitchen where I've been preparing a batch of mince, Iris, Patience and Jerry took all sick,

*and I attending to etceteras myself. Rain without inter-
ruption every body crowding in the house full of mud
the drivers disbanded,*

*Abel just returned from Powder Horn has been recounting
his "perils oft by sea & by Land". the ridiculous things
he has seen & vice versa, of the last his meeting with my
old friend & highly esteemed Pastor & adviser the Rev
RP. Thompson. Poor fellow, it seems the scourge carried
off thousands in Brownsville as well as Galveston, but
reluctantly left him among the living.*

*I've been as busy as a Bee in a Tar barrel, the past two
weeks selling goods making out bills cutting garments
for large & small, sick & poor making myself a general
benefit to my kind,"*

"Sunday   Rio de Tres Palacios   Jan 16ᵗʰ/59

*Friday I spent with Mrs Lunn, who sent her Horse down
for me to break to her riding. She is afraid of him but
he's gentle enough for any one with nerve, at all events
he carried me safely up and back again, It's been two
months since I last took a ride, the weather being such
one could not ride for pleasure and the Horses have all
been in use.*

*. . . Spring is coming Beef driving is almost at an end,
and I'll soon be scouring the country again. I do love to
ride Horse back, thought I'd go yesterday just to keep
my Horse in trim but they sent him after cattle instead
as they were collecting the drove turned out a few days
earlier.*

*. . . I chatted awhile with Abel who has just returned
from Caney, then came up stairs & mended a coat for
him, & twisted Yarn for Mother. After that I mended another Coat for Abel who left this morning with the Herd
the poor fellow would go ragged I reckon if I didn't look
after him. His Mother would thank me I expect if she
knew I some times helped her lone boy, but Manlike he
does'nt know that it is to my benefit to mend his clothes
now & then"*

"Sunday   Rio de Tres Palacios   Jan 23/59

Friday Brother came home just at night only to get hands & start early next morning. Abel is the only dependence left the poor boy has earned his money this winter if any one ever did, it seems as tho' there never was so much inclement weather to be encountered, as he has faced this winter. If he should chance to get sick all the driving would be at an end and I do not see why he is not as likely to as Messrs Moore and Kuykendall. But shipping is nearly over anyhow, the next trip is the finale I believe, but as Abel yesterday brought letters of the improvement in Market, maybe twill pay to ship poor as the Cattle are."

"Wednesday   Rio de Tres Palacios   Jan 26ᵗʰ 59

The Last herd of Beeves for the present Season are at Demings. Jerry has just returned from there saying Brother will return in the morning . . . We women folks have been entirely alone for a few days not a man on the place and to lighten the task of the negroes I've indulged my boyish propensities & rambled 'ad libitum' among Cattle & Horses unrestrained by staring eyes . . . a jolly time I've had nothing but fancy work the whole week. Yesterday I was up before breakfast helped Iris feed the Cows, fed 'Sam Patch' & the Oxen & calves, trimmed a bonnet for Auntie (mighty pretty) fed the Oxen & Horse, read & went to bed. I'm going to sleep perchance to dream and if so I trust it may be of something beside shipwrecks & Jerusalem Crickets as last night. Dear me I wish some body would do something for me to talk about, but I'm the only one of the family who ever stirs out of the Beaten track of Beef driving & sewing"

Jerry's wife Iris has gone into labor and Jerry has come up to the ranch house seeking help from Aunt Fanny who will send for Mrs. Lacy, a mid-wife. The servants know that she and Aunt Fanny are substitutes for doctors when a child is born and there is about to be a new addition to the Grimes community.

Between 12 & 1 oclock Jerry came in after Auntie to go down & see Iris. & between 4 & 5 Abel & 4 Mexicans took breakfast to start in the Prairie in quest of Beeves lost in the early winter, they had a cold time I reckon as the Sun glistened on the hoar frost when I awoke this morning.

Mrs Lacy was sent for at Daylight and this evening introduced us to the infant daughter of Iris & Jerry. I would say Heaven defend us from any more, did I not know that my Will is <u>not</u> Law, and this feminine Ebony must be clothed & fed & cared for whether I like it or not. Iris is doing well & so seems everyone else to be to judge from the sonorous breathing to be heard in every portion of the domicile"

Fannie relates below to the fact that cattlemen are obliged to carry on with gathering and herding cattle in all kinds of inclement weather and she also gives her opinion of just how important the continuing efforts of Abel are to the Grimes operation.

"Saturday   Rio de Tres Palacios   Feb 5ᵗʰ 1859

Abel came home Wednesday night sick & worn out with Beef driving only to commence again Friday & returned again to day to leave to night for some place to me unknown. Abel & the Mexicans four of them, Mr Hadden Mr B Kuykendall, Mr Sparks, Mr McSparran Mr Deming and I dont kno' who else accompanied by the most severe hail storm I ever knew in Texas, the stones half as large as a Partridge egg lay in piles on the ground & not cold enough to need a fire in the house. I wandered from window to window thinking how the poor Beasties were suffering & only wishing it would stop that not only they but my aching head might have relief"

"Sunday   Rio de Tres Palacios   Feb 6ᵗʰ 1859

I've just returned from Church tis the first time I've been in Church before since November. Abel came home this morning & overhauling him at the Creek he rode up & back with me. by 'moral discourses cutting shorter the way", we made a pleasant ride of it'

"Tuesday   *Rio de Tres Palacios*   *Feb 8th 1859*

Yesterday morning Abel & three Mexicans started for Lavaca Co, to search for the Beeves lost in the early fall heaven send they find some of 'em, there's been hunt enough for them to pay for them almost in expense to say nothing of the labor patience & hardship of the pursuit, which have been very great I should judge.

At Home we're building fences & getting ready for the crops, present appearances betoken an early spring but there is no telling a frost in April may effectively cut off all our expectations for an abundant harvest."

"Sunday   *Rio de Tres Palacios*   *Feb 13th 1859*

Abel came home this Monday morning sick, he looked as tho' he'd had a siege of Fever poor fellow how he must have suffered alone on the Prairie wonder what his mother would think if she knew how much he undergoes, little do parents kno' the lot of their children when they leave the home roof, they may Sin, Suffer, Sorrow & Die, and who cares. Very few!"

Fannie is now called upon to deliver the next slave child. This is her first experience in the birthing of another addition to the Grimes assembly.

"Monday   *Rio de Tres Palacios*   *Feb 14th 1859*

Well! the 'Glory' has come in a Lump. I am at last just about bed time called upon to supersede Mrs Lacy, was there ever an equal record made in the annals of young lady hood! I fancy not, I've lived it thro' quite bravely & so has my Patient tho' heaven alone knows whether my doctoring may not be the death of it yet. Patience rejoices in her second son as Peter is introduced to this mundane sphere under my inexperienced treatment I'm quite anxious lest he does not stay here, and pray heaven to deliver one from any more knowledge of like nature. I dont kno' as 'tis worth while for me to grumble about the nature of that usefullness but assiduously to set myself to whatever my hands find to do"

On a poignant note, Maria Louise spoke with the maturity and resignation of a pioneer mother. This quote from the same 1860 letter foreshadowed her death in childbirth a dozen years and ten children later.

"Oh I must say I went down to the grave yard the other day & had the earth dug up, some Abor Vitre seeds planted, rose bushes &c Iris got from Dr P the other day—& the place really looks pleasant to me—& I feel that I can be quite reconciled to be laid beside my dear children"—

Bradford Grimes and his wife Maria Louise had daughter Fannie Louise by the end of the year. In less than five years Maria Louise had borne three sons, only to bury two of them in the family cemetery. Only Bradford Robbins, the second by that name, lived beyond his first week. Young Braddie, or "Little Bub" as his mother called him, was born in late September 1857 and was clearly a joy to all his extended family.

"Abel has been so happy with his brother. It seemed as if he could not do enough for any one. He was toting Braddie round all the time

Jonathan & Frank are both hired for another year It seems to take most of the time to fix fences Hogs & cribs, on the odd drives they are making are gathering beeves,—I don't think B— has had time to find out how many beeves he has sold of his own or any ones stock this year—

The new School Master is coming with his lady . . . the latest news I know of Mr Syms of Georgia who appears quite like a Northerner in my opinion (not expressed) will come the next month to teach a yr for four hundred dollars & board his-self. The new school house between Mrs L & Mrs McC—house not built yet B— give twenty five toward towards it although he wants to know if I will get time to teach my own children here. I say I reckon,—I am trying regain my practice on the Piano for my little one while it is quiet & Bradford gone,—

Well this is all I can do for you so good bye
            with love your Sister   Louise"

In July, Fannie traveled to Connecticut with her mother, Charlotte, now in her late 60s is profoundly deaf, a widow in frail health and in need of increasing care. They were staying with Aunts Betsey and Nancy at Bradford Hill where they planned to stay for several months and then return to Texas in the Fall. Their return would be delayed indefinitely by America's deadliest war.

> *"Rocky Hill   July 15ᵗʰ / 60*
>
> *Dear Aunt Fanny*
>
> *Still I have not for a moment regretted my undertaking, for Mother seems much better than when she left home, she is now threatened with one of her old attacks, but during the trip she kept up wonderfully,—We were 12½ days from the Rancho here. I believe that is the quickest trip I've heard of in a long time.*
>
> *We all got along very well, tho' we were disappointed in accommodations on board ship, and also in coming up the River the boat being very much crowded and very warm, We were disappointed again in not finding Sleeping Cars.*
>
> *We left Chester & his family at Lynchburg Thursday morning about 4 oclock I suppose now they are 'eating & drinking & enjoying the good of thier labors' in company with all the good folks in Petersburg. We are to make a visit there as we go back if we go this Fall. Mother thought she could stand it to come on and I was anxious she should get here as soon as possible."*

By 1860 Abel has become a critical component in the Grimes operation. He seems to be part of every cattle drive but it is clear that Abel "Shanghai" Pierce has begun to have ranching goals of his own. The history books tell of the rivalry between this ambitious, larger than life ranch hand and his former boss, but for almost a decade these two men worked the cattle and prairies of Matagorda County as gentlemen and fellow stockmen.

By October of 1860, new talk of expanded cattle drives with bigger herds and new territory to the west in risky Indian lands and Aunt Fanny's letter back home tells of their ambitious plan to expand westward on to new rangeland.

"... *Bradford was gone Mr McDowell came to see him, for the third time, about moving his stock out West, almost out of the world, among the Indians, he (McDowell,) wanted a drove to start in ten days, Moore was afraid to start on his own hook or responsibility, but we started him off that day, just at night with nine hands, and expect him back tonight with his drove or a part of it, 600, head, Mc is collecting his own, he intends taking 8 or 900, in a drove, but B, and Moore think 600, better at a time, ... he was a stranger to B, as well as the rest of us, but all the Karankaway folks, speak of him as being a little extra, I hope the Indians wont catch him,*

Abel goes all over that country, and thinks it the best place he has seen for cattle raisers, his are going too, but it will cost a deal of trouble, and money, and take nearly all winter I expect, to move them, Mr McDowell says it will take 40 days to go and come, each drove, that it will want 6 hands to a drove, I dont know how many horses, but says he shall want eight hands, with four good horses apiece, all the time for a year or two, to take care of them after they get there, Bradford will help find horses or not, only pay him a certain sum, and let him pay his own expenses, just as he chooses, he is afraid (Mc) that the Indians will steal his horses I expect, for they are up to dat trick, but they have all been to see for themselves (Bradford, Abel, and Moore), and are so well pleas'd with the Country that they have determin'd to risk it,

Professor Gybbs is going to drive the cook waggon, and take baggage of all sorts, who goes as Boss, is not determined, Partin is the best hand he could get, and he wants to go, Bradford will send Mexicanos, mostly, to do the work

Abel has been home and made quite a stay, and is as much Abel as ever ... Abel's brother is coming ..."

Much to Abel's satisfaction, his brother Jonathan Pierce has at last joined him in Texas. Aunt Fanny writes that trouble provided by abolitionists has begun to strain relations between Texas and New England but soon the families in Texas will unite for the Christmas holidays.

Christmas came when the best of times were at their peak but with trouble just around the corner. Now on the brink of war, the slaveholding states are being plagued by abolitionists and their hard-won economies threatened. Meanwhile, the Grimes Ranch "extended family" including Abel and Jonathan, enjoyed a Merry Christmas respite. Fanny's letter to her niece Fannie and her widowed sisters Charlotte, Nancy & Betsey mention everyone by name: Frank Robbins, Abel and Jonathan, and each of the slaves: Jerry and wife Iris, Joe, Moses and Patience and the lady of the house, Maria "Louisa" Robbins Grimes. Jonathan will work for Bradford Grimes at various times before, during and after the Civil War.

"Christmas Day after dinner 1860

Dear all the Folks

Frank has gone home to Christmas to day, and we have had the stillest day that I have seen for months, our family is down to the old small number of 24

Abels brother Jonathan is here and has been for over a week, Abel has been, and is coming again soon, we expected him to day to take Christmas dinner with us, but he miss'd it,

It is obvious that the Grimes family has enough affection for Abel to have Christmas dinner twice just so he will be included and Fanny writes of the *"Encore Christmas."*

Friday morning

I expected to get a chance to finish this grand production yesterday, but we had to have another Christmas yesterday, Abel and his gang got home just too late to keep it first day, and he has talked and reckon'd, on coming home to Christmas, Bradford, wanted to give him, and the Mexicans, and Negroes, a good time all at once, so we had it all to do over yesterday,

Jerry kill'd the best pig in his flock, in the morning Jo, and M, a plentyful supply of chickens, Iris made an Old Virginia sweet potatoe pudding, Louisa made punkin, cream sweet potatoe, and other pies, she had plenty loafcake, and other small cakes, she rigg'd her table out with her new silver, cake basket and all, silver forks napkins and rings, goblets, citron, and orange sweetmeats, plum jelly and all the little fixins Mexicans and Negroes, had just as much and as good as anybody and a happier set never assembled to keep Christmas or any other thing, on the earth, after came the cream for eggnog is the par excellence of all things, we made twice, once for the Whites and once for the hands, I can see them grin now a milk pan full each time, (we could find nothing else big enough to mix it in) sent it out in our largest rainwater pitcher, and after their surfeit of nog they all went into the store and got their presents, Patience and Iris new dresses, and a heap of little stuff, children, toys, the men had, trousers and hats, penknives, razors, soap and brushes, handkerchiefs, stockins, shoes, fire crackers, candy, Abel gave Patience and Iris each a silk handkerchief, there was not one among them, or that could eat any supper, all got plenty"

"Christmas after dinner 1860

Dear all the folks,

. . . I suppose you want to hear of all the works here, Bradford has had a brick hearth put down like the one in the kitchen, in the store room, the table taken down in the kitchen and a door out through where the closet stood, the closet put up, a lock and key on it, (Mis Patience carries the key). In the front corner next the stove, a new table made to run from the side of the closet the whole length of the room, a window back and front, the big stove moved in there, and the old kitchen fitted up for a dining room sitting, washing, ironing room, gabbing, fiddling, talking, room. They have a roaring, ripping fire made there every morning, rain or shine, any body that wants to warm, or dry, always finds a good fire, and bushel or two of liveoak, coats to cover up at night,"

Men constantly on the range and spending days on end camping on the prairie were now wearing holstered pistols on their hips and Abel was no exception. Aunt Fanny refers to that as she describes Abel's bravery in going 40 feet down a well to install a new water pump.

> *"We have the force pump put down since Abel came. He went down with big end forty feet, and he is the only one that I know of, that would have done it, it took all the nigs and whites to fixt and hold it, but Abel just unbuckled his pistol, and went over the curb and down to the bottom with it and said nothing. Its different from any pump I ever saw, it goes with two handles and two hands to pump, and works with iron rods each side, from the base at the bottom of the well, and affords water for all purposes, horses and other stock included, ... FB"*

Able Head "Shanghai" Pierce around the time of his range war with Grimes.

Just when bad blood developed between Abel and Bradford and what it was over is not apparent until 1860. An incident described in Emmett's book tells of Abel being denied entrance to the home as dinner was about to be served. Bradford's version of the incident was: "I merely informed Abel that the hands would take their meals in the cook shack." As Fannie's diaries reveal, a relationship had developed but they also show that Abel was always welcome at the Grimes household with no mention of such an incident. An account given by Grimes to a Kansas newspaper in the '80's wrote of a confrontation between Abel and Bradford over wages owed prior to the war. These remarks by Grimes came after the feud and even if they were true, neither of these incidents were serious enough to have caused Abel's lasting hatred of Grimes; however, there can be no doubt that something much more personal made Grimes and Pierce bitter enemies for the rest of their lives. Something created Abel's burning desire to get even with Grimes. Whatever the reason, the feud would continue for years. Emmett also wrote:

"Any act, just at that time, which might lessen the social importance of Abel in the eyes of a feminine member of the Grimes family was certain to cause resentment, for Pierce found himself no longer inclined to conceal his love for Frances Charlotte, called Fannie, which brother Bradford obstructed with every artifice at his command."

Mrs. Ella Talbot, a long time Matagorda resident stated that Abel. Pierce spoke with eloquent contempt for Bradford Grimes as long as he lived. Emmett also wrote that Pierce spoke to the widow Ward about the incident and said about it: *"It crystallized the philosophy of my life: Punish your enemies, reward your friends."*

The course of Fannie's life diverges at the onset of the Civil War as does Abel's. Time and distance forged a life and eventually a marriage for Fannie in Connecticut, all be it an unhappy one. Abel fared somewhat better in love and on September 27th, 1865, he married Fannie Lacy. A daughter, Mary, was born in 1867 and in 1870, son Abel was born but died five weeks later. The death of Abel's son was followed by the death of his young wife in December of 1870. He would marry again but Mary, called "Mamie," would be his only child. Shortly after Abel married Fanny Lacy, his brother Jonathan Pierce married Fanny's sister Nannie.

CHAPTER SEVEN

Houston's Last Fight

When cattle operations ended in 1860, prosperity was at its zenith. Bradford owned the largest herd of branded cattle in Matagorda County and the WBG was surrounded by booming cotton and sugar plantations. The planters were among the best educated and most influential men in the community but as slave owners they were now the targets of abolitionists. William Lloyd Garrison, the most famous, dedicated and renowned abolitionist, publisher of *The Liberator*, and founder of the American Anti-Slavery Society, wrote in his Boston paper: "*Every planter has forfeited his right to live.*"

The idea of secession was conceived in response to Northern meddling but was being advanced not by the planters but by farmers owning few slaves, little land and little to lose. Ironically, it would bring financial ruin to the very same farmers agitating for it. By the 1850's one-third of the entire Texas population consisted of the slaves confined to large plantations where rich soils were bringing forth bountiful yields but the few men who could be called planters numbered only around two thousand. In spite of their wealth and prominence, they were helpless to overcome the growing sentiment of the majority and even though they had great influence on culture, manners and thought, they all knew that slavery was condemned by most of the civilized world.

Senators Houston and Rusk and Governor Pease were all Unionists but they too were caught in the trap between southern belligerents and northern crusaders. Neither of these groups had any concept of the problems inherent with living in the presence of a mass of racially different people in bondage, a fact never considered by northern society since it did not affect it in any way.

The slavery issue had been brewing before the Mexican revolution that led to the Spaniards departing in 1821. The Mexicans now in control passed a Constitution which prohibited slavery and that provision was used to curb further Anglo immigration into Mexican Texas. In the U.S., Senate leaders had thoughtfully balanced the divide between North and South by passing an Act that gave equal representation in the Senate between slave states and free states and kept the simmering problem tamped down.

The British Empire ended slavery by abolishing it and reimbursing slave owners under the Slavery Abolition Act of 1833. In the colonies, an attempt to end slavery had come from the pen of Thomas Jefferson when he had included strong anti-slave language in his original draft of the Declaration of Independence. Unfortunately, a majority of the other delegates insisted that it be taken out. In the 1820's and 30's, the American Colonization Society, with the support of Lincoln, Clay, Monroe and other prominent leaders, led a movement to return black Americans to Africa. Nearly all Northern politicians rejected the extreme positions of the abolitionists because slavery had touched the families of the most powerful. Abraham Lincoln, Stephen Douglas, John Fremont, Henry Clay and Ulysses Grant had all married into slave owning families but tried to remain moderate.

In 1854, Garrison publicly burned copies of the U.S. Constitution and called it *"A Covenant with Death"* and an *"Agreement with Hell"* while other extremists called the Constitution a pact with slavery. Calmer heads in the Senate, through one, brilliant piece of legislation known as the Missouri Compromise, kept both sides in check. This single Act permitted the ownership of slaves south of the Ohio River and prohibited ownership north of the 36° 30" parallel with the exception of Missouri. This carefully crafted Act gave equal representation in the Senate to both sides and allowed the industrial North and the agricultural South to co-exist politically from 1820 through the 1850s.

Over this same span of time great personal fortunes were made from southern soils and slave labor. Fehrenbach wrote of that era:

> *"The plantation system of the South produced more wealth, and greater surplus of capital, than the rocky soils of New England or the forests of the Middle Atlantic States. There were rich merchants in Boston, New York and Philadelphia, but none of these compared in*

grandeur to Harrisons, Carters, Rutledges or Middletons, baronial planters not only with vast estates, but impressive educations and law degrees."

Even as the system created great wealth in the South, it was dependent solely on agriculture. As that single source of wealth became more and more static it was producing nothing new while the industrial North grew ever more powerful and diverse. Lincoln, while openly opposed to slavery, never once called for its abolition in his campaign for election in 1860. Not until his campaign for re-election in 1864 did he finally solidify his position. Fehrenbach summarized Lincoln's position best when he wrote:

"The imperishable greatness of Lincoln in this period and afterward, rests partly on the fact that he never succumbed to the malaise. He recognized slavery as a dangerous problem no amount of moral frenzy would solve; he was prepared to damage slavery if he could but not if he had to damage the nation in the process. He considered slavery morally wrong but it could not excuse violence, bloodshed and treason. Lincoln was prepared to stand by the law, either as a private citizen or as President, even when he thought the law in error; he made this very plain privately, in his 1860 campaign and afterward. It was a distinction the South understood too late."

His position was not made apparent in 1842 when he married Mary Todd, the daughter of a prominent, slave owning, Kentucky planter. In his campaign for president in 1860, Lincoln openly agreed that the Constitution allowed slavery but was opposed to its expansion and even proposed a plan of compensation for states that would free blacks.

In 1854, as the country strained to expand westward, Stephan A. Douglas, a senator desperately aspiring to be president and thinking he could win the support of Southern Democrats introduced in the Senate a dangerous piece of legislation. The law Douglas introduced would allow new states to be admitted into the Union and then, after admission, would allow the people within those states to make their own election in respect of making slavery lawful. Douglas, elected to the Senate in 1847, had become famous by defeating Lincoln for his Senate seat in 1858. In that campaign he had distinguished himself and became well known everywhere for his part in the Lincoln-Douglas debates.

In the U.S. Senate, with the great protectors of the Union now removed by death, Douglas skillfully persuaded a number of weaker politicians to pass the "Kansas-Nebraska Act." The passage of this one, ill-conceived piece of legislation destroyed the long standing balance between North and South and opened the entire West from Iowa to the Rocky Mountains to legalized slavery. This single Act would result in the formation of the Republican Party, splinter and sectionalize the Jacksonian Democrats and put the nation directly on a path to war. An unintended consequence of his attempt to court southern support with bad legislation would bring Douglas down in defeat in the election that gave Lincoln the presidency in 1860.

Texas politicians were ardently in favor of Douglas' bad legislation but when the bill came to the floor of the Senate, Sam Houston saw the potential disaster it would bring and stood alone as the only southern senator with the courage to vote against it. Houston warned that the effect of the Act would do away with the brilliantly crafted compromise that had kept the peace for 34 years. Houston was the only giant left in the Senate as all of the other great leaders who had fought to maintain the Union at any cost were gone. Clay, Webster and Calhoun were all dead and Houston was the only one left to fight for the preservation of the Union and he did it alone, against all odds, and against the wishes of Texas. Passage of the Act immediately led to open warfare in the State of Kansas and, in the prelude to total war, weak northern politicians were now allowing northern ministers and abolitionists to frame the debate as a sinful, moral problem. Their fervent hostility toward the South only served to prevent further compromise.

In Texas, with a white population of four hundred thousand and with 95% owning not one slave, the secession sentiment grew ever stronger. It swelled to a point where the planters, in spite of their wealth and influence, could no longer hope to control the sentiment of thousands of white illiterate farmers. To add to their woes, the movement to secede was becoming popular among politicians and lawyers. The planters, appalled by this radicalism and uneasy as to where secession might take them, united with Houston for staying in the Union, for standing by the Constitution and for wanting the struggle to be carried on by any legal means. They leaned on the Supreme Court's decision in the Dred Scott case and hoped that its opinion would settle the matter as precedent as the justices voted to recognize property rights in slaves and it was now the law of the land. The Unionists believed that by staying calm and keeping Texas in the Union they would, over time, be able to suppress the radical fervor of abolitionists and the movement for secession. Unfortunately, the emotional tide had turned and hotter heads prevailed.

When Sam Houston was sent to the U.S. Senate in 1846 the giants who had shaped the nation were nearing the ends of their lives. Andrew Jackson was gone in 1845 and Henry Clay, Daniel Webster and John C. Calhoun soon would be leaving the stage. Clay had crafted both the Missouri Compromise, the Compromise of 1850 and had been Speaker of the House, Secretary of State, senator, and had run for president. Daniel Webster had been Secretary of State under three presidents, a member of the House and a U.S. Senator from Massachusetts. John C. Calhoun, was Vice President under both Jackson and Adams, Secretary of State, senator from South Carolina and even though best known for his pro-slavery views, voted in favor of the Missouri Compromise to hold the Union together. Houston entered the Senate as a battlefield warrior with a history few could match but he came at a time when the great leaders of compromise were fading away. Calhoun died in 1850 and Webster and Clay were dead in 1852. Sam Houston now stood alone in his fight to preserve the Union while his constituents were being drawn away from him by the ever more stringent efforts of the northern crusade for abolition.

Ironically, as slavery flourished along the river deltas, by the time men were going to war over it, slavery had already reached the economic limits of its expansion. Had the politicians come to the realization that rocky western lands were not suitable for the cultivation of cotton and sugar cane, a solution to the westward expansion of slavery might have been found without a war. Unfortunately, time would not allow men to recognize such limitations and the fate and destiny of the South fell to the majority. By the eve of the election of 1860, the true planters were panicked and desperately trying to keep Texas in the Union but resentment against the North by the general population was becoming ever more inflamed. Continual provocations brought on by sectional politicians, the ranting of northern preachers and abolitionists and the unrelenting, printed anti-slavery editorials in northern papers made it worse.

The planters, realizing that secession would be ruinous to them, huddled around Houston in the hope that he could lead Texas away from the impending peril. To most Southerners, not just in Texas, a Confederacy composed only of slave states was preferable to continuing in the Union under Republican rule.

Many of the hardliners had turned against Houston when he courageously voted against repeal of the Missouri Compromise and against passage of the Kansas Nebraska Act. During the debate before the vote, Houston rose to address the Senate. Portions of his address are as follows:

> "My anxieties increase . . . if this repeal takes place, I will have seen the commencement of the agitation, but the youngest child now born will not live to witness its termination . . . what benefit is to result to the South from this measure? Will it secure these territories to the South. No sir, not at all. On the contrary it furnished those in the North, who are enemies of the South, with efficient weapons."

As Houston concluded his address, he pointed to the eagle above the chair of the presiding officer which was still draped in black to commemorate the passing of Webster and Clay, and said:

> "Must this badge of woe also represent a fearful omen of future calamities which await our nation in the event this bill should become law? . . . I adjure you, harmonize and preserve the nation . . . give us peace!"

The bill passed four days later with Houston voting no. One Virginia newspaper labeled him a "Traitor" and in a time when state legislatures chose senators and not the voters, the Texas Legislature served notice to Houston that with the expiration of his term, he would not be returned to the Senate. Houston's term had until 1859 to run but his career in the Senate was over. Now he turned to other means to try to salvage Texas from the turmoil and with his first term about to end and without resigning his seat in the Senate, he returned to Texas to run for governor. For the first time in his career, the voters failed to support him and after being defeated by Hardin Runnels, he returned to Washington to serve out the last eighteen months of his term.

As his time in Washington was winding down and his

return to Texas imminent, Houston learned that Runnels had been re-nominated. He decided to run again, and announced his candidacy as an Independent opposed to both radical Republicans in the North and fanatic radicals in the South. This time Houston's fame, personality and a hard, rigorous campaign won over the electorate and gave the Southern extremists their first defeat in eleven years. He now had one last chance to keep Texas out of the Confederacy even though party leaders, empowered by Southern extremists in the Texas Legislature, were furious that Houston had managed once again to govern the people of Texas. In a time of great national crisis, the people of Texas had again turned to Houston for leadership.

Houston began to govern by focusing strictly on the affairs of Texas, as the Southern extremists continued to push the issue of secession to the forefront. While Houston sent Rangers to restore order on the Rio Grande, the Governor of South Carolina was issuing invitations to Southern governors to attend a convention to be held in Charleston on the question of secession. Houston, on behalf of the State of Texas, declined.

Since the time of its annexation, Texas had always been Democratic but the Southern complex was different from Texas. John C. Calhoun had been dead since 1850, but his Carolina legacy lingered and his pro-slavery poison now permeated the South and into Texas. Houston had been tutored by Jackson since their earliest association to believe in one great American Republic that would reach from sea to sea. He could not believe Texas would now forsake the idea he had fought so long to preserve and he struggled to create a Unionist base. But, by the time the Democratic Convention assembled in Charleston in April of 1860, the Calhoun Democrats had gained complete control of the party.

In September 1860, Houston gave an eloquent speech at a Unionist rally in Austin in which he pleaded for the citizens not to throw away all that they had accomplished over the previous twenty-five years. In his brilliant speech Houston said:

> ". . . The Union is worth more than Mr. Lincoln and if the battle is to be fought for the Constitution, let us fight it in the Union and for the sake of the Union . . . who are the men taking the lead in throwing the country into confusion? Are they the strong slave holders? No; examine the matter and it will be found that by far the majority

of them never owned a Negro and will never own one. I know some of them who are making the most fuss, who would not make good Negroes if they were blacked . . . Texas cannot afford to be ruined by such men."

When Lincoln was elected, Houston urged Texans to remain calm. When the date for a Secession Convention was called to assemble on January 28, 1861, Houston countered by calling the Legislature into session eight days in advance of the Convention and urging Texas to delay. His plea for calm and delay went unheeded and the Convention of men seething with rage against northern interference in southern affairs assembled and drafted an Ordinance of Secession. When it convened to vote on the Ordinance on February 1, 1861, Houston appeared at high noon and sat in silence as the votes were counted. The Ordinance passed 167 to 7 but it did allow time for a referendum to be voted on by the people of Texas. The referendum vote was scheduled for February 28 and Houston made one last speaking tour urging the people to vote to save Texas from ruin. He concluded his tour with a speech from the balcony of the Tremont Hotel in Galveston before an ugly mob. Friends warned Houston that the crowd was angry and dangerous but when Houston stepped out on the balcony above the heads of thousands assembled to hear him, his tall, magnificent presence brought silence to the crowd. He began to speak:

"Some of you laugh to scorn the bloodshed as the results of secession but let me tell you what is coming. Your fathers, your sons and brothers will be herded at the point of bayonets . . . You may, after the sacrifice of millions of treasure and hundreds of thousands of lives, as a bare possibility, win Southern independence . . . but I doubt it. I tell you that while I believe with you in the doctrine of state rights, the North is determined to preserve the Union. They are not a firey, impulsive people as you are, for they live in colder climates. But when they begin to move in a given direction they move with the steady momentum and perseverance of a mighty avalanche; and, what I fear is they will overwhelm the South."

South Carolina now sent out Commissioners to all of the Southern States to promote secession. The lone Commissioner sent to address the Texas Secession Convention was John McQueen, a Carolina lawyer who was referred to as "General." It was a questionable title since he had never seen war nor had he knowledge of the horrors that it would soon enough bring. One can only imagine the contempt Houston must have had for a lawyer with a phony military title sent to promote the idea of secession to a true veteran of two wars and a man who knew that war could only bring unimagined bloodshed and suffering to the South and the people of Texas.

Houston's knowledge of the battlefield was real and personal. Under the command of Andrew Jackson at the Battle of Horseshoe Bend in 1812, while engaged in hand to hand combat, an Indian arrow pierced his thigh and a bullet to his arm and one to his shoulder almost killed him. Andrew Jackson himself had witnessed Houston's bravery and ordered his evacuation from the battlefield so he might survive his wounds. Years later his leg was shattered at the Battle of San Jacinto. That wound too almost took his life when, after the battle, he was transported by ship on a long, painful, feverish trip to a New Orleans hospital where surgeons worked to repair his shattered leg. His wound was so severe that it took months for him to recover.

Houston now listened in silence when the Commissioner was introduced and spoke of the great honor bestowed upon him by the State of Carolina in sending him to persuade Texas that its honor was at stake and that their interests were identical. The idea that the interests of Texas and South Carolina were identical could not have been further from the truth since only about one-third of Texas was civilized and to the west its settlers shared a thousand mile border with wild Comanches bent on driving them back. To the South, the Texas Rangers had just returned from battling an outlaw army of Mexicans under the command of Juan Cortina along the banks of the Rio Grande on a still unsettled border. Now Texans were being asked to squander blood and treasure on the other side of the Mississippi River in a war that Houston knew in his heart would never succeed.

Nothing could change the minds of those bent on secession and when it came, Houston retired to his home in Huntsville and would not live out the war. In the end, the few brave men who voted against secession, the doctors, lawyers and many other professionals and citizens who fought to keep Texas in the Union, offered their services to Texas and fought loyally for the Confederacy. Those who were strongly opposed to secession were labeled as "Unionists" but, like most men whose home turf is threatened, almost all remained loyal to Texas. A stanza from Sir Walter Scott's "The Lay of the Last Minstrel" may describe best the hearts of the men who were fervently opposed to the war but remained loyal to their homeland when he wrote:

"Breathes there the man, with soul so dead,
Who never to himself hath said,
This is my own, my native land?
Whose heart hath ne'er within him burn'd,
As home his footsteps he hath turn'd,
From wandering on a foreign strand?
If such there breathe, go, mark, him well;
For him no Minstrel raptures swell.
High though his titles, proud his name,
Boundless his wealth as wish can claim;

Despite those titles, power and pelf,
The wretch, concentrated all in self,
Living, shall forfeit fair renown,
And, doubly dying, shall go down
To the vile dust, from whence he sprung,
Unwept, unhonor'd, and unsung."

CHAPTER EIGHT

War

W illiam Bradford Grimes wrote to his mother and sister stranded in Connecticut. The Civil War had begun.

"April—Evg 15ᵗʰ /61

The Boat that is to take this, brings news, that war between the North & South has actually commenced, What will be the result remains to be seen,—I know you have all the Political News much sooner than we get it consequently it is useless for me to give an opinion as to progress of events,—

The market in N.O. has verry much improved in the past week and consequently I am much better spirits than I have been,—

With kind regards to my friends & Love to Aunt Nancy & Aunt Betsey I will say good night from your affection-ate Son & Brother

Wm BG"

When the war came, the U.S. Army had 2,700 soldiers in Texas under the command of General Twiggs. The General was a Georgian by birth and his sympathies were with the South. From his small headquarters in San Antonio, Twiggs chose to resign his post and turned over all federal property and munitions. Many of his officers were Southerners and they too joined the Confederate forces. Cut off from northern firearms manufacturers, the Southerners were now dependent upon Europe for firearms and the

Texans for the most part were armed and equipped with their own weapons. The Texans seized all federal properties and provisions located in Texas and those federal troops who remained loyal to the Union retreated north to Kansas.

Hostilities reached Matagorda Bay as described in an account sent by Bradford from the port in Indianola. The conflict had just begun and cattlemen were scrambling to protect their interests.

"Indianola Apl 25th /61

Dear Mother & Sis

Maj'r Caldwell is about leaving here for Galveston on business & as there may not be a chance to write you again for some time I write you a few lines simply to say we are all well,—

There are about 600 U.S. troops in the Bay that came from the frontier expecting to take vessels at this place to go to N. York,—It seems that President Davis is under the impression, that, Lincoln intends to order these troops to stop here in Texas and try to reinforce them, and then try to retake the Forts in this State, In order to prevent this plan being carried out, Pres' Davis has ordered a large force of troops to this place to take the U.S. soldiers prisoners, consequently men are comeing here from all quarters from surrounding towns There are about 700 men here now that came here yesterday & reports from the interior state that more are comeing from every quarter,—

The confederate troops came here from Galveston last week & took the Steamer Star of the West by surprise & took her to N.O. This ship was to have taken the U. S. soldiers from here to N. Y.,—when the soldiers found their ship was taken they chartered two Schooners to take them to some place in Florida where they could get better transportation,—When the Schrs got to the Bar they found they were too much crowded & sent back here to get another vessel of some sort & in the meantime the confederate troops, that is men in the vicinity had got together & took all the officers that were here prisoners of war,—they then loaded some half dozen lighters & steamers and last night went down to the Bar to take the balance if possible Whether they will do it or not remains to be seen,—Reports are all over the country that the U.S. troops have possession here, & have a large force outside ready to land, but all of this is a mistake—

As I wrote you some time since I spend the most of my time at this place and by noticing the course of events I have made my arrangements so that I have no Cattle on hand at this place & but a verry few on the way here,— If I had been at home the past month, I might have had on hand at this time several hundred Cattle in which case I should have met with a heavy loss as there are no vessels left here for the last ten days with Cattle & it is possible there may none leave here for the next month,—Every other shiper has from 60 to 100 & 200 each there are here in all about 300 B's & 700 young Cattle waiting for Boats some of which have been here ten days & some of which are now on the way.

Love to all good bye Maj'r Caldwell can wait no longer-

Yours Truly & affectionately

Wm BG"

The Union response to this resistance was to blockade all of the ports along the Texas coast from the Sabine to the Rio Grande which meant no more export of cattle and cotton from Matagorda Bay. However, for all their successes in the war, the Union forces were least successful in occupying Texas. Where the Union sought to land troops ashore in Texas they were driven off as Bradford wrote of in his letter. The successes of the Texans in defending the coast from occupation allowed the planters to continue to pick and gin cotton and ship it over land through Mexico. At the port of Brownsville there were British and French ships by the hundreds waiting for cotton and willing to pay a premium price to get it to their mills in Europe.

News was traveling fast and Fanny Bradford wrote in her colorful way about the same incident from across the Bay on the ranch.

"Texas Friday 26th, April 1861

Dear Folks, all,

Sis, I receiv'd your last in due time and made my calculations to write this morning as the mail comes in tonight, but since Higher law Seward, has condescended to extend his pacific policy to benighted Texas, we have had a visit from a company of nincumpoops, at Powder Horn that took possession, and made every body prisoners, that were there at the time and every body that came in,

It was a thing so unexpected that everyone was taken by surprise, with no chance to resist, the troops loaf'd there three, or four days, and then started in one of Harris and Morgans, boats for New Orleans, 600 in number. I think they smelt powder, but were a little too smart, they staid a little too long, for folks got wind of it, in spite of them, and all this part of Texas was in a buz, They flock'd there by land and water, old and young, nigs and whites, along with Bowie knives they brought anything that would shoot, from a cannon to a revolver, they were here ready for anything and everything, but Moore sent word to Bradford to keep the last 6 shooter that he lent him on his western trip, . . . Kuykendall, and he weren't sure enough, Mr Lunn, B, H, BK, Spencer, Jones, Col Owen, and I don't know who else. Ned could not go because he could not get arms, he sent here but we were out of that article.

But Bub was more in luck and he was there when they came upon them, and he is there yet, which is the reason of my not writing, for we were hearing all sorts of silly rumors, and believ'd none, or only one, We knew there were soldiers camp'd at Texana to join Capt Vandorn, with plenty of arms that would reach Powderhorn last night, and today they were to try for mastery, but others got the start on them, but even if they were too late for the Sewards boys on land, they started after them in a steamer, and caught them and took all their arms, and have got them now as prisoners of war.

Such is the news brought us at dinner, Mr McIntyre went down with Downer, he has just got home and sent N. up to tell us that Bradford was waiting to see *what can, would be done, and whether New Orleans was blockaded as reported,*

I suppose you will hear all kinds of stuff, but I don't think they will swallow us in a long time yet, they will bother us, it will be bad to have no communication with New Orleans, it will make hard times, and perhaps no mails, all we can do is to wait and see"

Many of the Grimes cowboys including Abel and Jonathan Pierce would soon enlist to fight in Texas regiments. Grimes is becoming involved in wartime commerce by transporting cotton and goods of every kind along the coast to be sold through Mexico. The planters worked diligently to sell their crops whenever, however and wherever they could. Bradford was no exception and in addition to transporting cotton through Mexico he is selling beeves to the field kitchens of the Confederate Army.

Unable to return to Texas, Fannie and her mother are residing with her mother's kin and even among relatives Fannie seems unable to escape abolitionist fever. It has been apparent to Fannie that her Connecticut friends and relatives have no concept of life on the frontier nor the suffering of her brother's family and friends now isolated and fighting for their very survival in far-away Texas. Fannie has first-hand knowledge of man's dependence on guns and horses in a land where they constantly face hardship and death. Charlotte, in her deafness, did not hear or understand the constant criticism of Texas but Fannie knew well that Bradford, Maria and her friends are fighting for their lives.

The War officially began on April 12th with General Beauregard's order to fire on Fort Sumter in Charleston Harbor. South Carolina was the first to secede and six more southern states, including Texas, quickly followed.

Fannie's 1861 journal, on the eve of her anticipated return to Texas, began one month after the war started. She writes of her fervent support for her ranching family and friends in Texas and how much friction it had caused her in Connecticut.

"Rocky Hill, May 16, 1861

. . . there's dissension enough in this village without my helping it on; and, as I see more and more the spring of

action which control the emotions of its people, more and more I despise my native town. Less and less do I seek or care for the favor it has to bestow. Words cannot express the contempt I feel for these _friends_ who have unconsciously shown me _themselves_. Never again while life lasts can they have my confidence or respect; never again can they wound me . . . and with this page, my _respected friends_, I bid you a long farewell' henceforth we are acquaintances . . . I only wait for Mother to see with my eyes—and we will both be willing to give our parting and lasting benediction and seek a relationship where no ties of blood exist—not that they all have turned away—Oh no! My Father's relatives have shown their goodness in a thousand ways—there's noble blood in their veins."

"Hartford, May 20th, 1861

. . . this continual contention makes me _long_ for home (Texas); will no one ever learn that I've as good a right to my opinion as any other body—and, that I _cannot be turned_ from it, though I am forever annoyed by contrary theories thrust at me turn where I will for rest. So long as I continue perfectly quiet I think somebody should be found by this time—with common sense and common politeness enough not to insult me without cessation by a most extravagant display of opposition; but, I look in vain for such forbearance in this highly civilized northern land. Verily, I've traveled west and I've traveled south—I've mingled with foreigners and countrymen, the high and the low and now, here in the midst of Yankees, I'm ashamed of my nativity. For the first time in my life, I blush for my birthplace".

With Bradford, Maria and Fanny Bradford left to cope with the dangers and privations of war and with her friends in Texas taking up arms in defense of their lands and way of life, Fannie found herself in hostile company everywhere. She deeply resented being dictated to by friends and relatives totally unaware of life on the frontier and in Hartford with her mother, she again wrote of the intolerable strife.

"Hartford, May 20th, 1861

. . .had I remained away from them I should still, as I

*have ever done, have been proud to boast my descent—
now I see with mine own eyes, I can claim no honor—Oh
Connecticut, how thy brightness has dimmed; and, the
individuality of thy sons warped by this farcical, meddling spirit, this want of minding your own business.
How great is the discomfort and the misery, both individual and national brought by this everlasting bick-
ering with whatever is not orthodox according to your
opinion. The result of which is this unholy war—effect-
ed mainly through the preaching of New England Ministers!! Aye, 'tis true, true as inspiration and although I
cannot say on them be all this blood so uselessly spilt,
for I feel they have acted with blind zeal, I can still
pray that the time may come when their eyes will be
opened to see this moral witchcraft against which they
are fighting in its true light. Until then, my native State
'farewell'. I love thee not."*

Many Texans, having already fought a bloody war with
the Mexicans and having governed themselves for ten years
thereafter, were entertaining the idea of returning to life as
an independent Republic. Many had been strongly opposed
to joining the Union in 1846 since after defeating Mexico they
still faced continuous fighting with Comanches and Mexicans
on hostile borders with no help from the federal government.

Many Texans still resented the fact that in 1850, under provisions of the Boundary Act, millions of acres of Texas were sold to the United States for a mere ten million dollars in a sale which took away lands on the upper reaches
of the Rio Grande River. Those sovereign lands included
more than half of New Mexico, including the settlements
of Albuquerque, Santa Fe and Taos, one-third of eastern
Colorado and part of Wyoming. The Act was passed with
the help of Sam Houston who reasoned that they were giving up unsettled territory controlled by hostile Indians for
a settled border and enough money to allow Texas to pay
its debts and prosper without taxing its citizens. Long after
the establishment of the Rio Grande as the border between
the United States and Mexico, the Rangers were still being called upon to quell renegade incursions by Mexican
outlaws without any help from the Army. Texans began to
feel that they had made a bad bargain in joining the Union
since it now meant giving up so much of the land and sovereignty so dearly fought for and getting little in return.

During the entire time Texas was annexed to the

Union her citizens fighting Indians and Mexicans could not depend on the U.S. Army to provide the protection to its citizens they assumed they were entitled to. Time and again, Texans depended upon the Rangers to protect San Antonio and the other settlements. So knowledgeable were the Rangers in how to engage and fight their border enemies that in 1848, when the United States finally did go to war with Mexico, the Rangers were asked to come to the aid of the U.S. Army at Monterrey. These tough, seasoned fighters of Mexicans and Indians came when called, were first into the city and were instrumental in winning the battle.

For Fannie and her mother, the return to Texas was now impossible and they would remain in Rocky Hill throughout the war and the decade of the 1860s. It would be up to them to survive the hardships and separation and Fannie's anger and disappointment is revealed in her letters and diaries. The Union Government in May 1861 still allowed people trapped in the North to send letters to family in the southern states before all communications were cut off and in the letter below, Charlotte tried to reassure her son and sister Fanny Bradford that they would be alright even if they were separated with all communications cut off by the war.

"Hartford   May (1861)

To all the good Folks at home

. . . I hope you are all well and safe, I hope you Bub will have a chance to rest.

You need not be uneasy about us, we can get along with what funds we've got for a long time I would'nt run any risk to send money,—there must be something left after all your bills are paid, and with what Fanny was so good as to send Sis, will help us on a long ways—in the stile we shall live.

We are going to housekeeping at aunt Pollys with Henrietta and Caroline, the middle room is unoccupied, we shall take that I expect,— I had rather have a place where we can do as we like, if its not bigger than a turnip.

I had made up my mind we would go back early this fall, if the disturbance was settled so that we could do it safely. There's no telling now when that will be, All we can do now is to try to make the best of whatever comes.

Well I hope we'll all live thr'o the miserable times—and meet again in peace some day.   *Good bye,*

Mother"

The blockade had started to affect the mail as well as the shipment of cattle. Maria Louise continued to write regularly in hopes of news from her own family in Hartford. The mood was still hopeful for resolution but folks were preparing for the worst. Her letter reveals that the attitude in the South is one of belief that they can lick the Yankees.

"May 31ˢᵗ 1861

Dear Sister Fannie—

I take my pen in haste to write once more this morn intending to have done so before the last minute this week,

Bradford is very pleased with his new Buggie looks rather showy for hard times but he is obliged to have something strong, He has gone collecting Cattle that were bought & paid for & not fat enough to ship,—All his business has stopped nearly,—He has sent Abel with a drove of Beeves by land to N.O. I suppose he has lost about five thousand this spring if not more—

He will take care of things at home more I reckon now for Frank has gone to enlist at Old Virginia, wanted to see his folks first. Jonathan has been mighty sick but we work nowadays as we never did before to save & take care of what we can get—

Bradford against our will got up a paper to form a company round here to defend ourselves, but he got no signers & it fell through. I don't see what the northerners are after if they try to subdue us . . . as long as one man is left they never will . . . If the Northerners come down upon us we will be ready to defend ourselves . . . I do not believe the papers—& hope the excitement will abate & we allowed to govern ourselves as we think best,—

I never was more able to do more work or as much as I've done this spring & it seems to put a new existence in me I shall write to Mother soon & if she never hears from me again not to worry about me . . .

I don't know as we will have our house finished this summer—no money credit or health for Johnathan to work & I have to be in the store a good deal—I think Bradford will be home more than he has been—Good bye"

Stranded and cut off by war, Fannie received word of the death of Fanny, her namesake and her very favorite aunt. Deprived of her Texas home, the shock of Aunt Fanny's death overwhelmed her. Portions of her letter are included below:

"Rocky hill   June 2nd   1862

Dear Brother & Sister

Aunt Fanny was more to me than she ever knew or I either untill now. All this terrible year past in every emergency, when it seemed as tho' there was no way for me to get along the thought that soon I should have sympathy from aunt Fanny either written or verbal has kept me up. I have suffered as much before, but never with such utter hopelessness for I always had aunt Fanny to turn to and for twenty years naught has ever befallen me that she could throw no ray of light on. Now the brightest season before me is the hour of death and if I were certain I should be with her & Mother in a better world and that speedily—I should be content.

But now I do kno' too often her heart has ached and I might have cheered, how often she has been despondent and weary & I might have soothed, yes I kno' it now, and now tis forever too late to project by the knowledge, and what cannot be. Sometimes I think my heart will break, yet I am quiet as aunt Fanny but not patient as she was. No tho' I have industriously copied her for 20 years."

In April of 1862 New Orleans was occupied. In a journal kept by Kate Stone writing from Brockenburn Plantation just across the river from Vicksburg, she wrote about the consequences of the fall of New Orleans and control of the Mississippi River.

"Louisiana with her fertile fields of cane and cotton lies powerless at the feet of the enemy. Though the Yankees have gained the land, the people are determined they shall not have its wealth, and from every Plantation rises the smoke of burning cotton. The order from Beauregard advising the distruction of the cotton met with a ready response from the people . . . As far as we can see are the ascending wreaths of smoke and we hear that all the cotton of the Mississippi Valley from Memphis to New Orleans is going up in smoke. We have found it hard to burn the bales . . . They will smoulder for days . . . the planters look upon the burning of the cotton as almost ruin to their fortunes but all realize its stern necessity."

The burning of southern cotton created opportunities for those who would continue to grow it furiously on the cotton farms and plantations of Texas and it created opportunity for men like Bradford with an education in merchandising to seize upon the opportunity to capitalize.

One year into the war brought a near standstill to correspondence from Texas. One exception is this letter from Bradford written from Victoria in which he reveals that he is getting in the business of selling cotton by hauling it over the border and then out by way of Havana.

"Victoria   June 12th 1862

Dear Mother & Sister

I have this moment, late in the evening thought of an opportunity to send you a letter by a Gent leaving here for Havana,—I left all well at home a few days since,—I have bought a small lot of Cotton with a view to send it to a market, a part of the proceeds, I shall have sent to you when sold,— My Friend Caldwell is going with it to Mexico, and in case he does not find a market there will take it to Havana to dispose of it,—.

You can well imagine our loss . . . Louise gets along as well as could be expected in trying to make herself

contented with her situation,—she has Iris attend to
the heavy sewing & assist her in the management of
all the heavy work,—the two women I bought in the
winter do the heavy washing & assist in the field,—the
hands I got at that time have all thus far given general
satisfaction—

I wrote you in my last in regard to the war the progress
of which of course you hear long before we do,—you
can well immagine our humiliation at the loss of N. Orleans & the Mississippi River but still we are not willing
to admit that the enemy can ever conquer us, if he does,
one thing is certain he can never subjugate us—

Our State thus far has been exempt from invasion,
should that take place I presume every able bodied
man will then be called to the field to meet them, Up
to this time I have taken no active part in prosecuting
this war but my heart and purse have been with the
confederate Govt & had it not been for haveing Louise
at home alone as far as any white person being on the
place with 26 Negroes I should long since have been
with Beauregards command—

We have at home a moderate supply of clothing supplies of all kinds to last our family untill next spring,
if the enemy does not occupy our section and destroy
them,—Should the war continue untill that time there
will be great distress among our people for clothing &
other necessities,—Prints are worth 4- to 6- Brown and
bleached cost the same,—Coffee the same—Shoes 3 to
8$—Boots 8 to 12$—& 20$ all kind of goods brought
from abroad in the same proposition,—many persons
are making fortunes while others are loosing them-

I must bring this to a close however as I have to leave
for Lavaca,—I shall write you by my friend Caldwell
when he goes to Mexico,—remember me to my friends
if you think I have any there, Louise, Brady & Fanny
would join me in Love to all if they were here. Fanny
can not do much talking but she is making great efforts
at it,—goodbye with Love of you affectionate Son &
Brother-   Wm B Grimes"

Three women in this story: a Grimes, a Robbins and a Pierce were all separated from their brothers in the Confederacy. Fannie in the very heart of Yankeedom was isolated from her brother in Texas. Miranda Pierce in Rhode Island was desperate for news of her brothers Jonathan and Abel, both in armies on the Rio Grande. The Robbins brothers, Chester and Fredrick, were out of touch with their sister Sarah in Petersburg, Virginia and their brother Frank was in one fierce campaign after another with General Lee. Each sought and shared news in their friendships in letters preserved by Fannie.

Fannie's friendship with the Pierce brothers' sister Miranda is shown in this 1862 letter. Jonathan is working for Bradford on the ranch and Abel, now running cattle of his own, is still a regular visitor at the ranch before his joining the Confederate Army and Miranda is offering her condolences in respect of the death of Fanny Bradford. In the North they are now drafting men into the Army from nearby communities in Connecticut.

"I have thought often of you in your affliction and sympathize with you but there is only one that can give the wounded heart any relief any lasting comfort;

. . . Things are quite quiet here now that we have got over the drafting panic; we shall not have to draft now and I am somewhat relieved although I had no one to go. If I had, I should have been driven to the borders of insanity. It seems they are drafting men close to you in Hartford, I am sorry for the people for it is so dreadful to go against ones will; this town has made out both her quota's and we are more easy for the present. I hope this war will close soon if it does not all the people will be killed and all the money spent on both sides. My only hope is in God;

I don't like your brother's silence about my brothers . . . I do not let mother know that I fear anything to increase her anxiety. I feel a great deal more about Jonathan than Abel for this reason, He is not as hot headed as Abel and will let the South alone in every political respect if she will let him be . . .and I think it would be cruel indeed to make him go there; I would go over to Mexico or any other country to get clear of fighting; but I try to think that your brother and Abel will not let him go if they can avoid or any way prevent it. As for Abel I expect he had as love fight the North as not and maybe would not be afraid to fight.

. . . What would I not give for a letter from the boys if it would only say that they were both living and well, Have you any idea what they are doing? and whether John works for your brother this year.

God grant that peace and plenty may be restored to us all soon. I hope our folks won't lose their property in this contest; Abel's is all in cattle so I think he may save some. It is now near school time and I must stop. Remember me to your mother.

> *With much love I remain your friend,*
> *Miranda Pierce"*

Another letter from Miranda conveys the sincere affection and concern between the Pierce and Grimes families and mentions Bradford's gift when young Jonathan went off to join the army:

> *"Little Compton, May 19ᵗʰ '63*

Dear Friend Fannie,

I received your favor of the 15ᵗʰ last evening and was glad you could give some account of the whereabouts of the boys: but your letter has set me in a fever about Jonathan: Now seeing I am in such a fever, do not deceive me, is he sick the reason he is home? Has he the fever or ague, or has been wounded, or is the time he listed for out and if so can't he go back to the Rio Grande if he is compelled to go into the army: I hope he or your brother will be able to get a substitute or clear him from military duty. I should be pleased to hear he was settled at home.

Now don't deceive me, tell me all you know and send your letter so that I may get it in the same time I did the last and then if there is any unfavorable news I shall get it while I am at school and shall not let mother know a word about it, I will not give her any undue anxiety: but I can bear it and shall not be satisfied unless I can have the full assurance from you that you have told me the worst. I think your brother (William Bradford) likes Johnt for he wrote to us that 'Grimes gave him a fine horse and gun when he went into the army': and if Johnt is well and can stay at home I am glad and I had rather he was a little sick if he could live and ever be well again it would clear him from the service; you spoke of the boys fighting propensities: I don't believe they run very high: We are an awful set of cowards and they never would have gone into the army at all had it not been for conscription and being carried so far from their home wherever Jeff. Davis pleased to call them. I hope Johnt won't place himself in a situation to be drafted and brought to Richmond

. . . but, there is so much uncertainty in Southern life now and so many privations to endure that I don't believe I should be patient under them all. I suppose you wish yourself there if you did not get but one meal a day; and, no doubt I should if it was my home although, I suppose we know nothing of privation as to what the South does. However, I am not one that believes the South can't be starved out; that will take a long day I reckon. I must now close this promiscuous letter for it is near tea-time and I am still in the school house tired as an Indian's dog; but, I must finish up what I have to do here and go and mail this letter and then go home. You need not wonder that this letter is promiscuous for sometimes I have had two or three talking to me while I write. I finish this letter on the 21st; write soon. With lots of love to you and kind regards to your mother I close.

Yours truly, Miranda P.

Sometime in 1862, beleaguered and attacked for her sympathy for the southern cause, Fannie decided to fight back. In the North, the wealthy and many of the not-so-wealthy could avoid conscription by hiring someone to serve in their place. Fannie has used her personal funds to send money and packages to southern men who were captured on the battlefield and are now languishing in Yankee prisons. Some have written to her from their incarceration in Union prison camps and she is corresponding with them. One Texas friend writes from Ohio:

"Camp Chase near Columbus, Ohio
Jany 16th 1863

My dear friend Miss Fannie

Nearly or quite two years of war of battle and of bloodshed have intervened since last I graced the top of a page
with your name. But as you see they have had no power
to efface that name from my memory, or dim the remembrance of she who wears it. No wonder then, that encouraged by the hope of soon hearing from you, I am thus
engaged, when for the first time in those two years the
opportunity is now presented of sending you a written
communication.

As you may well have supposed I am a soldier in the
Confederate Army,—with the rank that of first Lieut—
which accounts for my being here a prisoner of war. I
have been in the service about eighteen months have
been in several battles but none so bloody and hard
fought as that of Memphis where I was taken prisoner.

Of course I am not allowed to say anything about pol-
itics, nor have I any disposition to do so, preferring to
call up and dwell upon those happier days, of our acquaintance and association—days of national peace
and prosperity which I hope may soon again return
to our stricken land. Here then am I in prison,—Those
most dear to me and whom I have not seen in a twelve
months a thousand miles off in the South and not a
friend that I love,—unless it be you on this side of the
line that divides our armies. Well, such are the fortunes
of war, and I can heroically bear all, and shall without a murmur,—but if from out the East should come a
warm soft and mellow light which the sun sheds not but
which in days gone by I have felt eminent from the sympathetic page of my friend whose eyes will follow these
lines,—that warmth and light methink would quite dis-
pel the cold and dreary look of everything around.

Less poetically, but not more sincerely—I know of hardly
any thing that would give me more pleasure than hearing from you as of old and before I get out of this place by
exchange or parole. Would write more at length if I were

certain this will reach you. Hoping it may and that I shall receive an early response believe me as ever

  Sincerely your Amm   *S. G. Etheridge*

To miss Fanny Grimes
Hartford Conn"

Fannie's response to prisoner Etheridge's letter was somewhat cryptic. In her handwriting, she uses the pseudonym "G O. Carter," and has sent a parcel to her friend by way of Captain Selkirk, another Texas friend and prisoner of war. Within the parcel she had clearly expressed her Confederate sympathies. We have no way to know the outcome of her ploy but someone had written over the text of her letter "Too bad for a Northern Lady."

"Hartford Feb 14ᵗʰ /63

Capt. J. Selkirk
Dr Sir

Please hand the enclosed Package to Lient S G Etheridge of 23ʳᵈ Ala if he is liveing. If not Please to open the parcel, burn the letter, and dispose of the balance as will most benefit the suffering Confederate prisoners. I should be glad to kno' of the Safe arrival of the venture,—And should be obliged if you would drop me a line for that purpose—and also to inform me of the welfare of my friend E. if he be liveing. Of course it will not be safe to allude to the parcel openly in writing thro' the mail, but I shall understand if I hear from you

If at any time during your detention within these lines I can render you any assistance, and by that I mean aid in any way the cause you espouse, or its supporters it would afford me pleasure to serve you to the extent of my abilities.

Ardently hoping that the cause in which the noble Sons of the South have periled life & limb pray be successfull, and faithfully believing that God will not suffer such heroic effort to fail.   *I am Respectfully Yours*
                 G O. Carter
PS. Please address G O. Carter   *Hartford Conn"*

Another friend and prisoner forced to wait out the war in Illinois was Thomas Nye who wrote to Fannie in hopes of getting money to buy clothing. He shared what little news of Texas he had:

"Barrack No 42   Rock Island Illinois   Dec 21 1863

Miss Fanny

I am a prisoner at his place and doing very bad of clothing I have taken the liberty of writing to you to let you know of it thinking that you would send me some money to buy some clothes with—

Miss Harveys was well the last time I heard from her which was last month. Mrs Hillard, Fran and Frank are dead. The Robbins were well when I last heard from them. brother Willie was not in the same camp that I was in but he got a discharge last year and has been at home ever since.

Write soon, be carefull to Direct any letter you may write to the above address and it will be certain to reach me

    Your humble servant   Thomas Nye"

In October of 1862, federal troops landed at Galveston and seized the island but men led by Confederate General Bankhead Magruder decided to retake it and in December the Union soldiers were driven off of the island. Afterwards, Admiral David Farragut with General N.P. Banks formulated a plan to land 5,000 troops at Sabine Pass but cannon fire directed by Lieutenant Richard Dowling prevented a landing force from coming ashore and drove the federal vessels back out to sea. They returned to New Orleans and never made another attempt to land in that area. At Brownsville, Union troops were driven offshore and in 1864 General Banks made an attempt to invade Texas from Louisiana intending to take control of the richer lands of the region and strike deep into the heart of Texas. They were met by the Texas cavalry under General Richard Taylor and with a force of ill-fed Confederates less than half their size. Banks and his contingent were soundly defeated at the Battle of Mansfield and Banks retreated back to the Mississippi.

Soon after the end of hostilities, an Army General sent to Texas to bring order during Reconstruction was quoted as saying: *"The trouble with these damn Texans is that they've never been whipped."* Union vessels entered Matagorda Bay and landed troops at Indianola, but wisely confined their activities to the immediate vicinity. Their few sorties inland were perilous and unhealthy as they quickly learned that fine marksmen awaited them and thereafter they elected to remain within the confines of the town and Matagorda peninsula.

Due to the naval blockade of Galveston, Matagorda and Indianola, a never-ending stream of cotton began pouring across the Mexican border. On the other side of the river, mule and ox trains, and Mexican carts all laden with cotton were coming from almost every plantation and farm in Texas. Matamoros became a great commercial center with cotton and other commodities pouring into her warehouses and Brownsville became the greatest shipping point in the South. Cotton, the fiber that had sustained the Industrial Revolution in Britain, kept commerce moving and hundreds of ships were sent to Texas to transport the staple so necessary to the mills of Europe.

The blockade was causing wild speculation and by the end of 1863, a Cotton Bureau was created to confiscate one-half of the product from the plantations for the war effort; the rest was allowed to go the Mexican route. Cotton was the life blood of the Confederacy but with its sale to merchants in Mexico eager to profit from the hardships of war, the Confederate government was losing revenue badly needed to purchase gunpowder. Meanwhile, a succession of wagons loaded with cotton rolled on toward Brownsville and over the river into Mexico. The wagon route south was through Alleyton, Texas near Columbus and further south to King Ranch where Richard King organized its shipment south another 125 miles further to the border. Another route of cotton to the border was through San Antonio where the merchants there were advertising the sale of goods coming back in wagons that had discharged cotton in Mexico.

The only way for the Confederate government to keep farmers planting, picking and ginning was to share some of the profits with the producers. Hundreds of cotton wagons were waiting outside of San Antonio to enter the Plaza to deliver cotton to haulers coming up from Mexico and returning with cotton on the trip back to the border. In Matamoros, cotton was loaded on river steamers and taken to

Bagdad village for trans-shipment to ocean-going vessels. There was so much cotton in Texas and so many willing to go to great lengths to sell it that some of it found its way as far south at the Port of Tampico. Boat crews could not keep pace with the demand from various nations waiting offshore to load on cargo. All along the coast, endless rows of cotton were waiting to be loaded and out of the holds of the ships came military supplies and goods of every kind including thousands of British rifles.

The Confederate government initially tried impressments of cotton in exchange for worthless Confederate bonds which angered the planters and they refused to exchange their valuable commodity until finally an arrangement was made to allow one-half of the cotton to be sold by the planters on the open market. Some of the more influential planters were able to avoid impressments altogether, prompting Col. Rip Ford to comment: *"it's a rich man's war but a poor man's fight."* In the end, those who were forced to accept Confederate bonds, notes and Confederate currency were going broke while some of the traders in between, like Richard King and Miflin Kennedy on the Texas side and Mexican custom agents, brokers and merchants on the other side, reaped enormous fortunes.

News from the war torn and blockaded South was getting especially scarce and was therefore always welcome. Bradford was cryptic when writing to Fannie and his mother in the North. He wanted to tell them about his situation and status of his family and friends but also tried to mask his location.

"Trespalacios Mexico May 4th 1863

Dear Mother & Sister

We have read several letters since I last wrote you, not knowing what was best to write you in regard to some questions you have propounded I have defered writing—It is a great consolation to know that Mothers health is improved and continues to remain so.

Death it seems has not confined its walks soley to the battlefield or to our vicinity, our relatives in every direction have been called to mourn the loss of Friends— Hasbrook is at present at home, . . . he expects to be

*called soon to start to meet his company,—He belonged
to Capt Selkirk's Co that was captured at Aransas Pass.*

*Able & Johnathan are on the Rio Grande in Yeagers Bat-
talion this Bt't'n is to be put under Colin Buchel . . . John
Moore, Wiley Kuykendall, McSparran & some other
Boys are there also,—We have a rumor that Wm Baxter
of Cashs Creek a member of Selkisk's Co has died in
Illinois or wherever the men are,—Also that in the late
fight on the Teche in La that Capt Wm Blair was killed
& L't Ben Ward had his leg broken, This was at the
time Banks came down there from Vicksburg and with
an overwhelming force drove our forces back,—*

*. . . Mr Jesse Gordon was shot in one of the fights in
Texas several months since, and is a cripple at home,
Jack Duncan has been in the army all the time but the
Co' Capt Alex Rugeley has not been in active service
at anytime except scouting in the vicinity of Mtgda on
the coast—Jack has now a Substitute, Chester & Chloe
Robbins are at present stoping at home during sheep
shearing They are not verry well pleased liveing at
Demings,—Deming is at last in the army at the mouth
of the Brazos at Velasco—*

Bradford continues his letter from the home-front with
a report on the help continuing to work as if there is no war
and gives a good description of the size of his cotton hauling
operations. Ever the merchant he has bought 25 more mules
to pull the wagons loaded with cotton bales south to the border and his slaves are working as if nothing has changed.

*"The Black ones are all moveing along as usual,—Pa-
tience for a change has been put in the field she was
subject to so many sick turns and afflicted so much
with sores we thought it might be caused from being
over the fire so much,— She is better this summer in the
field she has Ella, Nerva, Charlotte & sometimes some
of the Boys with her as hoe hands,—Jacob, Anthony
& Robert do the most of the Ploughing. Wm & Henry
are herding the Horses, Mares & Mules, I bot 25 of the
latter a short time since to work on the place, and use
on the road hauling Cotton,—Joe & Jerry are at work
nearly all the time at odd jobs, when I can spare the*

time from the field I have from three to five teams on the road hauling Cotton,—Mr T. Kuykendall has charge of what few Cattle we have left here,—I have him hired at $2—per day and furnish him two other hands, Nolan Keller is driving for us this summer & I have one of Judge Davies Negroe boys hired also, he has been with us now two years,—The Cattle here & also at the Leona are doing well this season,—we are haveing one of the most favorable seasons for Crops that we have had for several years, our corn some 30 acres of it is in tassel the balance is of all sizes, but all doing well"

In 1863 an article appeared in the Houston *Telegraph* dated February 17th printing an order from Confederate Headquarters for Texas as Special Order No.77 stating that Special Order No. 66 issued on the 8th February, granting permission to Messrs. Pool and Grimes to export two thousand bales of cotton to Mexico was revoked and stating further: *"This cotton will not be taken from the country"* by order of Major General J.B. McGruder.

During this time, Bradford has been offered an opportunity to come home to Connecticut to take over the Hartford piano business and become a Yankee again. He prefers Texas and now holds a grudge against New England as responsible for starting it all. He expresses his strong resentment of the government.

"You say Father Robbins and his family would like me to join Fredrick in buying out Robbins & Winship and reside in Ha'tfd—There was a time when my health would have permited me to have done so, that time is I think past—I am afraid however, I have lived too long in Texas, under the influence of its institutions to be able to conform to the ways of business that would be necessary in that of Father R's—If the Lincoln Govt succeed in overrunning our country, which I think they never can do, I shall never want to see the New England States again, And should we succeed in establishing our independence at an early day or rather before the representatives of the New E. States, have an opportunity to destroy my property, I trust I shall by economy, have enough to live on, without going North to go into business at an age when I aught to be able to think about giveing up active business,—

"You can assure them all that nothing would give me greater pleasure than to live near them, that is my friends in the N. E. States, provided they did not feel that they belonged to a party now seeking to destroy every interest I have on earth, or force me to submit to a Govt I am satisfied is not identified with my interests—If they are of the aforesaid party and willing to sacrifice my all, rather than admit that I am capable of self judgement as Government then of course they can be no friends of mine and I shall be compeled to seek others in a more congenial clime—

"We feel at times towards the N. E. States like the children of Ambitious, Arrogance and Headstrong Parents, who are driven, or kept from their childhood homes on account of some difference of opinion or perhaps because the children would not sacrifice all to gratify some unjust request of their parents-

"Matagorda May 11ᵗʰ   Since the above I have seen a Physician Docr Brown who says that the Glands of my throat are enlarged and are liable to become chronic— he gave me a Gargle of Cloride of Potasia I think it is—

"Louise has sent a Boy to Caney for me, consequently I must start home—"

On Dec. 30, 1863, word came that federal troops were erecting a fort on Matagorda peninsula and a company of Texas Cavalry commanded by Captain Edward S. Rugeley planned a night attack on the Yankee installation. His men were loaded into small boats and, while they waited for nightfall, an icy Norther with gale force winds struck and most of their boats were swamped and capsized. The mission failed and twenty-two young men were lost due to the freezing bay waters and the unforeseen intervention of weather. The Yankees built their fortifications but remained away from the mainland while the Texas blockade runners continued to evade Northern gunboats.

The men of Matagorda County, in defense of their lands and homes, constructed one small, coastal fort near the mouth of Caney Creek which eventually was bombarded by a Union gunboat but no real effort was made to take it. The mouth of Caney Creek would have been the obvious route inland for any force intent on seizing some of the richest plantations in Texas where the greatest percentage of cotton was being produced.

The American Civil War would become the bloodiest conflict in U.S. history and would claim the lives of more than 300,000 Union soldiers. The drain on manpower in the North was so severe and support for a negotiated peace so strong that had the South been industrial instead of agricultural, a Union victory would probably have been impossible. The South's terrible disadvantage was being wholly dependent upon cotton to sustain itself, but it held on to the plantations in Texas and continued to grow it and sell it.

Cotton was exchanged for things Texans desperately needed such as medicines, guns, shoes and coffee. Speculation in luxury goods along with inflation brought escalating prices. The men who volunteered to fight were gone and those later conscripted were old men and young boys. Some of the producers who were able to sell cotton for gold or trade goods made enormous profits.

Many years after the war, Bradford gave an interview for *History of Kansas City, Missouri* in 1888 about which the Editor wrote:

"The Civil War compelled a new course of action when, to meet the demand for general supplies in his section which the blockade had cut off, Mr. Grimes began sending cotton to Europe by way of Mexico. This cotton was brought hundreds of miles from the interior of Texas to the Rio Grande, thence freighted down the river and shipped to Havana, New York and Liverpool bringing supplies from all those points to the beleaguered Texans. This business was followed until the close of the war with pecuniary success."

None of Sarah Robbins McCulley's letters during the war survived but she hastily wrote a note to Fannie at the close of the conflict.

"Petersburg June 9th/ 65

My dear Friend Fannie

Brother Frank has just been writing to you and says if I feel inclined, I can enclose a note ,—I cannot under-

take to write a letter at this time as my mind is even now drawn off to some duties demanding my attention at the present time Though, but for lack of time I could almost fill a <u>volume</u> to tell all, we & others have experienced & suffered during the last four years,—I have often thought of writing to you but then were so many failures of letters going by flag of truce & other difficulties that I delayed doing so.

The news we've received from Texas at several different times, would be most interesting to you. Brother Frank I believe has given you a summary of the principal items. A sad account indeed,—the loss of so many friends, You also find yourself among the bereaved—and if you had not heard previously of your aunt's death it will no doubt be a sudden & sad information we break to you. We have all suffered a great deal of affliction. I have seen trouble that sometimes would seem to have crushed my spirits forever, but we'll not dwell on it now, except to allude to the death of our Mother & two sweet children & a noble brother in-law. My husband Mr McCully seemed near death at one time, from <u>Smallpox</u>, but it spared him to me, but not my darling '<u>Mamie</u>' so while I had cause to be thankful for his life we were left to mourn so lovely a child, but <u>tis all right</u> and we submit,

I hope you will let us hear from you soon and when I hear where you are I shall want to write again and make inquires after my former friends if you are in any place where I am acquainted. I am sorry I cannot write more now, as I could say a great deal, but must wait till another time—

Write soon—your true friend
Sarah Robbins McCulley"

One remarkable observation of the war years was the behavior of the Negro slaves. Thousands of able-bodied slaves were left in charge of the plantations and there was not a single incident of revolt. The Negroes were more docile and manageable during the war than in any other period; they labored peaceably throughout the war and many seemed to have been caught up in a feeling for their plantations and for a society in which they had no stake. In many instances, while mistresses directed the efforts of the slaves, no white woman or child was molested and fewer slaves tried to run away than in previous years.

Stephen Vincent Benet's masterful poetry created a wonderful description of the strength and determination of the women left behind when he wrote:

The gentlemen killed and the gentlemen died,
But she was the South's incarnate pride
That mended the broken gentlemen
And sent them out to the war again,
That kept the house with the men away
And baked the bricks where there was no clay,
Made courage from terror and bread from bran
And propped the South on a swansdown fan
Through four long years of ruin and stress,
The pride—and the deadly bitterness.

Let us look at her now, let us see her plain,
She will never be quite like this again.
Her house is rocking under the blast
And she hears it tremble, and still stands fast,
But this is the last, this is the last.
The last of the wine and the white corn meal,
The last high fiddle singing the reel,
The last of the silk with the Paris label,
The last blood-thoroughbred safe in the stable
Yellow corn meal and a jackass colt,
A door that swings on a broken bolt,
Brittle old letters spotted with tears
And a wound that rankles for fifty years—

Because of the coastal blockade of Texas ports, cattle numbers in the coastal plains began to build up until some five million range cattle were roaming the prairies of Texas and with no way to market them, their numbers rapidly increased. Meanwhile, economic conditions in Matagorda and elsewhere in the formerly prosperous parts of plantation Texas deteriorated until credit was non-existent and Confederate money became worthless.

The cultural differences between people living in the industrial North and those living in the plantation South could not have been more opposite, stark and misunderstood. Perhaps Benet said it best when he used the winter season to illustrate the difference in life lived in two distantly separated cultures and wrote:

For, wherever the winds of Georgia run,
It smells of peaches long in the sun,
And the white wolf-winter, hungry and frore,
Can prowl the North by a frozen door
But here we have fed him on bacon-fat
And he sleeps by the stove like a lazy cat.

CHAPTER NINE

Aftermath

When the war was declared legally over and federal troops at last felt it was safe to occupy Brownsville, Colonel Rip Ford, a former Ranger Captain, leading a ragged group of Confederate Texans, drove the Yankees off the mainland and onto an island. Old Rip had fought and won the last engagement of the war not knowing the war had already ended with Lee's surrender. Throughout the war, with the Union forces failing in their efforts to fight their way into Texas, the Texans generally fared better than most Southerners even though the Comanche continued to drive the settlers back until the war was over.

When it ended, men returning home were furious when they learned that while they were away fighting, corrupt politicians had been wasting Texas treasure and resources. Some returning veterans seized and distributed hoarded supplies from state warehouses and what few goods had not been wasted were distributed among military families. Politicians who had been elected to work for the people had been taking care of themselves first. All wealth was now gone, especially for the planter class whose primary assets had been their slaves. A great percentage of young white males never returned from the ferocious battles east of the Mississippi and the Texas economy was left in tatters.

On June 19th, 1865, General Gordon Granger landed at Galveston bringing with him the news of emancipation, and freedom came at last to the slaves in Texas. Along with General Granger came federal soldiers who had not been able to fight their way into Texas; and now, instead of proceeding to the frontier forts where there were still plenty of Indians to fight, they camped in the cities among defeated citizenry who were now the conquered and treated as such.

Exhausted, ragged and hungry men turned toward home

to begin the task of finding ways to rebuild their lives. A few of them returned defiant and bent on mischief and out of this group came the desperados, killers and criminals whose actions impeded and slowed adjustment to the reality that defeat was final. Most of the men who had fought bravely and survived now wanted only to rebuild their lives and forget about the past; but, only five days after Lee surrendered on April 9, 1865, Lincoln was murdered and the mood of the conquerors changed from forgiveness and tolerance to retribution and punishment. All local government in Texas ceased to exist and in the chaos and danger that ensued, its citizens went about armed for protection against lawless angry men looting Confederate supply depots looking for arms and invading private homes. Many of those who continued to defy and endanger the lives of the occupiers, in the main, were not leaders during the war but men who had deserted in the face of the enemy. Some were seeking recognition by killing from ambush and terrifying the weakest among the population. Unfortunately, there were enough of them to require military force to be brought against them in order to restore law and order.

With the war now over, most Texans seemed to be trying to regain some degree of normalcy. The Grimes family in Texas, eager to visit family so long separated by war, now had an opportunity to make the long journey to their native Connecticut. Things on the ranch would be vulnerable and Bradford had to make plans for the many contingencies that might arise. One major problem was the disposition of his former slaves and the future of his workforce. In the letter below he explained how he dealt with his former slaves and the entanglements of currencies in the post-Confederate economy.

"Houston July 16ᵗʰ 1865

Dear Mother & Sis,

I have put off writing to you so long, since the war has been at an end but I was nominated as a Delegate to the General Convention of U. S. of the Episcopal Church to meet in Philadelphia, and knowing that Louise would be so anxious to go home at the first opportunity, I accepted the position . . .

I have from past experience, lost all confidence in human calculations, consequently I think that my affairs may be just as well off if I take this trip. . . .

At the time I made up my mind to go North I had a Store in operation in this place, which needed my attention, I had some Cotton enroute to Brownsville . . . the troops were breaking up, and marauding, and stealing every thing they could lay their hands on both Government and private property,

In addition to this the Slaves were all set free, some of whom thought they were to have homes given them by the Federal Troops, Some expected they would be allowed to set up for themselves in Town or Country on any property they might select, A verry few of them thought they would still have to work in order to earn a living, Of course under that state of affairs I felt as if I ought to go home and get my arrangements made with my Negroes and remain with them long enough to see them through the change from Slavery to Freedom—

We had but little difficulty on our place, I called them all up, and told them that they were all free by the Military Authorities, but that the Authorities would not support them in idleness, and as they had to work for a living I would now have them and, pay them such rate of wages as the military Authorities should establish, They were after some little difficulty all agreed to this and I made a written contract with them for one year on these terms,—When I left home a few days since they all seemed to be well satisfied, I had commenced paying them for their work, and in some instances they seemed to think that as they were now at work for wages they could work with more interest—

For my own part I am perfectly sick of them and everything in the country. I suppose however, I am like everyone who has been completely whipped, as every Southern true citizen has been in the termination of this struggle, and especially those who witnessed the lawless acts of the C. S. Troops at the time of their desertion and break up, stealing every thing they could lay their hands on in some instances—

The only consolation I can find in the whole matter is that it is Gods will, consequently is for the best, and as everything seems to be beyond our control in this matter, I am ready to take my family and leave my business here for a few months in hopes I can by change of scene and life, recover my former spirits and health-

It looks like the moving of an avalanche for us to think of going away from home with three Children and a Nurse 'but such is life',—Louise expects to leave the house and everything on the place in charge of Iris and sorry charge I expect it will be, as Iris is expecting to be sick this fall—

Mr Pybus I presume will remain on the place—and perhaps Johnathan who is since his return from the army staying with us,—

Marshall Grimes was at this City when I went home last, but is I presume now at Galveston. . . . he says he has lost very heavily by the C. S. Govt, Everyone doing any amt of business has done that, expect the officials, some of them, have grown rich,—I am at present boarding at a private house in this place, there several Federal Officers who visit here, they say everybody has grown rich at the North during the war, in which case I shall be like a poor Boy at a husking when I get there, with my crowd of country folks, who have nothing new hardly for four years past—

You can read this to Father R's Family or send it to them with Love to All

Yours truly
Wm B Grimes"

Word of the aftermath of the Civil War was slowly filtering into Rocky Hill, Connecticut. Fannie received a missive from Sarah Robbins McCulley, the sister of Frank and Chester Robbins, about the tragedy her family had endured in the heart of the South. The scars of war would not fade quickly.

"Direct to Mr Caleb McCulley
Petersburg   August 23rd 1865

My dear Fannie

A false report saying letters were again stopped at For-
tress Monroe, and my not wishing to send my letter
unsealed caused me to postpone answering your letter
some weeks ago.

Frank and I were both very glad to hear from you once
more. Does it not seem a relief to hear from one friend
who seemed as if were to have been buried in oblivion
for the last four years. Oh it seems to inspire me with
new life when I feel as if I had been brought back into
a world where I find my former friend still living, even
though the heart faints again & again as I remember our
hopes in behalf of our Southern land lie buried in failure.

We have had trouble, deep trouble, More than I could
have thought previously I was able to endure, yet we
suffered as a family, less from the country's affairs than
many of our friends, (bro Frank suffered much hardship
of course). We were not made homeless & pennyless
from loss of property as many were. We had a life of ter-
rors & alarms & narrow escapes, especially after our city
was besieged, but while hundreds of shells passed over
and all around our house, we still remained in it unhurt
and though it was an awful state of dread & excitement
to live in for so long a time. Yet we heard of so many who
lost health & life by going into camp life, we were glad to
feel that there was a portion of our house so situated that
we could feel secure from harm if we could only hear the
gun go off in time to seek our refuge before the shell could
reach us. My baby with the servant girl had some very
narrow escapes, which I will not stop to describe.

It would take more than one sheet to describe all the trials I endured in our attack of small-pox which occurred
in the spring before our city was surrounded. Our situation was extremely sad. We suffered so much more
on account of being quarantined & not even my sister
& other members of the family would be permitted to
come to our assistance for fear of its spreading more

among them, even though <u>they</u> had <u>escaped</u> while <u>seven</u> of the children had it & all got well. However one of the boys would come to the door & do some errands for us or we would have suffered more.

But what a night I spent when Mr McCulley was at his worst and thought he was dying and gave me his dying messages to all the friends and giving directions about what I must do and so he continued all night not expecting to see the day dawn. And there I was, I neither had anyone to send nor any body to send to for help or comfort, but the night passed & the day dawned & he grew better & finally recovered So I was spared that affliction & felt that there was so much to be thankful for.

In the meantime My baby then about 3 months old was taken, I did not think she could live for one or two nights but she too got well & then when our oldest child was so ill, I suppose I had begun to think all would get well and did not think of such a thing as having to part with that small treasure. But one Sabbath Morning when I had been thinking she was growing better I suddenly noticed her eyes set as if in death, and in a half an hour she breathed her last. Oh I must not dwell again on that agony for it makes me sick. She was as dear to us as life itself & we were more than devoted to her, Her sweet loveliness of character & disposition everyone and with all the affection bestowed on her she was never the less amiable & obedient I do not think we murmured at the will of God for we know it was all right but it was long before my human heart could revive. I felt like someone crazy & could take no interest in anything & hardly had energy to live, but I had to try & arouse to action for in about two weeks my baby was taken sick again & hung between life & death apparently, all summer long when she improved, though in the fall & winter she had several attacks of chills & fever,—she now seems to enjoy good health, & is a smart active sweet child & a dear little blessing.

I may as well stop this subject here for I dont know the end of all the trials & painful circumstances connected with the troubles of the past year, I believe we wrote you about the particulars of our dear Mothers death,

*I have not written to my brothers in Texas yet as I have
been waiting to hear of communication being again established, but think I will start a letter within a week.
I intended leaving more space to ask all about your arrangements for the winter. Bro Frank imagines you will
start for Texas & if so I want to know when you will be
here to make us a visit, that long anticipated visit? Bro
Frank thinks of starting in September or October & so
if it would be as agreeable to you as to himself would it
not be a good idea to leave Connecticut in time to come
& see us & then all go in a party together, & so I suppose 'the more the merrier'.*

*Let us know your plans,— By the way I remember your
mother is with you, will she return to Texas? I imagine it would be a great undertaking for her, I hope her
health is improved. Give my love to her. Please remember me to all the friends in Rocky Hill & the neighborhood when you meet anyone I know.*

*Yrs truly
S. D. McCulley*

The greatest fear of the Texas leaders was that the
general lawlessness and violence would become a barrier
to Texas being restored to the Union. Because of lawless
bands that were forming, especially in northeast Texas,
General George Armstrong Custer was sent to Texas in August of 1865 and his cavalry regiment camped on the Brazos River near Hempstead, Texas until October of the same
year. He reported that renegades, especially in northeast
Texas, were attacking commissary trains and army patrols
and that the felons were protected by sheriffs still loyal to
the Confederacy. In Custer's report to the Commission on
Reconstruction he wrote:

*"In Texas it would hardly be possible to find a man who
had been strictly faithful to the Union and remained in
the State during the war. They forced all who were truly
Union men to leave the State. Those who did not were
murdered. The people of the north have no conception
of the number of murders that have been committed
in that State during and since the war . . . I would not
consider it safe for a loyal man to remain in Texas now,*

at least in that portion I have visited, after the troops are withdrawn."

There was a portion of General Custer's report that spoke to the mindset of the men who were to shoulder the responsibility of bringing order out of chaos, many of whom were opposed to secession but had gone off to fight for Texas anyway. In that part of his report that gave credit to these men he wrote:

"There are men who have borne a prominent part in the war but who fairly accept the situation in good faith, and do not do so from any selfish motive, but from a sincere desire and purpose to sustain the government. If necessary, I could name honorable exceptions of men who have, since the surrender of the rebel armies, labored energetically in support of the government and of government measures, notwithstanding the fact that during the war they were foremost as its opposers. This class of men adhere strictly to the terms and conditions of their oath as binding to the fullest degree."

These were the men who would lead during even the hardest of times. They would lead in support of maintaining law and order, leading in support of bringing the lawless to justice without regard to their prior leanings and they would shape the future of Texas during and after Reconstruction ended.

When the Radical Republicans finally gained control of Congress in 1867 they were bent on imposing their will on the defeated southerners and began by enacting the Radical Reconstruction Act. It provided for a new and more stringent oath which had the effect of disenfranchising most white Texans. Its passage further angered those already in a survival mode and, by refusing to let men govern their own communities, it made matters worse. Honorable men duly elected to Congress were not seated as none could take the revised new oath requiring that they swear that they had never fought for or supported the Confederacy; few could.

In 1867 citizens in a majority of northern states supported the denial by law of the rights of blacks to vote whereas, in the defeated Southern states, their right to vote was ordered by federal fiat as punishment for the conquered. In addition to enacting laws which made the locals more defiant, it made them less cooperative in curtailing and reigning in the violent. General Phillip Sheridan, in command of the 5th Military District in 1867, was reported to have muttered that if he owned hell and Texas he would want to rent out Texas and live in hell. Murders in 1867 and 1868 were now double what they had been in 1865 and 1866 before the Radical Republicans gained control of Congress.

Under Radical Reconstruction, military tribunals replaced the Texas courts and Union officers meted out justice as they saw fit. The better class of federal officers and men returned to their homes and families in the North leaving behind occupation troops composed mostly of the black regiments and lower class whites. Some areas were looted and any person who had fought for the South was humiliated while those claiming sympathy to the North took what they wanted. Union soldiers were out of control and no one was held accountable for it. Texans were subjected to this type of treatment for nine hard years sowing the seeds everlasting bitterness.

Freed blacks now expected to receive land and treasure. When it didn't come, they left disillusioned by northern promises that could not be fulfilled as the plantations were struggling for survival too. Former slaves now had their freedom but by no means equality. The Union army had overtly discriminated against blacks and the 200,000 black Union soldiers who had received unequal pay were openly discriminated against by northern officers in the occupation force. During the war, Lincoln himself had told a delegation of black leaders at the White House:

> *"There is an unwillingness on the part of our people for you to remain with us when you cease to be slaves . . . you are yet far removed from being placed on an equality with the white race . . . I cannot alter it if I would . . . It is better for us both therefore to be separated."*

To further disillusion the blacks, only five northern states permitted suffrage while Connecticut, Wisconsin and Minnesota voted down proposals to give them the right to vote. In Detroit, New York, Cleveland and Chicago there were riots against blacks while men in Congress, who posed as the great champions of blacks, wrote laws to limit their right to vote.

Now into Texas came the carpetbaggers and opportunists comprised of turncoat Texans and radical Unionists bent on disenfranchising all ex-confederates. They came from the lower rungs socially and were out to use their monetary advantage for cheap gain at the expense of the broken southern citizens. Those who came to take advantage also came to remake Texas into a northern state. The result was the election of men to power who would only prolong the suffering of Texans for years to come and cause further misery to its now free, black but pitifully impoverished citizens.

In October Bradford and Maria Louise decided to return to Connecticut for the first time after four long years of war. Bradford had not seen his mother or sister since they left the WBG in 1860 and Maria Louise had not seen her Robbins relatives for many years.

Grimes obviously had been able to survive by trading cotton and had done well enough at it to have the means for a return trip home to New England. An article appeared on October 30, 1865, in the Houston *Telegraph* written by its "Special Correspondent," who reported on the steamer *Magnolia*, up from New Orleans and described it as the premier in its class with first class accommodations. He reported that among the Texas passengers were Mr. Grimes and his family in a party of Texans who came on board at New Orleans off a steamer from Galveston bound for New York. They intended to disembark at Cairo, Illinois and travel to the East by train from there. In that same article the reporter gave a vivid description of his observations of the aftermath of war only a few months after its end.

"What a scene of desolation meets the eye everywhere on the Mississippi. The magnificent dwellings of the planters have disappeared leaving nothing to mark the spots where they once stood but tottering chimneys or dilapidated walls. Plantation after plantation may be seen entirely deserted, while upon those that are partly cultivated, there are only a few negroes and a multitude of children . . . When will the Valley of the Mississippi recover from the terrible shock it has received? When will we again behold the magnificent fields of cotton, corn and sugar which in other days greeted and delighted the eye of the traveler? . . . It saddens one to view the ruined condition everything and everybody in this once land of plenty and social enjoyment. Nowhere in the United States was there more wealth and generous hospitality than in the slave states bordering on the "father of waters". All gone! All gone! and the princely fortunes have taken to themselves wings and flown away while master and servant have both been made

to feel the horrors and privations attendant upon war".

The following year, in 1866, New Yorker Charles Morgan reopened his steamship service between New Orleans and the Texas coast and the ports began to recover as merchants once more found outlets for their goods. Cotton had reigned supreme prior to the war with strong demand for shipments to Europe. Now, with the great railroad building era which followed the war, it would go by rail to Chicago, Kansas City and St. Louis and some cotton was finding a way to the profitable northern markets.

This was the Texas that Fannie returned to in the fall of 1869, four years after the war's end and in the midst of the nine terrible years Texas suffered under Reconstruction. Upon returning to the WBG, Grimes had resorted to slaughtering cattle for their hide and tallow, a business which yielded a meager return and required the family to adjust to the hard times in the aftermath of war. In June of that year Maria Louise had written home to her mother, Emily Robbins in Hartford and the following portion of that letter shows what life on the ranch was like in 1869.

"Trespalacios June 19th 1869

My dear Mother,

I have been wanting to write to you all at home for a long time, but it was impossible to steady my mind enough for anything, so much to do & feeling so unwell,—I finally thought I would sit down & try & give an apc of one days work on this place. We have now between thirty and forty to feed all the time, men from everywhere Northerners Southerners Yankees & Western men, English, & Irish, Spanish, Mexicans, (Itallians, or Diegos they are called mixed) High Dutch Low Dutch & Germans besides the blacks, some are going all the time, some Beef drivers, Cattle drivers, ship Carpenters & house Carpenters, brick layers & Laborers—that dig & lift heavy work— blacksmiths Waggoners, Boatman, Cord wood cutters, & the Farm work attended too besides the work on a farm Butchering & tending stock of all kinds,—

I will try & write of one days work,— At day break Anthony rings the bell, Patience is paid a little extra a mo, gets up a little earlier & gets the Breakfast going, we have made a little change in the servants now & Miss Eliza sets the table & sees to having the bell rung & meals ready to the dot,—hangs up when necessary,— I was so sick every morning, could not get round so soon & baby to attend to after disturbing me so much in the night, but I'm generally up as soon as the Laborers, they have nothing to do but get ready for Breakfast & at half past 5 oclock generally 12 Men are down to the table & as soon as done ready for days work, 3 women go to the pen & milk a little from 25 cows so as not to starve the calves

Some Men go to fixing for Farm work, some saddling their Horses to ride, Bradford is round every where like Uncle Wm Goodspeed Eliza goes to the dairy skims milk washes pans & churns, this before Breakfast,— I have no regular nurse, nor seamstress, do as much as possible myself & all the mending most—& rainy days all the women help sew,—

I have just come from helping Eliza look after the sheets &c for 13 beds to be made every day,— Patience is putting a barrel soap away she makes once a month. Breakfast over for all I have to arrange for dinner, we cook bread by the half bushel cook meat every meal enough to last you a week,—we sometimes use 3 lbs coffee per day—& it is roast coffee, gather vegetables some days we have gathered prepared & eat 1 bu of peas & snap beans each, besides other things some work that, after dinner it is work in the garden gather things to eat for next day,—we cook half bu Irish Potatoes to time & then it is only a taste, we kill & cure a Beef once a week, That is work for Eliza two days-cleaning feed & tripe & cooking tallow . . .

Well, the bottom land that is between us & Mrs Wheeler is being cleared for cord wood (for machinery) & lanes are being fenced in to drive the Cattle from the Beef pen to the slaughter house, the House is nearly up, cellar dug,— 12,000 brick are to be set just to hold the boiler, & it looks like we had a sett of steamboat works down there smoke pipes &c, we have a Black smiths forge going, the Mowing machine is just mended & they have commenced cutting down weeds in the clover lot *in front of the house, We have a new ferry boat building seven feet longer than the other & 3 feet wider,*

The Gary Plough & Cultivator works fine this year,—& our field gives promise of 100 acres of fine corn, we have had a good season, for Irish Potatoes do not do so well, in hopes Sweet Potatoes will make up for their not doing so well,— As soon as the corn is ripe we want to plant Turnips by the lb—& peas by bu to help fatten Hogs—with the meat,—

At a little house we had built four cabins &c we have a white man & family keeping house for himself,—we would like to fix that way for others, then if the men come & work—will be more contented to stay to have a family with them, & such washes as we have 14 sheets & 2 or 3 table clothes & always a Doz shirts to do up at a time, & we make lots & lots of pants for the store, week before last I finished off besides cutting out & doing lots of the sewing—5 pr Pants 5 womens dresses 2 mens linen coats & the mending & new dresses (Calico) bought at the store to wear besides stuff for bonnets & shoes &c,—

Well Mother I've tried to think of everything on the bright side of the story, on the other hand there is many a hard thought among the folks towards each other, or about the table or something of the kind like at a Hotel . . . .

. . . I don't look for anything but suffering in this world, I started to write most particularly for fresh pictures of yourself & Father, those sent during the war through Mexico have become spotted. Yours nearly ruined, & I would be so glad to have some new ones. There is a prospect of a railroad being built clear through Texas to New Orleans soon now & I shall then, if I am here, expect you & Father to make me a visit for I am tied now with so many little ones although B says they will be scattered in good earnest by another year to get a living & I will die, well maybe I wont live for anything, but do write soon & believe me

Your affectionate Daughter, Louise."

CHAPTER TEN

Return to Texas

October 1869, Fannie Grimes was in New York bound for Texas. After a ten year exile, her sentiments about the war surfaced as she wrote in her diary about the way things were when the WBG Ranch was "Home."

"State of New York", Oct. 26, 1869, Tues. night.

The *long* talked of, fondly anticipated trip is at last commenced. Land of my nativity I bid you a glad fare-well, tho' the tears will come when I remember *who* not what I leave behind. I turn my face fondly, long-ingly toward my adopted country. Home, for so many years an exile, I wonder if I am going back to Home, friends, country; or, am I going forward to change—disappointment, strangers? The leave-taking is not *altogether* satisfactory, 'tis palpable the long antici-pated meeting with House and home scenes may not be; but, speculation is vain. I am on my way; so far so good. I left too hurriedly even for goodbyes; my lunch bucket following in Orpha's faithful hands came just in time to be handed on board. Not a soul on the dock to bid one Godspeed . . . too many sad thoughts of what *might be* during my absence came thronging to my mind . . . I reckon 'tis useless to dwell farther on the past, the present; or, the palpable future . . . faith ought to make bright the "long look ahead". It does so far as anticipations of much pleasure go, but some forebodings are comingled" . . .

Rail has been extended southward and Fannie records the details of her travel aboard a train to New Orleans.

"Oct. 31, 1869—New Orleans, Sun 'm'

Have been domiciled with Mrs. Norris on Magazine St. since ten o'clock this morning—this is quick work; too quick. The trip had nothing pleasant about it—hurried, weary & sick we came into the City this morning, glad to be at the end of our break neck journey . . . Boarded the 9.30 p.m. train; we barely had time to get our berths in the sleeping car. I was and am yet somewhat blind either from riding backwards in the sleeping car; or, over fatigue or sickness of which I suffered most singularly!"

New Orleans found Fannie awaiting the arrival of a steamship that would take her to Galveston where she would stay with Henry Journey and his family until a steamer to the port of Indianola on Matagorda Bay was available. From there, she was to find travel by boat to Palacios Point.

"Nov, 15, 1869—Galveston, Mon 'm'

Last Friday is a week since I arrived here. Left New Orleans on the steamship "Morgan" under the command of Captain Talbot. . . . Her commander proves to be an old acquaintance and friend of my father and brother and certainly has shown himself most friendly to me. . . . I learn, on personal inquiry at the Office on the Dock, that the Morgan is coming in today and will leave day after tomorrow. I find things here sadly changed; the whole City is changed but not for the better. Henry, a comparatively poor man, has been victimized by a Yankee and Carrie's health is miserable . . ."

For Bradford and his wife, 1869 had been a year of ups and downs. Bradford had conceived of a plan to improve their fortunes during their rough financial times. Legal and credit problems had beset them before but recently he had received encouragement from his sister Fannie and he alluded to his new strategy in this letter written while in Louisiana.

"Bossier City Jany 15 /69

Dear Sister

Yours of Nov 21ˢᵗ and also Sept 16ᵗʰ are before me, brought from home to be ans'd when opportunity should offer, I have a few leisure moments hence commence this,

you commenced yours Novr 21ˢᵗ by saying mine of the 3ʳᵈ gives me encouragement to hope I may get hold of something favorable in my business,—Now I am trying to arrange some plan, by which I can convert poor Beeves into money, the prospect, that we may get something more than the expenses, and it is the only chance I see to raise money, and our misfortunes have lost us our credit to a great extent, so that we must try to rely on our own resources entirely to get a start . . ."

In the summer of 1869, many things seemed not to be going well for the Grimes family in Texas. They struggled to get by and Maria Louise who came as a city-bred and fragile, nineteen-year-old bride is now overwhelmed with the chores of everyday life. Fannie has some idea of the struggle from the letter Maria Louise wrote home to her mother in Hartford in June. Bradford has plans for generating income in a failing cattle market but hard times have become the reality she will soon confront.

The Grimes operation now has a new rendering plant, a store stocked with merchandise including clothing sewn on the ranch, a new ferry boat house and a full scale workforce. Bradford had begun constructing housing to encourage workers and their families to replace the single men who often caused more work and headaches. Miss Eliza Avery had been both Louise's seamstress and companion since just after the war. Although she did go to Hartford shortly after this letter was written, she returned the following year and remained for many years an indispensable asset to the family. The Grimes Ranch Store was an additional source of commerce for the community and potential income for Bradford's family. Booth Jordan had been Grimes' bookkeeper for some time and managed the store operations as well. Both Eliza Avery and Booth Jordan were well educated close friends of Fannie Grimes and their extensive correspondence tells us much about life during this period on the WBG.

There was also a hint of difficulty in Louise's letter though. Much was at stake and they were both worried about the risks to family and fortune. Miss Eliza Avery has left for Connecticut and Eliza, the black woman who has helped in the kitchen, has gone to work for Shanghai Pierce leaving the household in need of a new cook and a nurse for the children. As if that was not loss enough, soon after her letter, their beloved Patience died.

"Sept. 10th 1869

Dear Sister Fannie,—

I have sad news for you and worse a coming I fear although if we can only have faith and trust in God, it may not be so bad with us. Patience is gone. She took her time for doing everything at daybrake—on the new of the moon. It seems that I've lost a mother. I mourn that I've lost such a faithful creature. She was buried at sunset of a beautiful day."

The absolute low point for the Grimes operation came in September as Maria Louise sent a clear plea for help to Fannie. Everything, even the weather, was going against their hopes for success. The desperation for herself and Bradford came through in her letter and their post-war troubles are too urgent to ignore. There is a hint of a different kind of trouble in the form of war on the range with Shanghai.

"Dear Sister Fannie,

Don't run now as though the Devil was after you because I'm going to send you some more of my blues—but by a special request from Bradford—who says if I give up, he shall too—that I must try & write you, that he is so troubled night & day trying to get things started & agony that his is worn out—& has left his business letters so long & you must excuse him for not writing & he also wished me to write for him as a special request, that if at all consistent to leave Mother G—& you could raise the means, & come out to stay & help a few months 2 or 3 at least—it was his only salvation left almost—he has strained his means & credit, till he is nearly crazy—

It looks like the day Mr & Mrs Williams & others came onto the place we were cursed harder than ever—& yet I hold on to her for I must have some white person to help push ahead & she will do better than no one—I could not send the nigs to the store all the time or even little Fanny for they will take advantage of the children, & Bradford Jr is out in the Prairie, no matter what, taking the place of a full hand.

Mrs Williams babe has been quite sick & it might yet take a change & die as Patience did, when I did not think her so very sick, but I think my two youngest already much sicker than hers, but I had to neglect them & work when I ought to have been in bed So things work—so much sickness, rain & sudden changes—we have had an awful time, till the blood commenced on me again yesterday, I could not keep on my feet from morn till night This morn we had 3 tables full, 12 sit down at a time, some have worked for us, some want work, some going & coming all the time, you have to keep on with them,

. . . . . . Oh dear Richard has got into Booths room & his bottle Ink & spilt it all over his dress & floor & broke a tumbler, while I have left to write. Fanny is clear used up with a cold this morn—

Our next trouble now is humbugging us about boats— These Diegos run off every other boat & then lie & promise & cut up so now we have freight to send off & raise our credit a little, can't get a boat . . . . cannot get hold of salt to go on with our killing . . . . . it cant get up the creek—but we have about a hundred barrels of tallow . . . some weigh 300 lbs ps—& about 250 hides I reckon, but bad weather made 40 or more of them spoil—

We have been fixing this week the machinery to pull off hides by steam, which will save hands time & labour I cant help but think B, if he lives, will get through & do something but we have mighty hard times & bad luck— . . . drunken Rows—till I feared blood shed last Saturday night—. . . & children so frightened could [not] get them quiet till ten oclock at night, . . . & then the sausage man left so I don't know as we will save any meat—. . . & we think the boatmen have grabbled & carried off most of our sweet Taters—

So you see things look awfully against us—. . . our chief

engineer leaves today, who has helped us much—... & the others too left, lead the nigs off at night & gamble ... not fit for work next day ... & I suppose they will leave soon, for want of whiskey or some other fight—John (Jonathan Pierce) wanted higher wages than Bradford could give & so he goes—... Germans are so vulgar & want Flour all the time. We have a Radical man coming, says he can get & keep to work all the nigs in the country—... have him get 15 so if one doesn't suit we will not be left without folks, but its coming & going all the time, ... you cant please so many—... grumbling all the time, ... all the noise on the place, ... get things cooked for all is mighty hard on me, & I don't feel that I can live through it.

I've almost lost faith in any & every thing there is no Sunday here B—still finds time to say his prayers—& if we have faith I've no doubt all will be right ... but I don't see why we are so cursed when others do well & better with less, Ben Ward kills as many as we do in a day—we could never get over 25 done, don't have more than a half dozen round him, but he doesn't have a family or store, Pierce is taking out this country 3000 head of stock a month Report says, calves & yearlings count fast.

Well babies crying, I will not try to write more—I do hope the tide will turn & let you come out & see us—but I have mighty little faith in such good luck—

... remain your affec sister Louise—

People on Caney have lost all their crops, most may pay expenses,—"

Fannie Grimes, always willing to help out, prepared to come straight away, leaving her mother in Rocky Hill with Orpha the housekeeper and traveled to Texas to the aid of her brother's family. By November Maria Louise wrote again to Fannie, by then traveling by steamer from New Orleans to Indianola, expressing both her gratitude and near desperate anxiety. She was herself, very pregnant with Emily Charlotte, who would be born in just a few weeks. Her attempts to coordinate Fannie's transportation, labor resources and to relay messages from Bradford were daunting challenges. Things had not gone well.

*"Friday noon Nov_*

Dear Fanny

I thank God to hear you have arrived thus far safe we hear by letter this morn from Capt Talbot—requesting B to meet you at Indianola if possible, I don't see how it is, for him to leave just now, as he gets off from going to court on acc of my expecting to get down every day, then the head foreman is or has been very sick, the cook leaves & the Radical man who get all the blacks to work for us, takes them all up to their homes in Wharton to vote,—right in the midst of push & at a time when the Beeves will fall off all the time . . .

Dear Fanny we feel that our salvation pretty near depends on your coming to us,—little Ricky is so sick—& has been since he fell in the fire I have got rid of that lazy Mrs Williams & been fortunate enough to get a young lady Miss Shultz from Matagorda, who takes Miss Avery's place & helps me much, but is not fitted to manage the doings in the Kitchen well.

I wish I had something pleasing to offer you on your arrival, but it is not all peace, we are gloomy & sad,—our dear little Fanny is just hunting eggs to save for Auntie when she comes is about the best news I have for you God grant you will not be worn out when you arrive,

I am not able to write more   Louise"

Finally arriving at the docks in Indianola, Fannie had completed another leg of the long journey home to Texas. She writes in her diary aboard the steamship *Morgan* at its moorings but she still had to find a local vessel to deliver her across Matagorda Bay to Palacios Point and up to the ranch.

"Nov. 20, 1869—Indianola

. . . Yesterday when the ship got in Mr. Fromme, my brother's agent, came on board, delivered letters from

my brother, expressed his willingness to render any assistance needed and advised me to remain on board ship overnight and left. Brother advised me to take a boat to Trespalacios and I'm lucky in finding the boats all in. 'The Sea Gull' is the most commodious and best. 'The Josephine' is commanded by a person who has the reputation of being a murderer and horse thief and the 'Louise' is commanded by another no better. Rather than go over to Palacios and ride up with Abel's hands (Shanghai Pierce's cowhands)—Mr. Fromme says 'I think Mr. Grimes would prefer your going by one of the boats tho' they are not very nice. You kno' there's some difficulty between himself and Mr. Pierce.' And so I decide on the boat not without some irrepressible reflections to the effect that 'tis not a very generous feeling which subjects me under the circumstances to traveling in any one of these three greasy, hide smelling, filthy boats with very questionable crew, rather than consent to the alternative of receiving a favor of an enemy—well now and here is not the time for judgment."

Fannie has become aware that bad blood had developed between Bradford Grimes and Abel "Shanghai" Pierce. Her brother is no longer the largest cattleman in Matagorda County. Since returning from the war, Shanghai has been intent on surpassing Grimes in every way and has formed a partnership with his brother Jonathan. They have built a ranch across the Trespalacios and up-stream that they call "Rancho Grande." In his ambition to accumulate more cattle, he is expanding his operations over the free range domain that Grimes had controlled for years and is working hard to shrink Grimes' reach. This was the unhappy situation Fannie found when she finally arrived at the Texas home she has longed for.

After deciding to travel aboard the *Sea Gull*, Captain Talbot was getting her luggage aboard. She wrote further:

"Capt. Talbot is averring that 'The Sea Gull' was 'no place to ask any lady to get into.' . . . No more delay could be made and turning me over to Captain Shepherd who also was and is a friend of father and brother, Captain Talbot put my trunks on the wharf, bid me a friendly farewell and went on his way. I knew, as long as I was in a sea Captain's charge, I was in good hands."

Now that Fannie would travel on *The Sea Gull*, she was been made to feel welcome by Captain Shepherd's wife. On the morning of the 21st, the Captain informed Fannie that a fair wind had come up and that if she would get aboard *The Sea Gull* they were ready to set sail. The condition of the boat and its crew was appalling as she described it:

"I descended at the risk of my neck to the dirty deck of 'The Gull' and not wishing to add to the anxiety depicted on the countenances of those who were seeing me off, I smothered my apprehension and sat serenely down on one side of the companion way, directly between an open barrel of salted meat and the top of the stove pipe, with nothing to support my back. Only the omnipresent smell of tallow and hides to suppress my nerves, thus commenced my last sail homeward in company with two Americans and two foreigners, all men I'd never seen before that I know of. For six mortal hours I kept my post, but my trepidation vanished early—the men all knew me I found and were disposed to be very courteous. I quite enjoyed the cup of coffee Commander 'Joe' made for me and the lunch Mrs. Shepherd put up for me. Arrived at the flats where the 'Gull' stuck fast and I was transferred to the skiff and rowed to Downers. A very kindly greeting awaited me and Anne went out immediately and brought the horses; and, as soon as they were ready we started for home. 'Twas just dark and we accomplished the six miles in very good time tho' I rode a badly worn down horse . . . someone else coming up the bay having taken the better one. 'Twas 8.30 when we got here and had supper. Anne and I are to occupy my old room but it isn't homelike."

Fannie had longed to get back home once again to the life she had known before the war. She was not prepared for the changes the war years had brought to the ranch home and headquarters. When she arrived after dark, she knew what she saw was different and made a quick note in her diary.

"After an exile of ten years I write 'Home' in my diary— but 'tis hardly home in my heart. By lamplight things look not very familiar and I miss, oh how much I miss. I was prepared for change, but imagination never pictured what I find; I'll wait until daylight for judgment."

It was not until January, 2 months later, that Fannie finds herself in a frame of mind to write about her post war impressions of what had once been her safe and cherished home:

"Jan. 21, 1870—Trespalacios

No! a thousand times No!! 'tis not home ... I have none now. I'm very weary tonight yet 'tis a long interval between this and the last date. In brief, two months have passed since I arrived—months of work and weariness, not of pleasure. I cannot help it if the words are ill chosen ... they are written and they are true. Care and sickness have been my portion and disappointment. The reality of evil to be found here greatly exceeds my wildest thoughts and my severance from home now is perfect."

By now she had learned the full extent of the range war that had begun between her brother and his former employee. She and Abel were old and dear friends and there was no reason to immediately take sides until the facts presented themselves. Abel had married their mutual friend Fannie Lacy in her absence and she remembered him fondly.

Abel Pierce was setting himself apart from Grimes in his vision with respect to the advantages of owning land. When Bradford and the Captain started out in the cattle business there was so much open range not belonging to anyone and so many wild, unbranded cattle, there was no need to take title to the vast tracts of land. Bradford was a free range cattleman but now, with Shanghai buying herds from others, forming partnerships around Grimes and with a large crew branding every maverick the crew came across wild, unbranded cattle on the free, open range were getting harder to find.

Shanghai was determined to rapidly build the size of his herd to become the newest and biggest cattle king in the land. The Civil War left few sources of credit around but at Indianola, Abel had learned that his friend Dan Sullivan was the owner of a thriving, general mercantile business. To Sullivan he laid out his plans for expansion and petitioned him to provide the credit he needed to make his plan work. In addition to branding mavericks, he intended to purchase brands from others and form partnerships with shippers and transporters. Sullivan saw the merit

in Shanghai's plan and eagerly supplied all the credit he
needed.

Pierce began testing Grimes at every turn and building cattle numbers at a rate that required more territory
crowding Grimes and hiring men away from him. In order
to establish a base of operations, brothers Abel and Jonathan commenced building their Rancho Grande. Jonathan
would live there, anchor the ranch headquarters and own a
one-fourth interest in their cattle operation. Shanghai took
the monetary risk and moved among potential sellers while
his brother-in-law, Wiley Kuykendall, married to their sister Susan, ramrodded the branding crews. After sealing
their agreement, the brothers had stationery printed that
read: *A.H. and J.E. Pierce, Stock Raisers and Cattle Dealers.*

Ranch headquarters of Jonathan Pierce located 3 miles up river from
Grimes on the east bank of the Trespalacios. It burned in 1904.

In 1865, shortly after returning from the war Abel
married Miss Fannie Lacy and put out the word that he
intended to surpass Grimes. With financial backing from
Sullivan he could buy cattle for cash and he put together a
crew of hardened cowboys to make it work. In 1866 brother
Jonathan married Fannie Lacy's sister, Nannie and together the brothers would build a sizable, valuable empire.

Fannie Grimes quickly became aware that the activities of her old friend Abel were causing great pain to her

brother. She was also feeling great sorrow over the loss in 1862, in the midst of the Civil War, of her beloved aunt Fanny Bradford. Her namesake and her mother's closest sister had given up everything to live in Texas with the family during most of Fannie's childhood years. Now she lay buried in the ranch cemetery, recently joined by loved and ever faithful Patience. Fannie had been putting off a visit to the burial ground which now held the earthly remains of her dearest loved ones: her father, her aunt Fanny, three of Bradford and Maria's small children and now Patience.

"Jan 21, 1870—Rio Trespalacios

There's only one bond, that spot I have not yet found courage to visit. I dare not allow such a strain on my nervous system when __all__ my strength is needed. All and more, since I came another has been added to this already large family . . . six children to do for."

"Jan. 23, 1870—Rio Trespalacios

All day long I've been trying to find a moment to visit the one spot of __rest__ this place has ever afforded. For two long months I have longingly looked toward that quiet nook but have not dared to go to it, if duty had not given employment for every moment in the house. My strength is not now equal to strain but if I could leave the sick long enough, the sad indulgence should be mine.

Two boats are in today—contrary to my usual favor I have but one letter by this mail. We are having sickness and trouble enough here for the family one would think. There seems only trouble continually thro' all this stricken land."

Adding to the routine activities of ranching, Bradford started killing older beeves and those less desirable for the live market. For this purpose he constructed the "WB Grimes Trespalacios Rendering and Packing House" during the summer of 1869. It was a bloody and smelly operation but with emancipation and thousands of returning Confederates looking for work, Grimes employed a great and diverse number of laborers in his tallow operation.

At Indianola, there was a market for salted hides and

kegs of tallow to be shipped to other ports. In an article that appeared in *The Cattleman* magazine in 1944, Mary Whatley wrote:

"A visitor to the town during those years said the cattle were driven into chutes, killed, hoisted by their hind legs and skinned. The meat was hauled beyond the city limits and dumped. There the town's poor helped themselves to beef, and the roving hogs of the country-side gorged themselves while vultures by the hundreds hovered in black clouds over the decaying meat."

The Grimes Rendering and Packing House strung the cattle hides along the wire fence to dry and the tallow was packed in wooden barrels. The product was shipped to Indianola by barge and from there to New Orleans and other parts of the world. It was a tough, labor intensive operation but the rendering plant made enough to sustain Grimes in the late 1860s and early 1870s when his cattle business was faltering. Although it was the largest tallow factory of its kind, there were two others west of the WB Grimes operation on Carancahua Creek.

The rendering plant Grimes built was designed to include a boiler and four wooden tanks large enough to hold the deboned meat from eight large beeves. The wooden tanks were filled to capacity and then hot steam forced into the tanks causing the tallow to melt and come to the surface where it was shoveled off into barrels or hogsheads. The cuts of lean meat were given to anyone wanting meat and the steamed residue called "hash" was fed to hogs. Grimes' operation could process around one hundred head of cattle per day. Later, Bradford would add a cannery to pack the better cuts in large tins for delivery to the U.S. Navy. The Grimes cannery was the only one of its kind in Texas.

Fannie had become a refined lady living in polite society over the past decade and the coarse and distasteful realities of her brother's business were not what she had expected to find. The tallow operation was not at all to her liking and she records her observations of this vile business in January:

"January 24, 1870—Trespalacios

The Tallow Factory which is saddest of all innovations and most deplorable, tho' it may bring in money—query

*however, keeps thirty or forty hands employed, mostly
white and because white 'good as anybody'—at least
in the way we stand—they must eat with us, though
heaven knows how, in crowded condition of the place.
Neither they nor we have privileges. Over twenty men,
drunk or sober, as happens, crowd three times a day
into our dining room; and, tho' decency and propriety
pervades the motley crew from all nations, which sur-
prises me, I cannot affiliate comfortably with them.
They are marvelously good of their kind, but I don't like
their kind. Ah! No."*

Fannie took time to record her feelings about the decline in the style of living that existed before the war. Her
sentiments about the illness and poverty she finds are re-
flected in her description of the worn furnishings, so familiar
to her as a young girl, and the sadness of the hard times
and desperate conditions brought on by losing the war. Everything and everyone was suffering from the lack of former
prosperity and in January, after nearly two months back on
the ranch she finds time record her observations of "Home."

"Jan. 24, 1870—Trespalacios

*Time speeds on its mysterious way . . . Here I stay qui-
etly in the old familiar room but there's only here and
there a glimpse of its belongings. The old high bedstead
which long years ago, with much labor and perplexity,
I made lower by crookedly sawing off its legs, stands
once again in its wanted position. In the latter years of
my occupacy of this room it had given place to a nic-
er couch, which too is gone with the former prosperity.
The teester Mother made still adorns the four-poster
and from it hang the same cords which beautified its
pretty bar in former times . . . that bar is gone . . . the
beauty has been eaten from the cords by moths . . .
the tassels have shared the same fate . . . the crystal
rings are so discolored they might pass for iron . . . and
even the teester, which has marvelously borne the ravages of time, is a little torn and moth eaten. Of these
days, nearly all the animate are at rest. The inanimate
are gone—I hardly know where. Only I am left of the
former—only the bedstead and sideboard of the latter,
time worn and battered that shows little of its pristine
glory as it graced Mother's parlour in her 'acting out'*

*nearly fifty years ago. Poor old sideboard—it has lit-
erally weathered many a gale—it has housed many a
treasure. I bid it sadly farewell. If I live to locate for
myself another household it will hardly go with me, tho'
I fain I would have it. The day has been a sad one for
me. I have been gathering a few of the valuable noth-
ings around which I have fond memories, saddened
and made sacred by death, still cling. I have not felt
well but I've been very busy nursing Fannie, sewing
for her, washing and twisting wicks on candle rods, my
novitiate at the latter 'never too old to learn!!'"*

In her next entry she again writes critically of her impressions of the distasteful tallow operation.

"January 26, 1870—Trespalacios

*Well, I've taken my first lesson in the Tallow Factory
tho' I went no nearer than the dining room. How Miss
Anna retains her gastrical equilibrium day after day
is a mystery to me. Last night I turned coffee for our
28 white laborers and though they are marvelously
careful in making their toilets for the table, and only
one ever forgets his coat, the odor was at times almost
overpowering. Spirit of Lubin, what must it be like in
hot weather. I am sorry for my sister (in-law); I'm sorry
for all connected with this vile business. I wish I could
see any way out of it—at any personal sacrifice—other than coming here myself. Thank God most sincerely
and fervently that is not required of me but it would
have been my portion had I been 'cursed with the curse
of granted prayer.' Here was the 'Home' I've longed for,
cried for, upbraided Providence because I was denied
it. Merciful Father!"*

Fannie finally finds time for socializing with friends
and neighbors. Her discriminating and critical nature has
not changed from her writings ten years earlier as we can
see from the next entry about one of the Lacey sisters. Jane
and Nannie are the two sisters of Shanghai's wife Fannie.

*"Mrs. Jane Pybus—nee Jane Lacey—called today. I
don't consider that I've much estate to rejoice in but*

*I don't care to exchange with her, tho' she does think
she's lucky in possessing such a nice looking English
husband. If he is a bit of a tyrant according to English
style, and their boy is like unto him, 'the light of our
household' she calls him. I must confess to a <u>prefer-
ence</u> for Kerosene if gas is not attainable. I wish I did
love children, <u>but</u> <u>I don't</u> and I can't well make myself
can I?"*

After weeks of hard work, of pitching in and trying
to help make things easier for Bradford and Maria Louise,
including nursing young Fannie Louise, who was ten and
in ill health, Fannie was anxious to get away from the un-
ending problems at home. She made the decision to go to
"Tadmor," the Robbins family's Colorado River plantation,
where she visited often prior to the war. It was from there
that she had easy access by ferry to her favorite place, the
delightful port city of Matagorda. Chester had died the preceding summer leaving Chloe a widow with several small
children and Fannie records the changes in her diary with
shock and sadness at what the war years had wrought:

"February 6, 1870—Saturday night Tadmore:

*. . . Four months this day since I left Connecticut and
tonight I sleep for the first time in ten years on the Colorado. I strike still the same note, 'tis so changed, yet
destruction and ruin are less apparent here than elsewhere.*

*Ah, the changes which ten years have brought. How
much I have fretted and arraigned both God and man
in my secret soul because of the evils which have come
upon <u>me</u>. And behold, on almost every side my old com-
panions <u>have suffered</u>. . . . 'The evil of the past has
been all sufficient to its day'.*

*Now full of trouble is this world; especially is it so in re-
spect of my poor, suffering homeland . . . I often feel like
cashing in my lot with her as the load, one which I cannot lift, I might at least lighten. Sometimes I think that
even the chaotic existence which has taken the place
of what was once 'Home' itself might, after long years,
assume a <u>systemized</u> cheerfulness somewhat similar*

to the Home of former times . . . Tomorrows <u>will</u> be if I live to meet them."

One of the evil realities Fannie found upon her return was the hanging of four cattle thieves by a group of vigilantes comprised of cowboys from all the surrounding ranches. Three of the thieves hanged were the Lunn brothers, sons of Betsy Lunn, who befriended her before the war. Her sons have now turned into thieves and outlaws. The fourth man hanged along with them was an outlaw known as All-Jaw Smith. There are several accounts of this particular instance of open range justice including the recollection years later by Fannie's nephew BR of having seen the bodies of the dead cowboys left hanging from ropes. In Fannie's 1857 diary, there were numerous references to the kindness of Betsy Lunn and the Lunn family as close neighbors, so the fate of the Lunn brothers must have had a shocking effect on Fannie's view of how things had changed.

Fannie wrote in February about a visit to Mrs. McSparren, Betsy Lunn's sister. She observed that the children of the sister, now married to McSparren, also had failed to morally measure up to the upstanding code of their deceased father.

"February 16, 1870—Rio Trespalacios

. . . their worthy mother is but poorly repaid for all her care and anxiety—God grant there is a reward yet in store for the estimable woman."

Betsy Lunn had died in her absence but here Fannie is recording her thoughts about Betsy's wayward son Wilburn, the only one to survive the lynch mob because he had been able to crawl away from the scene into some thick brush. Ben Lunn, now a doctor, was the only other hope of salvaging the family's reputation but she has her doubts about Wilburn.

"Her sister labored too for sons and daughters who do not mind bringing reproach on their mother's name, she left them for a home where there is no sin or sorrow I trust. Others say she was worthy of the children, whose characters are abhorrent to all good citizens. God only knows the heart. She was my "Betsy" and I trusted her. I think her prayers for the welfare of her children will <u>yet</u>

be answered, tho' it looks like the time was far distant. With a sad heart I marked the changes since every nook and corner of the now neglected place was familiar and a source of pleasure to me. Wilburn is recently married and is improving the premises again. Perhaps he plans now to turn a new leaf. Last night he gave a house warming which was well attended and decorously conducted so far as improvement, but I counted as I rode by—over 30 carcasses of cows or beeves which had been killed for the hides. If they were owned on the ground where they die, surely their owners are improvident. If others owned them, then are the base charges true, and these, the children of my wholesome friend are all unworthy of their parentage? God forbid that they should die as they are living. One is more careful of his mother's house. God grant that Ben, may truly live the life he has commenced, that he may prove to his enemies his right to the character he has assumed—a professional Christian—a licensed physician. May God, 'lead him not into temptation but deliver him from evil'—make him the best of human friends a Christian Doctor."

Later in February the whole family was anxious to attend church to hear Brother Savage, the Methodist preacher from Matagorda. They were travelling in a "buggie."

"February 25, 1870—Trespalacios

. . . half way on our route, facing a brisk norther, we met the intelligence that Mr. Savage had failed of his appointment. The buggie ahead of us has already turned off its course . . . getting home about 1 p.m. and not finding the head of the house returned we kept on down to Moore's in quest of the mail . . . we found no boat up; however, one arrived after dark . . . but I found no letter from home in Connecticut though there was a very large mail."

In spite of the struggle between Bradford and Shanghai, Fannie remained close friends with Jonathan and Nannie and in February she recorded spending two nights with them at Rancho Grande.

"Feb. 25, 1870—Trespalacios

On Wednesday I rode up the creek and arrived at the Pierce ranch just before sunset—spent a very pleasant, sociable evening—enjoyed a good nights rest and started Thursday morning in company with Nannie to spend the day with Sue K. Sister drove up in her buggie with something of the air of the old days, a pair of mules and driver. Fanny with her they made a long call at Pierce's and followed us to Sue's where we found Miss Eva O'Neil already visiting. There were ten of us to dine but Sue speedily baked us a turkey and fitted us a table." . . .

The fact that she was joined on this trip by Bradford's wife Maria Louise shows that the women folk were not letting the feud between Shanghai and Bradford affect their long standing friendship with Jonathan and Nannie. Little Fannie Louise was also traveling with her mother and now fit enough for the trip in the buggy. There was no mention of Abel anywhere in her journal during this time. Fannie continued . . .

"With Nannie back at Pierce I enjoyed another evening of sociability. In the morning Nannie and I sallied forth once more and rode 7 or 8 miles up the creek and called on Mrs. Garnet, poor, poor woman. The merest hovel serves herself, husband and three children—three more lie quietly in their narrow beds 'neath a pretty cluster of trees in sight of the house, if 'house' I can call the windowless shanty. On every side is evidence of poverty and worse. Coming then down the creek we stopped at Anne O'Neils—the honest, industrious woman's blood is visible there. We dined with Anne and spent a pleasant hour afterward. Next we called on Mrs. Pybus . . . then to Mrs. Partain's with many professions of satisfaction from all that I have taken the time to call . . . my horse travelled splendidly all day and I so much enjoyed it."

Fannie had ridden up to Nannie's on either a very old or a badly "rode down" horse which she refers to as "crow's bait" and upon her arrival was loaned a good mount by Jonathan's brother-in-law, Wiley Kuykendall. She continued her ride up and down the creek with Nannie on the borrowed horse. When she returned home she wrote more about the sad condition of what was once the happy home of her youth:

> *"Jonathan gave me a letter and sent Henry to lead my 'crow's bait' down (downstream to the WBG ranch corral). Just at dark we arrived at the ferry to find the rope broken, but Captain Reeves happened on hand and set us over in a skiff—he had brought a large amount of mail—luckily a letter from cousin M.T. for none came from either Mother or Orpha, but I learned of their welfare, a letter too from Betty after a long time. 'Twas late when I exchanged a cheery word with the gloomy ones on the place. . . . There are so many festering hurts on this place 'tis in vain I doctor with cheering words, with expedients, with hard work—I can but give temporary relief at best, no radical care is effected and I get well nigh discouraged."*

In March Fannie had again found time to ride over to Tadmor and then on to what remained of the past glory of Matagorda.

> *"March 4, 1870—'Tadmor'*

> *Tis almost a week since I came down and I find things so much less changed here and fall so readily into the quick old ways that I seem hardly to have been away. The ten years since last I enjoyed the hospitality of 'Solomon's Temple' seem to have passed in a feverish dream. I am my old self again if I but shut my eyes for a moment."*

When she finally crossed the Colorado to the port of Matagorda where she once found style, grace and gaiety as a young lady of 22, she was shocked at the changes war had brought.

> *"Of all the sad sights which have met my gaze in the sorrowful experience of change that had been mine since I left New England, the dilapidated town of Matagorda, which once marked it as the abode of wealth and refinement, are fast dropping to decay. Their beautiful*

yards and gardens are exposed to ravages of hogs and cattle. The families who once occupied its living are reduced to want. Of the many who once gave me kindly greeting in that happy little town, only about a dozen remain and those so changed, in all but good will, that I could scarcely recognize them. Death, War and Time have done their worst with the doomed town it would seem. When I called at Judy W's, Nellie met me at the door. The kind loving Nellie of yore—but older—care worn and the only member of that numerous and happy family left to give me welcome. All are not dead, some are gone from home, but six sleep in the narrow bed prepared for all the living. In the neglected graveyard, which I visited in company with Nellie, I found all that remains on earth of those who made life pleasant in my early absence from home. My school mates most of them are 'gone home.' A little branch of Myrtle plucked from her grave is all that remains to me of 'Narcissus'. Miss Eliza, little changed, is the sole surviving representative of the family unless the life of long absent Jim is spared . . . of that no one knows. Miss Eliza has Narcissus' little India, a fair picture of her mother and bearing some resemblance to her dissolute father who so singly failed to make my dear friend happy."

In Fannie's 1857 diary she had recorded the pleasures and happy times spent as a guest of Mrs. Hilliard when, before the war, she had written:

"If there is any place in the world I'd like better to stay, 'tis here at dear Mrs. Hilliard's. She is so kind and goes on so finely."

In her long absence from Texas, Mrs. Hilliard had died and Fannie paused at her grave in the old Matagorda cemetery to reminisce and later recorded her feelings:

"Dear Mrs. Hillard sleeps quietly in her long neglected grave, not one of her name or blood is left to care for the spot where she, with her little ones, was laid. Mr. Hilliard is now on Caney and the saddest wreck of what was once a noble man. And this is the history of nearly every family of this once populous and prosperous town. I stopped at Mrs. Hodges' and the once overcrowded Hotel (Colorado House) is empty, desolate

and falling to ruins. Without help—without the stimulus of boarders, Mrs. Hodges still keeps her table well set, and her guests well satisfied. She has not forgotten to be hospitable either, as when I stopped with her coming from the North before, so now she refused any remuneration. Mr. Hodges has grown younger rather than older, but I presume has suffered pecuniarily—his store can hardly bring him in much, the Hotel less, and Mrs. H's store will break them, I'm afraid."

Among the legendary characters employed from time to time by both Grimes and Pierce was a young man named Charles Siringo. This colorful character wrote in his famous book, *A Texas Cowboy,* of the slaughtering of cattle for hides and tallow on the WBG and of being put in charge of rounding-up and taking care of horses on the ranch for $15 per month. Siringo too was a casualty of the range war. He worked first for Grimes as a 17-year-old cowboy and then for Shanghai Pierce in Wiley Kuykendall's branding crew. When Shanghai suspected that some of his crew might be branding a few mavericks for their own account, Siringo left before he could be fired.

After leaving the Pierce outfit, Charlie was out mavericking on his own in a cow camp with another cowboy when a known killer by the name of Sam Grant came to the camp and shot Charlie while he was seated on the ground. The shot, intended for his heart, struck him in the knee. At that moment Siringo's friend, Leige Dennis, came riding out of the brush and Grant quickly departed. Leige's timely arrival saved Charlie from a second deadly shot. He was taken in by Jonathan and Nannie and allowed to recuperate at Rancho Grande. Chris Emmett recorded the shooting in his book about Shanghai and wrote that Siringo always believed *"a certain wealthy cattleman hired Sam Grant to kill me on account of my boldness in branding mavericks."*

In the late summer of 1870 Fannie returned to Connecticut with young nephew Braddie and niece Fannie Louise with her. She had taken them north to attend school and live with her in Rocky Hill and with Maria Louise's sister Emily Childs in Hartford. The arrangement would allow for an education as well as the family society so sorely lacking in Texas.

Maria Louise used the letterhead stationary of Bradford's rendering and meat packing business to give Fannie news from the Ranch and a bit about her children Emily,

Lottie and Willie. The harsh lawlessness, labor shortages and ugliness of the work continued.

WM. B. GRIMES,
Tres Palacios Rendering And Packing House
P.O. ADDRESS, BOX 20, INDIANOLA, TEXAS

*"Saturday afternoon
Trespalacios, Sept 10ᵗʰ 1870*

Dear Sister Fannie,

Booth received a letter from you last night saying you had not heard from us but once since your arrival home. I know Bradford has not written until last week but I have several times, but amongst the rest of the wickedness going on, I know that some of my letters that I have sent home what they write back—have not been received . . . News just come Fanny Pierces lungs both gone—no hope—don't know whether time or not—. . . Bradford keeps up wonderful—has a bed in the west corner where the bureau stood & sleeps better than I do,

I am so afraid of the ugly men. They drew 35 barrels tallow yesterday, the most in a day ever drawn— spreading Hash in the field in every direction. The Farmer John takes the field another year builds himself a house furnishes his own hands down the field, B—furnishes lumber & team, B—goes up & down in spirits sometimes not enough cattle & then not enough men

B—has been setting down some awful rules about the Whiskey at the same time I want to fix up some bitters that you made when you left with Morphine Camphor &c & we dare not send for liquor & I will try & have him decide what or how you can fix it—we have nothing for a snake bite & dare not—& don't want any one to know

Just washed Wills head. If you were married you never would have a little curly head more like yourself than Emmie. She has awful boils from hear &c is getting better, but so sweet, grows every day like little Fanny & seems bound to take Fanny's place in her Papa's heart. Somehow Lottie can try all her life I don't think she can fill it & she will be the smartest in the family. I am very glad to think she is going off to school like Fannie—Old Miss Harvey sent excellent reports of her good behavior"

Another hard year passed for Bradford Grimes. The first year of his rendering business had been a struggle; finding enough labor was a continuing headache and never enough cattle or boats to ship out hides and tallow when he needed them. Finally, with a little luck, his fortunes were improving. Maria Louise had reason for optimism too, as expressed in excerpts from a letter to Fannie and her two oldest children now in Connecticut.

WM. B. GRIMES,

Tres Palacios Rendering and Packing House,

P.O. ADDRESS, BOX 20, INDIANOLA, TEXAS

"Trespalacios, Nov 10ᵗʰ 1870

Dear Sister Fannie,

Two nights ago a letter come from you & Fannie L. &c &c, the first good mail since quarantine was raised. The boat whistle has blown & its bell rung—Bradford hurrying some letters for the mail so I will try to scratch a few lines,

The boarding house in the distance is being finished & the new packing house must be finished first. The new Scottish Woman Mrs Ward arrived to day—it does seem to me for the first time in my life, I believe I shall be satisfied & delighted, she seems so womanly & motherly kind good & smart—lost all her children, of 8 but one who was sent back to Scotland to school. Her husband has been one of the best working men Bradford has had all the year—well we have the parlor filled with beds—Mr McRenolds has at last arrived from Ohio, the

*grand Beef Packer for us—came Sunday night, on him
I suppose depends whether we sink or swim, but Bradford is as much pleased with this great big person with
his good kind smart ways—&c as I am with Mrs Ward
hope it will all go on good—*

*Mr Harvey the man who has been packing meat for us
has been for his Wife & they arrived by boat this morning. I had to turn out Murphy & his comrads to camp on
the floor over to the boarding house, & he was mad, &
the family have gone to house keeping in the Mexican
ranche. Mr Van Ingen left after few days since he could
not stand the crowd, so Booth our <u>soule independent</u>
again Book Keeper, though one is expected from N.O—
& a business man from New York soon so you see the
whirl we must live in & the changes of the past week—*

*You will have a new correspondent I presume in Miss
Eliza—I fear she will be disappointed for I tho't the
crowd would be away—& I fear she will not like what
Bradford wants now—but I've had my orders, & shall
try to obey—*

*Mrs F. Pierce alive yet—Sue not well am going up to see
her if I can for Booth next week—Hope this will find you
better soon—Love to everybody*

*Mr Harvey the man who has been packing meat for
us—has been for his Wife & they arrived by boat this
morning"*

Bradford had originally begun the hide, tallow and
packing business to provide a means of profiting from less
marketable cattle. He and the cattlemen in the area were all
now looking at the developing market for the better quality
cattle in their herds with the emerging rail heads in Kansas
and Missouri.

The hanging of the Lunn brothers and an outlaw
named All-Jaw Smith brought rumors that Shanghai was
the instigator behind this rough justice. With some of the
blame being directed toward him, he decided to absent
himself from Matagorda County until things could cool off.
He had also learned that the hangings had offended friends
of All-Jaw Smith who were operating on the western fring-

es of the Grimes-Pierce range. Smith had been part of a band of questionable characters operating to the west in DeWitt and Gonzales counties and the alliance with the Lunn brothers was probably what got them all hanged. Another reason would have been that the Matagorda County cattlemen wanted no competition from groups operating farther west.

Included among the friends of All-Jaw Smith was the notorious gunman and outlaw John Wesley Hardin who, while on the run, rode with the Taylor and Clements outfits on their cattle drives. Hardin and James Taylor had already gunned down Jack Helms, a U.S. Marshall and a former employee of Shanghai Pierce. James Taylor killed John Sutton in front of his wife after the couple had boarded a ship in the port of Indianola and Taylor's brother Billy shot down Gabe Slaughter who was traveling with Sutton. Perhaps this unbridled gun play had unnerved Pierce and prompted his impromptu vacation to Kansas City.

Booth Jordan, Grimes' erstwhile bookkeeper-turned-drover by summer 1871, wrote from Kansas to his friend Fannie. He spoke of herding cows in to Kansas for Abel Pierce and of his boss's return from a visit to Rhode Island. Abel had evaded his troubles with the law in Texas but in her letter to Booth, Fannie expressed disapproval of her old friend's way of life.

*"Bradford Heights, Aug 31*st

I was glad to learn you were 'well & in fine spirits'—Did Abel's arrival cheer you so much? I've never learned to call him 'Shang', never shall I reckon, I don't admire the soubriquet, shall not mention his sojourn at Abiline in any of my letters south. The 'natives' are vowing vengeance on him. Harris threatens dire misfortune to himself & property 'wherever he hides' All this is moonshine I don't doubt, don't presume Harris can do any thing with him but they may annoy him.

I'm sorry he has made himself liable to so much censure & unpleasant comment, 'twere better not to have 'made haste to be rich'. Riches are but a poor exchange for peace of mind & personal security.

I hope I may hear from you soon and with something

*more than your recent prolixity & also with more of detail,
as your surroundings are all strange to me, you should
introduce your 'locale' as well as your history to my apprehension. James is calling—'Mail Time' Miss Fanny!*

With kind remembrance to Frank—"

When Shanghai returned in 1871, tempers had cooled
and he again took up the matter of throwing Grimes off the
range. At Rancho Grande, under Jonathan's management,
things were running smoothly. B.Q. Ward, who had purchased large tracts of rangeland west of Grimes, was further restricting him and to make matters worse, Shanghai
had begun to buy cheap land between the Colorado and
Trespalacios. Shanghai's expansion now included rangeland on all sides of Grimes and his gradual encirclement
of Grimes became known as the "Shanghai Circle" and
Shanghai was overheard boasting *"I bought the land right
out from under the hooves of Grimes' cattle."*

As the Shanghai Circle cut off a herd of choice Grimes
steers from his main range, Grimes made a quick decision to
deal with the problem by driving that herd to a Kansas railhead. This risky plan netted him a surprisingly handsome
profit and Grimes became keenly aware that trail drives
might now provide enough profit to answer his changing
fortunes. He began emptying the range within and around
the Shanghai Circle and, with ranchlands newly acquired
in Kansas and the Indian Territories south of Dodge, his
incentive to continue the fight for Matagorda territory less-
ened. Grimes and others were setting their sights on the
railheads and elsewhere.

Fannie received an informative letter from her good
friend Booth Jordan about Abilene, Kansas. His was a
fresh description indeed of what the Wild West was really
like in 1871, not the dime store version portrayed even a
decade later, but a giant magnet for cattlemen and their
money. With its principal railroad hubs for shipping cattle,
Kansas was also famous for gambling houses and prosti-
tution. The city of Abilene was such a place when Booth
wrote to Fannie. He and his friend Frank Hilliard were out
of jobs, almost broke, and ready to return to the prairies
of Texas. Staying at the best hotel in Abilene, the "Drover's
Cottage," they must somehow settle their accounts before
they went home. Booth vividly described some of the details
to Fannie.

"'Drovers Cottage'
Abilene Kansas
8 P.M.- September 19th 1871

Dear Fannie

I have just returned from the Post Office but I have re-
turned just as I went without anything . . . for you know
that I am miserable when I do not hear from you,

. . . Pierce is still buying a few fat Cattle & shipping
them to St Louis & Chicago but as yet he is unable to
give either of us anything to do. . . . and we are here flat
broke Pierce loaned us $100 and that is all gone now.
After settling up all our debts here there was not a pen-
ny left. Frank went down with some Cattle to Chicago
last Wednesday, and he will make enough on the trip
to settle our Hotel bill.

I had an offer today to go back to Texas and I think I
shall accept it if I can persuade Frank to go too—There
is a party here who knew me on the Creek, I sent him
some money which was due him for Cattle which Mr
Grimes killed of his. This gentleman brought to this
market some 4000 Beeves—a portion of which he in-
tends to winter. He also intends to drive here next year
some 10 or 12,000 and he wishes Frank & I to either
take charge & winter his Cattle that are here or go back
home with him and each one of us bring up a drove for
him next spring. Pierce recommended us to Barge very
highly.

I am in favor of going back to Texas. I think that by far
the most preferable field for me to operate in, but I shall
not leave Frank come what will we stick together, and
if, with our habits, we don't succeed then none will,
Neither of us drink and I am almost quit swearing, it is
now only on Especial occasion that I ever utter an oath,
and Frank never swears, he smokes as much as usual
though."

Booth's unfinished letter continues the next day and
contains assurances of what a straight arrow he is and that
he has not been tempted by all of the vice around.

"September 20th 1871—3, P.M.

I have just finished my dinner, and now I will make an attempt to finish this. I would have done so this morning but as our Post Master was arrested last night for opening letters & taking money out of them the Office has been closed all day in consequence. So I thought I would wait until matters were sorter settled before I mailed this.

I suppose you would like a description of this place. Abilene is situated on the Kansas Pacific Rail Road and like all other Kansas towns about 20 years ahead of the country. the inhabitants number about 2,000- and transients about the same, this is a great point for Texas Drovers, who are the main support of the place. There is one first class Hotel, the name if which heads this sheet, like Newton there is plenty of Gambling, I have seen men meet on the street & one would propose a game of 'Seven up' and if the other accepted he would out with a Deck of cards and they would go at it then & there using a Dry Goods box for a table.

There is one portion of the town, known as 'McCoys Addition' which is set aside for the habitations of those of the 'fair Sex' who would rather have 'Stamps' than virtue and that portion of the town is in a truly a deplorable state, the women are all diseased, of course you know the nature well as a natural consequence the disease is communicated to those with whom they have intercourse, and there are hundreds of Texas boys who are sorry that they ever saw this place. For they can never marry that is if they have any respect for the woman they love for you must know that the disease is hereditary and will spread from Husband to Wife and from them to their children and so on for two or three generations. Horrible to think of isn't it? I have never been out to the Addition, don't presume I ever shall.

The principal local business of this place is Gambling— the number of Houses engaged in this business exceed those of Newton, of course there are plenty of dance houses, and the supply of women on hand is not equal to the demand there are living here one or two respect-

able families, but the lady portion of them never stir outside of their Houses for fear of being insulted.

I am heartily sick of the country, the people and their ways. . . . I am not sorry that I came here though for I am more & More disgruntles with certain modes of gaining pleasure, which before I had only seen in their best colors. I would give almost anything if I possessed it if I was only settled down in this world with a course marked out for the future . . . I am going back to Texas, away off in the wilds of Texas at that. and if I can get me a wife—to accompany me one who will be willing to live the life I wish to, that is one of solitude, I think I shall try it. I shall build a log House with three rooms, one of which I shall furnish & leave vacant for you should you take a notion to pay her boy a visit, who knows.

Frank has just returned and I will have to quit for the time being."

"September 21 1871—Morning

. . . I was ashamed to tell you that all our efforts at procuring something that would pay have up to this time proved fruitless, ... Frank has agreed to accompany me 'home' and we will start next Monday—Our intention is to return to Matagorda County and take the 'prairie' for it, we will work around home until about March & then we will go to Bargis and bring his cattle through for him.

My reputation here is unspotted, a minister of the Gospel would not have been more careful of the places he visited or with whom he went than I have been since I came to this town,

My acquaintances are amongst Texans of influence & with them I associate and none others, amongst the acquaintances I have made here there are several who possible you know and who may some day be of great help to me at home. Capt King of Corpus, Finley & Hensley of Lavacca, Tom O'Conner of the Neueces, Judge Simpson of Columbus, and Maj Breckenridge of San Antonio. these are the principal men then there are many others. I never drink or carouse around buy nine oclock evry night I am in bed.

But enough I am going to close this My head aches terribly in answer to this please address your letters to the care of S. W. Fisher, Matagorda, so hoping to hear soon from you, I close. Rememberance to all <u>particularly</u> to Duckie.

With love as ever   Your loving '<u>boy</u>' Booth"

After Fannie's return to New England in the summer of 1870 she never returned to Texas but remained in touch with family and friends there. The Grimes-Pierce range war continued unabated for several more years. Grimes was unwilling to give up his traditional grazing land without a fight and, despite his aversion to owning large tracts of land, decided to buy 3,074 acres in the middle of Shanghai's Circle. He combined this land with adjoining tracts belonging to his neighbors until among them they controlled around 10,000 acres. Grimes then constructed a plank fence at great labor and expense from the Colorado River to Wilson's Creek. The effect of its construction was to include behind one fence about 50,000 acres including joint rangeland and cattle either owned or claimed by Grimes or Shanghai or both.

Shanghai's reaction was to complain loudly that Grimes was overstocking the range and resorted to the courts for redress. He hired D.E.E. Bramen to file suit for an injunction against Grimes with the attached affidavit of Pierce declaring that Grimes was *"proceeding with a cruel and reckless disregard of my rights and is forcing great numbers of cattle and other stock within the enclosure against my urgent and continued protest."*

Pierce sought an injunction which would give him the authority to eject Grimes' cattle from the enclosure. Shopping around for a court with a friendly judge, Bramen decided on a forum in a different county and ended up filing suit in DeWitt County where an affable judge entered an Order favorable to Shanghai. Before the ink was dry on the order, and before the matter could be litigated further, Pierce cowboys began chasing Grimes' cattle out from behind plank fences that enclosed lands belonging to both. Grimes however was not quitting and due to the fact he could also claim residence in Kansas by virtue of his ranch ownership there, claimed diversity of citizenship. Therefore, under laws of Federal Procedure he now had the right to remove the case to the U.S. Federal District Court in Galveston.

In the meantime Shanghai's cowboys swept the enclosure clean of Grimes' cattle and the matter became moot. Grimes was then advised by his lawyer that his only recourse lay in filing a separate suit in State District Court for damages. By now conscious of the opportunities offered in trailing cattle to the Missouri markets, Bradford chose to let the matter die and turned his efforts full time to rounding up and branding cattle for the trail to the Kansas railhead.

In the end, Pierce's holdings far exceeded all others for sheer numbers of cattle on the Matagorda prairies. When Shanghai died on Sept. 26th, 1900, his holdings were listed in the inventory of his estate as 178,300 acres; and, although his holdings far exceeded those of Grimes, all of the books written about them speak extensively of their good and bad relationship before and after their feud.

CHAPTER ELEVEN

Fate from a Hurricane

The port at Indianola gained real prominence in 1844 when waves of German immigrants on their way west were landed there. Their sponsor, Prince Fredrich Carl of Solms—Braunfels, promoted the establishment of the first German colony in Texas. He purchased land on Matagorda Bay for a port of debarkation to be named Carlshafen. From there the immigrants travelled inland to 1,300 acres on the Guadalupe River where they settled in a colony called New Braunfels. Prince Solms provided for their crossing but failed to provide funding for shelter at the landing or for transportation inland. Deposited on the shores of a wild, new land, these poorly equipped immigrants were left to fend for themselves and their improvised shelters were the beginning of a town. Unfortunately, they were unprepared for the harsh winter that came soon after their arrival and many of them perished. Nevertheless, a port was born from their makeshift camp and by the 1850s it was second only to Galveston and threatening to surpass it in maritime commerce. The port had great influence on the development of Texas by providing the most westerly access to the overland route to California. The port that was to be named "Carlshafen" was named "Indianola":

> *"Over her wharves moved the necessities and luxuries of life for the inhabitants of Western Texas as well as the ordnance and other supplies that shielded Texas from the untamed Indian tribes. Scores of towns in Western Texas were born from her womb and nourished at her breast."*

It was here at Indianola that a terrible storm would change the relationship of the Grimes and Poole clans from friends to family.

The man most responsible for the growth of the port was Charles Morgan of New York, founder of the Morgan Steamship Line. His company operated steam ships from New York to New Orleans and Galveston and in the Morgan fleet were ships that could transport live animals as well as comfortable passenger ships. Great numbers of sailing ships owned by other shippers and individual captains were coming in and out of the port supplying inland towns with goods and returning with cotton, dry cow hides, tallow, pecans and other locally produced goods in their holds.

During the rapid growth of the port, the Morgan Line transferred Thomas J. Poole from its New Orleans office to Indianola as Agent in Charge. In 1860, the election of Lincoln caused credit and lending to dry up and growth of the port slowed. Poole joined with others in petitioning Governor Houston to act in restoring credit for the city's growth as Indianola already had two shipyards doing a booming business but lacked credit for ship building and rail. Poole, as Secretary of Morgan's Gulf, Western Texas and Pacific Railroad, was trying to bring rail from Victoria to connect with Morgan's steamship line but with the election of Lincoln and talk of war, rail would not come.

Tom Poole, Sr. had formed a business partnership with W.B. Grimes, one of the principal shippers of cotton during the Civil War. Later they traded in dried cow hides, kegs of tallow and live cattle, and Poole and his wife Irene were regular guests on the Grimes' Trespalacios ranch. Poole lived to see the arrival of rail from Victoria and points west but died in 1875. Later that same year, a devastating hurricane would completely destroy the Port of Indianola. His widow, Irene and her small son Tom and daughters Mary and Frances would somehow survive the fateful storm. Indianola records show that among a group huddled together during the blow was "*a child of Mrs. Thos. Poole*" who survived the hurricane in one of the few houses not swept away. The home of Irene Poole is listed as being one of the many destroyed. Irene and her children, having miraculously survived the killer storm, made their way to the WBG Ranch when the waters subsided. It is not known how long they remained under the care of the Grimes family but during this time Irene's young son Tom Poole II would fall in love with the Grimes' oldest daughter and his future wife, Fannie Louise.

Mrs. Thomas Jefferson Poole, recently widowed, having lost her home in Indianola to the hurricane of 1875 wrote to her friend and her late husband's business partner:

"New Orleans June 5 1876   '24'

Mr W. B. Grimes

Dear Sir

Your letter was received a few days ago and you must excuse me for not writing sooner, (as I was in the midst of moving),—and the letter remained in the P.O. till advertised—

I have purchased a little home here, and concluded to remain, as upon thinking it all over concluded it was as well for the children here as any other place, besides there are more ties here than anywhere, but, poor forsaken, dear, old, Indianola but of course that is no place to live now,

My place is way up in the upper part of the city, nice and cool with large shade trees, and very comfortable, if you or Mrs Grimes ever come this way, do, stop and make me a little visit. I know you are always in a hurry—. . .

Give my best love to Mrs Grimes and also the children, should like very much to hear from Mrs Grimes.

Direct to Corner Napoleon Avenue & St Charles Avenue

Respectfully

Mrs Irene T. Poole"

The following year, in 1876, tragedy struck again but this time within the Grimes family when Bradford's wife Maria Louise died giving birth to twins. One of the twins, Nellie, also died and the family burial ground now held six of Bradford's children, the Captain, his wife's sister Fanny Bradford, a former slave Patience and now his wife of 21 years. W. B. Grimes was suddenly alone in deciding how to best care for and secure a future for his seven surviving children. One can only imagine the grief and despair Grimes felt as he laid his beloved Maria Louise and a newborn daughter into the ground on the banks of the Trespalacios. Now 51 years old, he was somewhat late in life to be left alone and responsible for such a large family.

Grimes, now wifeless, with ranches to manage in Texas, Oklahoma, Kansas and the Dakotas, and, having been out-spent and out-lawyered by Shanghai Pierce, began to focus on his long harbored thoughts of a permanent move to Kansas City. Over the years on annual cattle drives to Kansas, he had cultivated business and social contacts in Kansas City and knew that it was fast becoming a center for commercial expansion and a hub for cattle trading. His son BR was now a seasoned trail boss and could gather cattle for future drives and manage the WBG ranch in Texas while Grimes would handle the northern ranches from Kansas City. His two younger sons, Will and Richard, were young cowboys bred to ranch life and on their way to becoming ranchers in their own rights.

Grimes, now a grieving widower with seven children to raise and educate, was ever the practical, forward thinker and in summer of 1877 he wrote of his plans in a letter to his sister Fannie in Connecticut. In these excerpts, he shares his reasoning and gives us some insight into his future plans.

"Orleans June 14 '77

Dear Sister

I have been in New Orleans canvassing the matter with Mrs. T J Poole in regard to her taking the place of our Dear lost loved one, I found Mrs. P. in trouble and needing the assistance of a business manager for her affairs as much I do a manager for my domestic affairs, and believing her to be the most suitable person I have ever known to take the care of my children and to take the place of our Dear Mama, I have arranged for her to share her future destiny with mine, She has no personal attractions as to beauty but has truly consistent Christian traits of character that make her better fitted to have the care of my Dear little ones, than any Lady I have ever known. She is now the same age that Mama would have been, no, I am mistaken she is nearer your age.

Her late Husband, and myself were connected in business transactions for many years and our families were very intimately acquainted and you may recollect of Mrs. Poole spending some time in our family during the War, during which time she, of her own accord took Braddie & Fanny in hand and taught them, she feels a great reluctance in taking so great a responsibility as the care of my large family of children and this too in addition to her own three. She is the only person that I have ever known that I would dare wish this great responsibility with, she is not a Northern Lady hence has not the thrift of ours yet I do think she has as little desire for making a display as any Lady I have ever met.

I shall expect to be at Swannee, Tenn at a meeting of "Trustees of the University of the South" about the last of July, and shall expect then to go to New Orleans to Unite my destiny with that of Mrs. Poole, So that if you would be present, you can commence to make arrangements at once.

Of course if I had not known Mrs. Poole so long a time and allways of such a mild retiring character, I should not have been so ready to risk my future happiness and that of my large helpless family, so soon after the death of our Dear Mama, but my whole affairs are, and will be in an unsettled state untill I get a home, and [place] someone at the head of it.

Mrs Poole seems pleased with what I have told her in regard to Kansas City,

. . . Of course our locating there must depend to some extent upon the disposition I can make of my affairs in Texas, the prospect of selling, thus far is not flattering at all and at present I can think of no one suitable to run the Ranche even let alone, the Ranche Store, Farm & Works, though I have every reason to be satisfied with my preliminary success since I stopped running my Tanning Works and left the Ranche in Feby, 75.

I would like to hear from you at once on the subject as I inferred from a remark made by you you had thoughts of Mrs. Poole in connection with my situation, and also have your views as to your being in N.O. and also as to the Girls being there at this important event, I would also like to have you write Mrs Poole at your earliest convenience

Love to all the Family of your affectionate Brother

Wm B Grimes"

On August 7th, 1877 in New Orleans, Louisiana, Irene Poole married William Bradford Grimes. It was the union of two families brought about by tragedy, loss and the hurricane of 1875. They would soon thereafter make their permanent home in Kansas City. Several years later a daughter Grace was born to Irene and Bradford.

The challenges facing Irene in raising all ten children of their blended family were unusually daunting. BR, the oldest of Bradford's children, was 20 years old and a grown man while baby Louise Robbins was barely a year. Despite Bradford's worthy recommendations and the decades of familiarity, Irene, the "stepmother," was never loved by her new wards. In a 1937 autobiography, William B. Jr. wrote: *"In 1879 my father married Mrs. Tom Poole who had two girls and a son. My! What a mistake! He moved the whole bunch of us to Kansas City."*

In 1881, Grimes and his wife Irene would witness the marriage of his oldest daughter, Fannie Louise, to Irene's son Tom Poole II. As a wedding gift Bradford gave the newlyweds title to the WBG ranch and there they made their home. In 1882 a son, Tom Poole, Jr. was born followed in 1886 by their daughter, Irene.

In Grimes' absence from Texas, Shanghai tried, through third parties, to buy Bradford's Matagorda ranch lands but Grimes, sensing that Shanghai was behind the offers, refused to sell any of his holdings. This refusal was really of little consequence to Pierce since the range-land held title to by Grimes was now small in comparison to the Pierce holdings. Having won the war with Grimes, peace reigned. As if to gloat or have the last word, Pierce is reported to have said: *"I've beat him, put him on the Black Hills and so peace to his ashes."*

Grimes however, was by no means finished in the cattle business and had moved his cattle operations on a grand scale to the Indian Territories south of Dodge City, Kansas. Henry I. McCallum wrote about the open range before barbed wire in *The Wire that Fenced the West.* In it he described how both Grimes and Pierce were committed, open range men and slow to come to the realization that wire would win the day. About Pierce he wrote: *"His cattle kingdom spread across the Texas counties of Matagorda and Wharton bordering the Gulf of Mexico, and the parts of this region which he didn't range were lands controlled by his one-time employer and all time enemy, W. Grimes. Between them, the opposing forces of Pierce and Grimes ruled an enormous area of lush, unfenced coastal grassland centered around Trespalacios Creek."*

About Shanghai's declaration that he had forced Grimes to the Black Hills he wrote: *"Shanghai felt that at last the score was settled in his favor, and he was able to escape a little from the clutches of anger which had gripped him for so long. But he had only a brief respite, for Grimes was not yet moved so far away that the two could stay clear of each other forever."*

In the Indian Territories, Grimes had formed an alliance with Major Andrew Drumm in a partnership with Indian Tribes in control of permits to pasture cattle on the open range in what became known as the "Cherokee Outlet." This was a narrow strip of valuable pastureland for cattle that needed fattening after the long drive from the Texas Gulf Coast. It was choice cow country and in the spring and fall it offered the indispensable feed and water which trail animals desperately required. The Grimes-Drumm partnership operated with Indian permits on these prime range lands which were situated athwart the trail where the upcoming herds from Texas were bound to pass to get to the Kansas markets. When Shanghai's cowboys arrived at the Cherokee Outlet, armed Grimes' cowboys were there to block their passage and Pierce was forced to route his cattle on other trails to other markets; and so, Grimes, on his own turf, had the satisfaction of meeting out a little justice of his own making. The Cherokee Outlet was his answer to the Shanghai Circle!

The enterprising and adventurous legacy of the Grimes family continued forth with W. B. in this next phase of his long career. His ventures entailed far more than ranching. In Kansas City he would call upon on his early mercantile training in New York when in 1883 he founded and incorporated the W.B. Grimes Dry Goods Company. He built a prominent six-story building in downtown Kansas City known as the "Grimes Block." Soon after he opened its doors for business, it became a widely known wholesale house that would rival any of its kind, even in St. Louis. After launching his mercantile business, Grimes entered into the banking business. In 1937 an article appeared in the *Kansas Citizen* praising the accomplishments of W.B.

Grimes as an early leader in the city's business community and stating: "*History and prophecy march side by side in the first president's annual address to the Commercial Club, parent of the Chamber of Commerce. William B. Grimes, reporting to the Club's membership in an address delivered November 15.*"

The many accomplishments of William Bradford Grimes included bringing rail to the city, forming an insurance company, organizing the National Bank of Kansas City, the Kansas City Electric Company, the American National Bank, the Kansas City Deposit and Savings Bank. He was a director of the Kansas City Board of Trade and a Trustee on the Board of Regents for Sewanee University. These contributions secured his legacy in a city representing all cattlemen and earned his high standing in the region. Shanghai Pierce's victory over the Matagorda range and W. B Grimes' pioneering in Texas and Kansas City closed an historic chapter for both of these remarkable men.

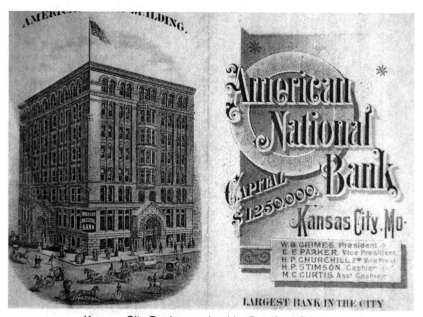

Kansas City Bank organized by Bradford Grimes,
a founder and its first President.

Cattle Drives to Kansas

While the Civil War raged, the blockade of the Texas ports interrupted the cattle, cotton and sugar trade, and thousands of cattle drifted into the coastal region ahead of every norther and sleet storm. Afterward, with the slaves freed from farming, opportunities opened for men ready to work at gathering cattle from the open range. After the war, the northern markets opened with a dramatic demand for beef and the planters turned from trying to farm with hired labor to their grasslands and cattle in an effort to regain their lost fortunes. The stage was now set for a spectacular epic known as the "Trail Movement." Byron Price, in his history of *The Trail Drivers of Texas*, wrote that twenty-five to thirty-five thousand men trailed six to ten million head of cattle and a million horses northward from Texas to the Kansas railheads between the end of the Civil War and the turn of the twentieth century. In his history of these times, he wrote: *"Judging from the literary remains housed in range archives and libraries, memories of the experience lingered far longer in the minds of the men and boys involved than did the tracks of bovine hooves upon the landscape of the Great Plains and beyond."* There would always be a silent kind of respect when anyone was heard to say that they had been *"up the trail."*

The earliest cattle drives before the war had been to New Orleans but the big drives came when the railroads began pushing new rails out from the Missouri River and across the plains of Kansas. Grimes' cattle drives were among the earliest with his cowboys trailing herds from the WBG Ranch to Abilene and Ellis on the Kansas-Pacific line and to Newton, Wichita, Great Bend, and Dodge City on the Santa Fe. The experience of trail driving was mind bending when imagining thousands of longhorns herded northward day after day with little time for rest. Weather was always a factor and lightning from thunderstorms could, and often did, excite entire herds into thundering panic. When a stampede happened, a rider's horse was his best hope for survival by letting his mount run with the herd as a fall meant sudden death. River crossings caused casualties trying to force hundreds of unwilling cattle across raging currents that could terrorize men as well as animals. Trail adventures could bind men together for a lifetime and define the remainder of their lives and stories of the great cattle drives would be told and retold as long as these men lived.

Grimes' oldest son Bradford Robbins would become a key partner with his father in the cattle drives to Kansas. The joyful occasion of his birth on the Trespalacios ranch was recorded Fannie's diary on Oct. 1, 1857 and when Fannie returned to the WBG in 1869, BR, as he was known, had just turned 12. When she departed for Connecticut the following summer she escorted him all the way back to New York City where he would live with her and his Robbins relatives and attend a proper school. Before his return to the WBG ranch there would be six long years of homesick longings, study, pleasure and a notable change from his early days as a young cowboy in Texas.

BR recounted details of his trip north and the new life he found there in a 1942 Biographical Sketch. He recalled that his first journey to New England required three weeks and started from home on the ranch boat dock landing where Fannie, BR and his little sister Fanny Louise boarded a small sail boat for the trip down the Trespalacios and across Matagorda Bay to Indianola. From there they traveled by steamer to Galveston. BR remembered the trip on the coastal steamer, *S.S. Harlan,* and the experience of having supper on its upper deck dining room where he tasted new and wonderful dishes for the first time. In his memoire he wrote that the "piece de resistance" was real sardines and when he was served a pink blancmange for desert, he felt that he was really living.

Another Gulf steamer took them to New Orleans where they boarded a Mississippi river "side wheeler" to Cairo, Illinois and then a train for the final leg to New York. There in the city, no better home could have been had for the small, earnest Texas boy than that of his Aunt Emily and Uncle Harry Childs. In the home of his mother's sister, he was welcomed as one of the family by his cousins May, Emily, Carrie and Harry, Jr. There he found love, kindness and guidance through five teenage years. The never failing interest of his mother in his mental and moral growth came in her frequent letters replete with clippings and words of good advice. He also felt the wise counsel of his Uncle Harry to be of great importance.

He told of his schooling in New York that began when he was enrolled in the boy's school on 13th Street known as Grammar School 35. Backward he must have seemed at first with his inadequate foundation but he advanced rapidly up to the standard of others. Away from the classroom, polish was added with frequent visits to Central Park, the Museum of Fine Arts, the Musicale, or the theater, all of which were encouraged by his Aunt Emily. Vacations were spent in Rocky Hill with Fannie or in Hartford with his grandfather and grandmother Robbins. In Hartford he developed a friendship with Collie Colt, a lad whose father manufactured the famous six-shooter for Texas frontiersmen. Completing in four years the work of Grammar School 35, he continued by enrolling in a commercial course at the College of the City of New York.

Over these five years Braddie the young lad had become BR the young man, standing 6 feet tall in his stocking feet. In 1875, word came by telegraph that he was to meet his father in Great Bend, Kansas, where he would be bringing up a herd of cattle from Texas. They were reunited on June 23, 1875, for the first time in five years and having now attained the stature of a strong young man, was assigned the work of a drover. Then and there BR began the life of a cattleman, first in the service of his father and later for himself in the only business he would follow throughout his life. After his first drive in 1875, he made several more up the trail with Grimes cattle.

The Grimes herd at Great Bend was summering on free range Kansas grass and was to be moved to winter in the Indian Territory south of the present town of Kiowa, Kansas. BR's memoir also told of his introduction to the life of a cow hand. He remembered that throughout the nine months following his June arrival and on into the harsh winter, he never knew the comfort of a bed or the shelter of a roof. All of the cow hands slept in the open and cooked over a chuck wagon campfire and winter came early that year. Bitterly cold northers swept across prairies covered with snow and he recalled the cruel, cold nights, when he slept under a bank in a hole dug back in a hillside where mornings would find him stiff and exhausted from the cold. By the first of the year, he returned, after an absence of six years, to his loving mother, family, and home on the WBG Ranch in Texas.

The following spring Bradford organized a drive that started later than the customary drives in April and one of the cowboys, Frederick Cornelius, left an account of that journey in his memoir of life and times along the banks of the Trespalacios. Cornelius had emigrated from Germany in 1870 at 20 and worked first for Grimes in the Rendering and Packing House, where he recalled that they were killing 125 cattle per day in the canning operations. Later he worked for R. A. Partain, a cattle boss for Grimes, gathering cattle to go up the trail and left the following account of that experience:

> *"I was not dreaming to leave my young wife so soon, but I was persuaded by Mr. Grimes to take a couple of hands and sufficient horses and overtake the herd, which had gone nearly a month before, and go with Mr. A. Dawdy, who was in charge of the cattle, to Kansas. Overtaking the herd above Austin on the St. Gabriel River about ten days after I left home, everything went on nicely, only at Valley Mills we had quite a lot of rain, raining for about three days off and on, so we were not able to move. Soon after we heard of that fatal and terrible storm which swept Indianola and the entire coast country of many men, women and children and animals of all descriptions. This was my first encounter with a storm in Texas. After that we moved along very slowly, our horses and cattle not being able to be moved very fast. After reaching the Indian Territory, we camped early in the evening, in order to gather "Buffalo Chips" for fuel during the night to keep those on guard with the cattle from freezing. They would come in, one at a time, to warm, you know; that time of year, about the middle of October, is getting pretty chilly up towards the territory and Kansas. Getting to Wichita, Kansas, about the middle of December we never lost much time there, but started back as soon as we had turned the cattle over to a Mr. Joe Jackson, who was in charge of the cattle Mr. Grimes had taken up there in spring."*

Cornelius wrote about life on the "Creek" and the difficulty in visiting neighbors around the Trespalacios as his limited mode of transportation was a yoke of oxen pulling a "slide" from place to place. He recalled that Grimes had the only covered hack in the vicinity and described Grimes as a "packery magnate."

B.R. Grimes Cowboys around the Grimes chuck wagon in Oklahoma Territory

BR, now well-seasoned from nine months of living in a cow camp in the Indian Territory, was made "top hand" and in the spring of 1876, took part in this same drive with Cornelius that ended at Dodge City. While on this drive, BR's mother, Maria Louise died shortly after delivering twins but her death was unknown to him for several weeks. That same 1876 drive was written about by Charles Siringo in his first published book about the life of a cowboy. After Siringo's book was published, he was considered the best known cowboy author in the United States. He wrote many books over the years but in his most popular book, *A Texas Cowboy*, he gave the following account of going up the trail for Grimes:

"W.B. Grimes gathered 2,500 head of 'mossy horn' steers from five to fifteen years old and placed them under Asa Dawdy, the trail boss. Most of the cattle in the herd were wild timber cattle. While gathering the herd, the cattle were kept in pens until the herd became too large and then had to be night herded.

"After the herd was gathered, the road brand "G" was burned deep into the hair of each steer to identify it up the trail. The trail crew consisted of twenty-five cowboys, a cook, and the trail boss. There were a number of steers that stampeded so often that it kept the cowboys up all night. The striking of a match to light a cigarette or a pony shaking a saddle would often set the herd off on the run.

"The so-called Chisholm Trail was struck at Austin. The many trails from the Gulf Coast region merged into the Chisholm Trail at the fort on the Colorado River three miles below Austin. The trail at Austin was a roadway several yards wide and extended seven hundred miles to Kansas. At Austin half of the crew returned home. Only twelve cowboys with six horses each were left to take the herd to Kansas.

"The marauding bands of Indians in the Indian territory were a constant source of trouble. The Grimes outfit was besieged time and again by roving bands of redskins demanding beeves. Before the herd got out of the Indian Territory they encountered a more difficult situation than the Indian menace. The cook wagon, which was traveling in front of the herd, crossed the Salt Fork River just ahead of a big rise. By the time the herd arrived, the river was bank-full and one-half mile wide. The herd was pushing right on into the water. The leading steers became frightened soon after taking the water when the horse of a cowboy leader refused to swim and went down. The steers turned back, and the cowboys could not get them to take the water again. There they were on one side of the river and the cook wagon with all the food and bedding on the other. It was a case in which the cowboy's ingenuity had to be relied upon to take care of the situation.

"On the seventh day, with the river still too high to cross, conditions began to worsen; their darkest hour was upon them. It was decided that a scouting party should try again to locate a settler's home, another herd, or someone who had food. After several hours the party located a United States army camp on the opposite side of Wild Horse Creek, a tributary of Salt Fork River. Wild Horse Creek, like the river, was a raging torrent two hundred yards wide. The army captain told the cowboys that he had plenty of food and they were welcome to all they needed, but they would have to come across after it. Siringo, thinking drowning no worse than starving, put his horse into the water and succeeded in gaining the opposite side. A wash tub was filled with flour, bacon, coffee, sugar, and salt, and Siringo started back across guiding the tub by the side of his swimming horse. He thought to bring along a large tin can in which to make coffee, and a smaller one to drink out of. That night the boys feast-

ed, for it had been seven days and nights since they had eaten anything but beef—without even being salted.

"The sun came out of its hiding on the eighth day, and the stream lost part of its roaring, swirling waters. The herd was rounded up and put across without mishap. Thirty-five miles out of Wichita, Kansas, they reached the Nimiscal River at the mouth of Smoke Creek, where Grimes had a permanent camp. Grimes was there to meet them, having arrived by rail a few days earlier. He ordered the herd divided into three groups and held over the winter. With each division he assigned one boss, four cowboys, a cook, and a chuck wagon, and five ponies to each cowboy."

On BR's first trip from the WBG he recalled being paid as a regular cow hand at a salary of twenty-five dollars a month and grub; the following year he was made "Boss Man" in charge of the herd at a salary of one hundred and fifty dollars a month and grub and by his third trip, he was in complete charge of a herd of steers at that salary of a hundred and fifty dollars a month and grub on the 1,500 mile drive from the WBG to a Grimes ranch in the Dakotas. The journey was recounted by BR in a memoir written toward the end of his life which he dictated to his wife Daisy; this memoir was originally published in the *Clark County, Kansas Historical Quarterly* and a portion is recorded below:

"The WBG ranch kept from eight to ten men busy branding the year around. The annual round-up began in early spring for it was traditional that herds start north not later than the first week in April. The Chisholm Trail lay about ten miles distant from the ranch. Let me tell you about a drive I made up the trail to North Dakota.

"One day my father told me I was to be top man or trail boss in charge of twenty-five hundred head of cattle he was sending to our ranch in North Dakota, and that he would pay me twenty-five dollars a month and grub. Of course, I felt mighty important as any boy in his early twenties would.

When we started the round-up, thirty or forty men covered an area fifteen miles wide and rode between the different creeks, and rivers, the Juanita, Colorado, Chranahua, Tres Palacios, and others. It didn't take long before we had three thousand or more head milling and bellowing close to the ranch, but it took us some time to cut out those we were to drive north and brand them with our trail brand "G" in addition to the WBG ranch brand they already carried.

"All cattlemen used a trail brand as an extra precaution and for quicker identification of stock that might stray, become stolen, or get mixed up with other herds along the way.

"We also rounded up a remuda of one hundred extra horses that were pretty wild. We placed them in corrals so that they could become acquainted with each other and lose some of their wild notions before becoming a part of the trail outfit.

"A remuda was always placed in charge of a horse wrangler who accompanied a drive and remained at the rear of the herd He was responsible for them. At night he tied the horse he was riding with a long rope which he attached to his arm so that if the main bunch strayed while he was asleep, as it always did, his horse would start to follow it, pull the rope and awaken him.

"When the cattle were to be counted, six men formed a lane, through which the animals passed, sometimes singly sometimes two, three, or four at a time. We used peas, beans or tied knots in string to keep tab of the number of head. When twenty-five hundred had been accounted for, we turned the others loose and headed them for the range.

"When all was in readiness for the drive to begin, our crew consisted of fourteen riders, Oz, our cook, who was in charge of the four mule chuck wagon, the horse wrangler, who would not only have to look after the rumuda but rotate remounts for those horses that would become galled or tired out, and myself; seventeen men in all.

"Oz was one of our slaves. Where he got the name of Osborn Williams, I never knew until he told me one day *he had 'just picked it up'. He was a flat nosed fellow, a fine cook and a happy spirit. I can hear him singing, and I can hear the tunes he played on his ten cent harmonica which he always carried with him.*

"My father had furnished me with money with which to buy foodstuffs to replenish our larder on the way. Oz always felt important when telling me of what was needed. He was an important member of the crew, for upon him rested the responsibility for having meals ready to bolster up the riders who were often tired out from lack of sleep and hard riding enervated by the hot dust-laden winds that blinded them and cattle alike, or wearied by rains that made the trail a quagmire, they found the going trebly hard.

"When we left the ranch we had about one thousand pounds of food supplies consisting of, in part, green coffee which we parched in a Dutch oven, several sacks of sugar and flour, bacon, rice, hominy, beans, and dried fruits. Oz always had soda biscuits and flapjacks on the menu. Of course, we didn't have any printed menus. We just took what Oz gave us and ate it or went hungry. Eggs were few and a great luxury. Rabbits, prairie chickens, and antelope could be killed on the way if you were a good shot. As I've said before, I don't believe I was ever considered a good marksman.

"The smell of frying bacon, the odor of 'dried sal't, which was the name we gave pork slabs, and the aroma of boiling coffee, never failed to whet our appetites. We used tin cups and tin plates.

"A twenty or thirty gallon barrel was lashed on either side of the chuck wagon and filled with water for drinking purposes. As we didn't have any ice, you can readily understand how warm the water became. A poncho, or dried hide, was slung under the wagon and filled with kindling. It was the duty of Oz to replenish the supply of kindling with dried chips picked-up on the way as in many districts, wood was priceless, and we had to use it sparingly. But it was water first, last, and all the time for man and beast alike.

"The crew ate in turns as they changed shifts, and Oz knew he would be busy from sun-up to sun-down, and while lots of times the boys would wake him up at night and tell him they had to have grub.

"Our average move did not exceed twelve miles per day. We always timed a drive so as to reach a creek at about noon and another before dark, at which times we'd throw the herd off the trail to graze and water. When the noon stop was made we left the herd in charge of just a sufficient number of men to handle it while Oz went on ahead several miles and prepared dinner for the others. When the men with the cattle reached Oz he was ready for them and the herd would be turned over to the boys who had already had their dinner and the trek continued. Night riders took charge immediately after supper.

"Each rider had a yellow slicker, or rain coat, two blankets and a tarpaulin which he laid on the ground, if damp, or used with his blankets when nights were cold. And each had his favorite horse.

"The trail was about one-fourth mile wide and deeply rutted by the hoofs of the cattle which were always wild and hard to handle at the start, but much more docile by the time we reached Austin, Texas. Unless stampeded, they held the trail fairly well. Always at the start one animal would take it upon itself to be the leader of the herd and no matter how often we stopped for water and feed that critter would head the bunch when we started.

"We left the ranch one afternoon at about four o'clock. Fifteen hundred miles lay ahead of us. None of us knew that we would, but we hoped to reach our destination alive. Dust storms, tornados, Indians, and renegades, were no strangers in those days. We bedded down the first night we were out, and sunrise next morning saw us well underway. We timed the day's drive so as to reach the Navidad River before sundown. We reached it that evening, threw the herd off the trail, and bedded down for the night. In due time we passed close to Lockhart, Texas and while the herd continued on its *way, Oz and I bought about one hundred dollars worth of supplies. Lockhart was then a non-descript settlement of a few hundred people.*

"We reached Austin, Texas, about one hundred and fifty miles from the ranch without anything special happening. I paid off and turned back six riders as the cattle were giving little trouble. Some of the boys who received part pay bought overalls or shirts or other wearing apparel, while others visited saloons and returned to the outfit in a more-or-less worse-for-wear condition but still quite able to sit in their saddles and nurse the herd. We remained in Austin thirty-six hours during which time additional foodstuffs were bought. The city then had a population of between twenty and twenty-five thousand people.

"Leaving Austin, we passed close to Temple, Texas, without stopping, and when we reached Fort Worth, about four hundred miles from home, we rested the stock and purchased enough grub to carry us through to Dodge, Kansas.

"When we crossed the Red River at Doan's ferry, so called after a man by that name who operated the ferry, we found ourselves in what was spoken of in those days as The Beautiful Indian Territory.

"Quanah Parker, a half-breed was head of the Comanche tribe. Quanah was waiting for us when we stepped into his land. I knew what was expected of me so did not hesitate to hand him fifteen good dollars as pourboire for good will; which would permit me to feed and water the herd without being molested as we passed through the Territory. He was most polite, spoke excellent English, and when thanking me he assured me we would not be harassed by his tribesmen. I have always believed he must have had scouts out who promptly reported to him when a herd would reach the river. He always met them on the north bank and collected tribute."

In later years, Quanah Parker was reputed to be the wealthiest Native American in North America.

"When Indians asked cattlemen for an animal they asked for a *wohaw*, a word they had picked-up from the bull-wacker's call to their long string of oxen freighting to different army posts. '*Gee*' turned the lead oxen to the right. '*Wohaw*' swung them to the left. It was therefore easy for the Indians to connect '*wohaw*' with beef, or cattle.

"A few days after I had settled with Quanah we were bedding down for the night at Cache Creek when several Comanches rode up and demanded *wohaw*. Their spokesman was a little yellow-faced half-breed and as evil looking as you can imagine. I didn't appreciate the demand for I felt I had already settled with Quanah and that should be all that could be expected. I told the Indian I had nothing to give him. He didn't seem to care what I said, and when I finally told him I had made peace with his chief it had no effect. His demands became more insistent and I became equally stubborn. In the end, he evidently thought he could win me over by being more polite. He began to palaver, and addressing me with the customary Indian salutation, said: '*You heap good chief. You good Texan.*'

"I emphatically denied the compliment. I thought I might scare him by letting him think I was the worst bad hombre ever turned loose on the cattle trail, and would stand no nonsense. But he wasn't taken aback. He continued to tell me what a heap good chief I was until I decided to get rid of him by riding to the rear of the herd. But when he rode alongside me I wondered what the outcome of the interview would be. I bandied words with him as we rode. Before we reached the tail end of the herd one of my riders overtook us and told me the other Indians were talking about cutting the herd. I immediately rode back to find the Indians bunched together and holding a pow-wow.

"It wasn't long before the Indians demanded, in one voice, '*wohaw*,' and looked at me in such a way that I felt cold chills running up and down my spine. Because of my inexperience I determined to take a chance. I again refused the demands. Had I been wise I would have given them a steer and they would have been satisfied, while my refusal to do so might have as I *afterwards realized, resulted in having the herd stampeded. Ringed in by riders, who had their revolvers ready to shoot, we talked and argued until I finally told them that if they caused me any trouble they would have to make peace with Quanah. Whether or not Quanah would or would not do anything I didn't know, but having taken a stand I was determined to maintain it. What effect Quanah's name had on them, I don't know to this day. Anyway they finally decided to leave. I returned to camp and laid down.*

"I became conscious during the night that someone was moving close by. Opening my eyes I saw that evil looking spokesman creeping up to my horse. Reaching it, he drew my revolver from the saddle morral, a receptacle for odds and ends, where I had foolishly left it. I could see him twisting the barrel around to see if its chambers were loaded, and they were. I thought for sure my last hour had come. I sat up. My movement caused him to look my way.

"'You good chief me good chief,' he remarked, meaningfully, and his ugly look emphasized his words.

"I made no reply, and when my silence must have nettled him he continued to assure me in lurid language that I was a good chief.

"'You shoot, Me shoot. Me die. All same you die,' he bluntly informed me, and I jumped to the conclusion that he thought I had another gun. I didn't tell him I didn't have one.

"It was probably just as well, if not better, that I was unarmed for I would have been tempted to shoot that red devil right then and there. Nevertheless, as I had not threatened to shoot him I was plumb locoed when he spoke of killing me. If he shot I knew I'd never know what hit me. I wished I had given him the entire herd. It was the first and last time for me to leave my revolver where I couldn't easily reach it. I didn't dare call for assistance lest he shoot and I be beyond the necessity of having it. I watched him in silence as he again twirled the barrel so slowly that I knew he was debating just what he should do. I was helpless and knew it, but he didn't. Just what that red skin was prompted to do after scaring me to death I'll never know. He dropped the revolver into the morral, glared viciously at me and hurling a score of choice epithets upon my innocent head walked off.

"Upon later occasions when an Indian asked for wo-haw, I gave him a steer or a cow without argument, even though I had already paid tribute to his chief.

"The Indians must have been hungry all the time. They invariably showed up at meal time. The morning following my experience with the Comanches, a band of Arapahoes appeared for breakfast. Of course, we could have dispensed with their presence but we didn't even suggest they go for reasons you'll now readily understand. The Arapahoes may not have been as wild as the Comanches but they were wild enough. Having been a party to the 1867 treaty with the government they evidently thought they were Sunday school children in comparison with their Comanche brothers. During the meal they ate ravenously. Oz was sure we wouldn't have anything left. One of them spoke of the Comanches saying: 'Him go, go all time. Me sit down.'

"Having had enough of Indians to last me a life time I readily agreed that his tribe was a much more peaceful one than the Comanches, and I didn't stretch the truth. When they were through eating they asked for a wo-haw and I very willingly gave them a calf. When they parted I told them they were good Indians but didn't add I hoped I'd never see them again.

"Cache Creek was not as shallow as I would have liked. However, I decided to ford the herd. Fortunately, it got across without the loss of a single head. But Oz and his chuck wagon didn't fare so well, although he knew his mules and his mules knew him.

"The north bank was steep. Oz was confident the mules could climb it. Four men as outriders ran ropes from the pommels of their saddles to the wagon to assist the mules which forded the stream in safety, and with vociferous shouts, in which Oz, from his seat on the wagon, joined lustily, were encouraged in their efforts to climb the bank. Just as the bank was reached one of the riders failed to do his share of the pulling and in less than it takes to tell the entire outfit was a tangled mess in the river. Oz came up sputtering. He hollered his head off at the mules and the riders alike. The adjectives he used while we were rescuing him and his precious mules, and afterwards while we were retrieving what we could of the supplies brought laughs from everybody and materially eased the situation. But Oz couldn't be prevailed upon to attempt the ford again at the same place.

"'I ain't aimin' to take mor'n one bath this trip,' he observed, 'onless I takes it of a mah own free will'.

"We had to go downstream quite a distance before we found a place to suit him.

"Stampedes invariably occurred at night. Very often slight sounds such as a horse shaking itself and making the stirrups rattle, or a rabbit [trying] to weave its way through the herd, was all that was needed to cause the sea of flesh to become terrified and break loose.

"But it was when thunder crashed, streaks of lightning flashed, and a deluge of rain fell that cattle forgot to be ladies and gentlemen and became panic stricken. It was then a real stampede where the herd was sweeping across the prairie. And it was then that the intelligence of the cow pony demonstrated itself. Each rider had his special night horse, usually a white one as that color could be more easily seen, and chosen because of his intelligence. They could see through rain and darkness what their riders could not see. They could stop and turn on a dime to follow a recalcitrant critter, and knowing they could the men had to anticipate their every move and be prepared not to be thrown to the ground. My men were not the dressed-up-for-the-occasion cowboys. They were riders who knew what to do in a crisis without being told, and did it.

"My first experience handling a night stampede which was caused by the premeditated acts of others, was shortly after we left Cache Creek.

"Cattle thieves, or timber wolves, as they were called, would lie in wait in a timber clump and watch their chance to steal as many from the herd as they felt they could safely handle. They then branded them with their own brands.

"One night when we were bedded down the herd began to get restless, a sure sign to a cow hand that something was wrong. Before we could find out what was disturbing them, the herd started off across the country in all directions on a real rampage. With tails up they tore here there and everywhere, bellowing with fear. It took us all that night and the next day to round them up and another day to count them. Our loss was small. On some of those recovered were fresh brands which convinced us we had been the victims of cattle thieves whose deserted camp we later found in a nearby wood and who, had the stampede not occurred would have waited until we had gone our way and then disposed of the stolen cattle as their property.

"That stampede didn't help the herd which continued to be restless for several days and doubled the work of the riders.

"It wasn't long before we met another band of Arapahoes. I was riding about a mile ahead of the herd when the Indians accosted me. I recognized one of the band as having been one of those who had breakfast with us. He pointed me out to the others, saying: 'Him chief,' whereupon one of them greeted me: 'You chief? Howdy John.'

"'How', I returned, and we got down to business.

"They didn't want wohaw. They wanted money. I gave them three dollars which satisfied them and me. And I had come to the conclusion it didn't pay to do much, if any, arguing.

"As there were always many herds on the trail they had to be kept a safe distance apart to prevent being merged. We frequently saw the camp fires of outfits ahead, and upon one occasion those of my men who were off duty and I rode forward and joined in an im-

promptu dance. Men in slickers represented the women. Harmonicas furnished the music, and to the tunes of The Arkansas Traveler, The Irish Washerwoman, and others I've forgotten, we danced all night.

"At Fort Supply, a government post located near the junction of Beaver River and Wolf Creek, we passed onto the Dodge fork of the trail. As there were quite a number of soldiers stationed at the Fort, a stage coach operated between it and Dodge, a distance of about one hundred miles. Upon reaching Clark Creek post office, a lone building stocked with odds and ends, we forded the Cimarron River to get into Kansas.

"We reached Dodge the later part of July with the herd in good condition, although we had lost about one hundred head that had dropped on the way including those lost in the stampede I've told you about.

"Only two of the riders and the horse wrangler decided to leave the outfit, they having lived up to their agreement to accompany the herd as far as Dodge. I paid the riders off in full and they started back to the ranch.

"The horse wrangler was a Mexican by the name of Ortiz. After buying him a ticket, which I told him I'd give him when he was ready to leave, I gave him ten dollars and a credit slip for the balance due him which he could cash at our store. I did this because I knew he was a booze fighter and wouldn't have a cent left when ready to leave.

"When train time came I waited for Ortiz to show up. When he failed to appear I started out to hunt for him. My search which took me into all the saloons and through the red light district was without result. No one had seen him and to this day I have never learned what became of him. I have always believed he was lured to the banks of the Arkansas River and murdered by men who knew he had left the herd and must have thought he had a considerable sum of money on his person or perhaps he found a resting place in Boot Hill.

"Dodge was a wide open border town of tents, slab board shacks and unpainted buildings. Gambling,

wine, women, and song ruled it. Its population consisted of a hodgepodge of humanity, the worst element pre-
dominating. Brawls were many. Life was cheap. Murders
were frequent, and yet nobody thought anything was
wrong. Unmarked graves dotted a nearby area known as
Boot Hill, so named because those unfortunates who died
with their boots on were unceremoniously buried there.
To-day, Boot Hill lies in the heart of Dodge City, Kansas,
as a memorial to the good and bad men who rest under
its sod. Tourists view it with much curiosity and no doubt
try to conjure up what must have happened during the
days when the inhabitants of the town facetiously told
each other: "They planted him in Boot Hill."

"It was in Dodge that every advantage was taken of
the innocence of the cowboy. The worst liquor, marked
cards, loaded dice and rigged gambling devices of every
kind beset him on all sides. He never had a chance. Like
the proverbial lamb that was led to slaughter he was
fleeced not only of his money, but all too frequently of his
entire outfit, gun, saddle, and even his cherished pony.

"Our camp was on Mulberry Creek, about ten miles
distant from town. Early one evening a youth whose
name I never learned drifted into camp for supper and
to spend the night. He was in his early twenties and
a likeable fellow. It was while he was asleep that a
man rode up and shot him without a word of warning,
and as quickly rode back to town. When the Marshall
demanded his surrender he refused to give himself up
and was shot in turn. Before his death he said he killed
the boy because he believed he had been following him
all the way from Texas, a belief no one shared. Both
filled graves on Boot Hill.

"Pasturage was limitless and free. We remained on
Mulberry Creek for about two months during which
time I bought and sold cattle before continuing north
to Ogallala, Nebraska, where I was to turn the herd,
which now consisted of three thousand head, over to
the foreman of our Hot Springs, N. D. ranch.

"We reached Ogallala without trouble and while there
I contracted with the Yankton, N. D. Indian Agent to

deliver six hundred head of four year old steers at the Agency, which was located on the Missouri River, ninety miles north of Yankton, a drive I'll never forget.

"The steers were as rambunctious a bunch of critters as I ever handled in all my experience on the range. They stampeded nightly for six consecutive nights. It seemed to all of us we were never out of our saddles. Just what got into those sea lions I don't know. Perhaps they knew they were headed for the end of the trail that had no turning. But we finally reached the Agency and my job was finished. Some of these steers driven all the way from Texas became so foot sore, we roped them and bound the feet with rags. On this trip we once drove 50 miles without water for the cattle.

"After arranging to return Oz and the riders to the ranch I disposed of the remuda, chuck wagon and mules, for two thousand dollars which, with a check for sixteen thousand dollars received for the steers, I place in my belt and started for Kansas City to bank both and incidentally enjoy the bright lights before returning to Texas. I reached home Christmas Eve, or just nine months after starting north."

In his memoir BR recounted another story unrelated to the drive of '76 in which he described how horse and cattle thieves operated along the trail:

"One winter I was running about four thousand head of mixed stock in the Indian Territory close to the Kansas border. I had cut the herd in two, and about thirty-five miles separated the units. At about dusk one evening Barney O'Connor, one of my riders, and I were riding from the south to the north camp when we saw a group of men bunched in a draw about a mile distant to our left. We assumed they were Indians "making medicine" or, to be more explicit holding a pow-wow, as no whites other than those wintering their stock in the Territory were supposed to be in it, and we saw no cattle.

"As the trail we were following did not run in the direction of the group, we paid no attention to it until Barney happened to look back in time to see the men deploy

and ride toward us. This unfriendly maneuver not only surprised but convinced us they were Indians on the warpath, otherwise they would have ridden in groups or single file. Having a good lead we didn't wait for them to catch up with us but galloped forward at full speed.

"I was in the lead with five horses attached to a long rope. Barney was in the rear keeping them speeded up. When one of the animals became entangled in the rope, fell, and snarled up the others, we didn't waste any time trying to straighten them out but kept on going. We thought, of course, our pursuers would be glad to have the horses but when they didn't pay any attention to them and kept after us we were dead sure they were Indians after our scalps. It seemed to us the faster we rode the faster they rode. We couldn't shake them off, much less lessen the distance between us. We were glad to hold that.

"The chase of five miles ended when we reached the dugout of a nester which we entered quicker than it takes to tell. Its owner was absent but there were several guns and rifles of the old fashioned octagonal barrel ram-rod type. Each of us loaded a gun and waited for whatever was to happen. When the riders came to a halt about two hundred yards from us we saw they were whites. They could have shot at us, but they didn't. Barney was so hopping mad he wanted to shoot right then and there but I told him there were too many against us and that we had better wait for developments.

"We could see the men talking with one another and concluded they were renegades for at that time all the riff-raff white of the country was making the territory their hide out. However, it wasn't long before one of the men came forward with a white handkerchief tied to the barrel of his gun, and we stepped into the open. When he reached us, the fellow said they believed us to be horse thieves when they saw us riding by with the horses, and were doubly sure when we galloped off; that they would have shot us as we rode had they been able to get within firing distance; that lynching was too good for us and that we might as well give ourselves up. By this time our other men had ridden up; they proved to be Kansas vigilantes who were de-

termined to put a stop to horse stealing. We told them who and what we were and offered to take them to our camp to prove our statements. They examined the brands on our horses and on the five we so unwillingly left behind. In the end they were satisfied we were peaceful citizens and rode off without even apologizing for their mistake. We didn't ask them to apologize. We were tickled to death to be alive."

On yet another subject in his memoir, BR talked about justice for cattle thieves:

"Cattle stealing. . .was indulged in by nesters and nondescripts who lived precariously in Texas, the Indian Territory, and Kansas. Upon more than one occasion I left calves dropped on the Chisholm Trail with different ones with the understanding that they could keep half the number if they'd looked after the others until I called for them. Out of anywhere from a dozen to twenty head I'd expect to get when I returned I'd invariably be told all had died except two or three. Of course I knew the man lied, but what could I do? I was always so disgusted that I told him he could keep them.

"It was in Texas that cattlemen suffered the greatest depredation at the hands of cattle thieves, white renegades whose thefts assumed such proportions that the cattlemen formed their own vigilante committees.

"What I'm going to tell you happened way back in the early seventies. I was not party to the lynching but saw the result.

"A wooded area known as Newell's Grove had been watched off and on for a long time and it was suspected to be the rendezvous of a band of marauders who removed the hides from cattle they killed and took them to Indianola for shipment to eastern points where they sold them for six dollars each. Sometimes they buried the carcasses. If they didn't they just dumped them into a nearby creek or left them to rot on the prairie.

"The first clue to the identity of the Newell Grove bunch was when a cattleman chanced to see a number of

hides being placed aboard one of the Trespalacios creek boats. He inspected them and convinced himself they had been taken from stolen stock. Further investigation showed that the captain of the boat had known for some time what was going on and had helped the thieves get several prior shipments aboard surreptitiously.

"News of the discovery reached the cattle rustlers who were evidently afraid the captain would tell on them. They visited the boat one night, gagged and bound the captain and tying a small cook stove around his neck dropped him into the creek. But that murder didn't save them. A few days later the five members of the gang were swinging from the top cross piece of a gate. Yes, I saw them dangling, dead as herrings. They were buried with their boots on. There were no repercussions and cattle stealing was no longer a nightmare for the cattlemen in that part of the country."

A herd of B.R. Grimes cattle in the Oklahoma territory in the 1880's.

This rough justice involved the hanging of the Lunn brothers, the children of Fannie's friend Betsy whom she wrote about in her diary after the war. Another account of the hanging was also published in *Historic Matagorda County* as follows:

". . . soon after the close of the Civil War, two or three of the Lunn brothers worked for Shanghai Pierce. About 1868 they quit and went into the cattle business for themselves. They had their headquarters at Newell's

Grove on the Carancahua Creek. The ranchmen in the western part of the county soon noticed that these brothers were making rapid progress in their new undertaking. Their suspicions aroused, they instructed their cowboys to watch the Lunns. It was not long until they were at Well Point near Turtle Bay putting their brand on cattle that did not belong to them. About seventy-five or eighty cowboys who worked for the different ranchers raided the home of the Lunn brothers at Newell's Grove and hanged them. One was given his freedom after he promised to leave the county and never return."

The memoirs of B.R. Grimes were colorful and real as he related stories spontaneously from memory as his wife Daisy recorded them. One story he recalled was about a time when he spent thirty-nine hours in the saddle looking for water for 700 head of cattle. He said he started his cowboy life with kid gloves, carrying a prayer book and a pocket edition of Shakespeare. The kid gloves were soon discarded, Shakespeare replaced with a six-shooter, and the prayer book found needed practical use when BR read the burial service for cowboys buried by the side of the trail.

Bradford Grimes and the men who went "up the trail" with herds from the WBG Ranch to the Kansas rail heads.
Top row: Charles Sringo, Ples Dawdy, and Fred Cornelius.
Bottom row: Bradford Grimes, B.R. Grimes (oldest son), and Asa Dowdy.

The WBG outfit, according to BR, was sometimes known as the Sunday School Outfit. Several rules of conduct were enforced such as not killing strays and it was the custom of the Elder Grimes to accompany any cowboy to church at any place he might meet the drive in places like Austin, Ft. Worth, Great Bend, or Dodge.

BR concluded his memoir with the statement that: "*Following the trail was always a man's job.*"

CHAPTER THIRTEEN

Cattle in their Blood

In 1888, a year when Grimes' Kansas City accomplishments were at their peak, tragedy again struck on the WBG when Bradford's oldest daughter Fannie Louise died giving birth to her third child. Fannie Louise Grimes Poole, only 29 years old, was buried in the Grimes Ranch cemetery alongside so many of her siblings. She left behind young Tom Jr. and Irene and their father, now a widower, sent them away to Kansas City to be cared for.

Fannie Louise Grimes Poole—Eldest daughter of Bradford and mother of Tom Poole Jr. and Irene. She died on the WGB at age 29.

By this time Bradford owned a large and comfortable Kansas City residence purchased in 1877 to accommodate his large family and in 1888 it became home to two small, motherless grandchildren sent there by their father. The person given the responsibility for their care was Irene's daughter Frances Eleanor Poole who apparently was a poor choice and didn't want the job as Tom, Jr., then only five years old, remembered that he and tiny Irene were not made to feel welcome and were often hungry and left to fend for themselves. In 1890 their father, Tom Poole Sr., married again and continued to pursue his career in banking but his new wife Martha had no desire of seeing Tom and Irene back in Texas and they were left in Kansas City.

Tom Poole Sr., who married Bradford's oldest daughter Fannie Louise and with his son Tom Poole Jr., founded the Poole Cattle Company.

In spite of the unhappy living arrangements, there were definite advantages to Tom Jr. growing up in Kansas in a cattle ranching family. His grandfather was bringing along his sons BR, Will and Dick to manage cattle spreads on thousands of acres south of Dodge City in the Indian Territories that are now part of northern Oklahoma. Young Tom was to learn well from his cattle savvy uncles and together they would all become men with cattle in their blood. His Grimes uncles and his grandfather Bradford would tutor him and teach him to handle cattle the "Grimes way" so when the time came for his to return to Texas, he would have the skills of an all-round cowboy and businessman. He would also have the added advantages of an education in Kansas City schools and privileges of being the grandson of a leading Kansas City businessman.

Will and Dick, before entering the cattle business full time, were obliged to apprentice in the "Wm. B Grimes Dry Goods Co" store on Delaware Street and when their father started the Kansas City Power and Light Company, Will was made secretary. In John F. Valentine's book, *Cattle Ranching South of Dodge City: The Early Years 1870-1920*, he includes lengthy write-ups on the history of W. B. Grimes and his ranching sons. He traced their operations on several ranches south of Dodge, in the Indian Territories, the Black Hills of Dakota and wrote about the cattle partnership the elder Grimes had with a Major Drumm in the Cherokee Outlet. As his sons matured, Grimes took a more active role in helping them to establish their own cattle businesses.

We know little of Bradford's married life with Irene beyond the expressions of the children. Clearly the older sons did not think well of her and may have resented their father's generosity toward her. In William B. Grimes Jr's 1937 autobiography, he wrote about the earlier state of affairs around 1893: "*By this time my father's home was broken up. He gave Mrs. Poole 3,000 head of cattle and all the ranch equipment, horses and all . . . the only property he had left that wasn't encumbered.*" These hard years coincide with the "Panic of 1894" the equivalent of a financial depression. Whatever the intervening events, Irene Twitchell Grimes was laid to rest in the Grimes Family plot at Elmwood Cemetery in Kansas City on September 19th 1896.

According to Will's recollections, while his father was riding in a buggy, the horse in harness was frightened by a train and caused a wreck in which the elder Grimes was seriously injured. While recovering from the accident he developed pneumonia and thereafter, his health continued to decline until he died in Great Bend, Kansas, in 1904. Ironically, he would leave life from the same place where thirty years earlier he had met his son BR while bringing a herd of his WBG cattle up the trail from Texas.

William Bradford Grimes had been married for a third

and final time to Lillian Cornell, and with her, he led a peaceful and productive life in Great Bend until his death in February 1904 in his 79th year. The history books and newspapers are full of accolades and praise for his extraordinary life but the following are excerpts from a letter by son Richard "Dick" Grimes to his Aunt Fannie about her older brother's death.

W.B. Grimes, Pres and Treas. F.V. Russell, V. Pres Carl E. Stromquist, Sec.

The Grimes Light, Phone and Power Co.

CAPITAL STOCK $20,000

"Great Bend, Kansas 3/1 1904

My dear Aunt Fannie-

This is the first opportunity I have had to write you since father's death, & of course you know the particulars, & from the papers sent you know the feeling of the general public towards father, which to me is more than gratifying, for a good name is more to be valued than great riches.

We are well, & Lillian, fathers wife, (this is the title by which she insists I shall call her) is recovering slowly, although the strain & packing on top of it to go to her home, has almost used her up. And before I go any farther will say that I feel greatly attached to her, in that she made fathers last years a source of great help, pleasure & comfort. I rec'd a letter the Friday previous to his death, in which he stated that they were both well & happy & had so much to be thankful for, and that was the trend of all his letters to me. There too I have been here several times, & each time I noticed the love & attention on her part to do for him, so many little things that were a great source of pleasure to him, such as, having his slippers ready for him when he came home, & you know his failing for clabber, well she kept little vessels large enough for a meal for him at all times, & so on, she is certainly a noble little woman, and am only sorry I am unable to do for her now in return but she wishes to go back to her folks for a time, & says some day she will make me a visit.

Now to business I have gone over everything I can find, but the Light plant & $10000.00 stock in the telephone plant is all I can find. His insurance was all turned over to some one as collateral to secure money to handle the plant with, one piece of which was from all I can find made over to you, can not say now as to what Co. it was in, but will put the particulars in when I go back to the house. Find the plant in excellent condition everything of the best, & a good man hold of it as Manager, so that it will not be necessary for me to come over & stay for can run over anytime & see how things are going.

Hoping this will find you in good health & while I am a very poor correspondent, still you are not nor have been entirely forgotten by your nephew. I have often wished (& expressed it so to my wife), I could get enough ahead to bring on my family & make you a visit. But am afraid that will be a good distance in the future.

With love & best wishes I am   Your aff. Nephew
Richard Grimes.

If there is any further information you desire, address me at Ashland Ks. & I will gladly do anything in my power. Leave for home in the A.M—RG—"

Bradford Robbins "BR" Grimes established his own main ranch headquarters near Ashland, Kansas and from there managed operations in Clark, Harper and Woodward counties and in the Cherokee Outlet. In Valentine's account of BR's ranching, he wrote that at one time Grimes cattle ranged over the hills and valleys of some 80,000 acres under nine different brands. His operations just south of the Kansas line in the Oklahoma Territory were conducted on open range from the Spade Ranch. When this area of open range was opened to settlement, BR moved south of the Clark County line on a strip of leased, government range twenty miles long by ten miles wide near the town site of Buffalo. BR, Will and Dick also jointly owned an outfit known as the Ten Cattle Company and in the brand books of Clark, Harper and Woodward counties, they recorded their own brands as well as bought brands on hundreds of cattle they would turn onto rangelands north, south and west of Ashland, Kansas and in the Cherokee Strip.

William "Will" Bradford Grimes Jr's autobiography records that when he came home to Kansas City from college, he still had the cattle business in his system. Even though he and Dick were obliged to work for a while learning the mercantile and banking business, they soon joined their brother BR back on the open range and in the business they were born to. In his autobiography Will recalled that in one year in the seventies the elder Grimes drove several herds totaling 21,000 steers from Texas to the railheads in Kansas. He also wrote: "*My father's calf branding in Texas went as high as 5,000 head. Quite a bunch of calves! And, they were all roped and branded on the prairie and never had been in a pen. My, how I did enjoy the work! I got to be some roper by this time.*" Whether driving cattle up the trail or working on the range, it meant long, hard days in the saddle since the objective was to end the drove with most of the cattle they started with and to do it right, it took experienced men accustomed to hardship.

When Will finally got the chance to be on his own, he got right into the cattle business in a major way buying and pasturing steers south of Dodge and handling cattle for the Seigel-Sanders Commission Company out of Kansas City. Working for the company out of Dodge City, Will would handle over 60,000 head in one summer. About his work for the commission company he wrote: "*I had to cut all the herds that passed through that part of the country, and it was all done on horseback. I was then thirty-two years old and rated high financially, but badly over rated.*"

BR remained a rancher all of his life and just before he died in 1948 he remarked: "*I never quit the cattle business though there were times it nearly quit me. As an instance, the Fall I turned 1,600 big steers on the Dakota Ranges came one of those killing winters; I gathered just 60 head in the Spring.*" His youngest brother Dick, born on the WBG Ranch in 1868, began his own cattle operation in 1894 in Clark County and managed the Ten Cattle Company for himself, Will and BR. A 1905 census showed Dick as also having some 3,400 acres under fence in Clark County.

Meanwhile, young Tom Poole Jr. was growing up; and, having inherited the WBG Ranch from his mother, he returned to Texas at seventeen to rebuild the Texas operation and earn a stellar reputation as a cattleman. Coincidentally, when Tom returned to claim his part of the Grimes legacy it was the same year that Abel "Shanghai" Pierce died. With two thousand acres inherited from his mother, four

thousand acres from Captain Richard Grimes on Carancahua Creek and lands purchased around the homestead,
it was small compared to the original range controlled by
Grimes but it was enough.

CHAPTER FOURTEEN

Up the Trail by Rail

W. B. Grimes would never return to the WBG but his grandson Tom would carry the mantle of the Grimes family in Texas while BR, Will and Dick would continue the Grimes operations in Kansas. From the time of his return to Texas, Tom was ever expanding his cattle operations and would become well known for his success in shipping steers to fatten on Oklahoma and Kansas grasslands.

When Tom returned to the WBG, his banker father recommended that he attend business school in San Antonio. Ever an obedient son he took his father's advice; but, with his solid Kansas City schooling, he would to remain only a short time and he later remarked to the author:

"Each day as I walked to and from the school, I passed a saddle shop with a saddle in the window that I admired and really wanted. After a while, I decided I had had enough business schooling, that I had learned all I needed for the cattle business, so I bought the saddle and caught the train."

Tom would prove that there was still life in the WBG and with his father away in the banking business, the decisions were now all his and with the skills learned in Kansas, ranching came easy. Bachelor life on the ranch was another matter and he began to ride over to the Logan ranch on Carancahua Creek where he had developed a keen interest in John Logan's youngest daughter, Jessie. Tom had asked for her hand in marriage and was certain Jessie could share with him the hardships of a ranching life. She was descended from a frontier family that had suffered the hardships of war and she would be a strong and fearless companion. Her father, John L. Logan, had survived four years of fighting for the Confederacy at Shiloh, Corinth, and Vicksburg and her great-uncle, William M. Logan was the same Captain Logan who had led a group of militia under Sam Houston at the Battle of San Jacinto.

Jessie Logan Poole. Wife of Tom Poole, Jr., and a descendant of Capt. William Mitchell Logan who led his 80-man Liberty Militia into battle with Sam Houston at San Jacinto.

In 1904 Tom and Jessie were wed and settled in to the old WBG home on Trespalacios where Jessie fit easily into ranch life, bringing her cooking and gardening skills to give new life to the old ranch home. When the men were working cattle, Jessie would hitch a horse to a prairie sled, load it with food and deliver meals to the cowboys on the round-up and when their first child arrived in 1907 she would be named Fannie Louise in memory of Tom's long dead mother.

Tom, with a desire for more land and more cattle, seized upon an opportunity to lease land from a neighboring rancher, Ed Kilbride who owned several thousand acres east of the Colorado River. Kilbride and Tom talked it over and made an arrangement under which Kilbride would lease the entire ten thousand acre ranch to Tom and his expansion was started.

Livery stable built and operated by J.L. Logan, father of Jessie Logan Poole, wife of T.J. Poole Jr.

The Kilbride, with ample summer range and salt grass pastures during the winter months, allowed a meaningful increase in the number of cattle Tom could manage. The Kilbride ranch house was enlarged to accommodate Tom's growing family and when it came time to move from the original WBG, Tom sent ahead a ranch cook named Sam and two other hands to prepare for his arrival with his family. In recalling their move and the all day trip to the Kilbride, Jessie later told the story of the move to one of her daughters who wrote it down, in her words:

"Driving to the ranch in a buggy, I held Bea on my lap and put Fannie Louise on the back seat. As time passed, Fannie Louise began to cry for her supper but the ranch was still quite a distance away. Crossing the railroad near the station at Wadsworth, Tom popped his whip and we streaked across the prairie with no beaten path and only his rancher's instinct for direction as night began to fall.

After sundown, I became worried about going in the right direction and Fannie Louise continued to cry. Finally Tom said, 'If we can only make it across the creek, we'll practically be home.' Then, at a great distance, we saw a dim light and following it [we] reached the ranch house tired and weary.

The men at the ranch had been worried about us traveling so late and had thoughtfully placed a lamp in the windmill tower as a beacon. Sam, the cook, had heated some milk for the girls, set up furniture, and had the bedrooms made up and waiting, all of which looked more than inviting to us as newcomers."

Tom expanded once again in 1910, with the purchase of George Sargent's cattle. In partnership with his father, he formed the Poole Cattle Company and leased the nine-thousand-acre Sargent ranch east of the Kilbride, and in 1916, the partnership bought the twenty-three thousand acres joining the Sargent ranch to the east bringing, under Tom's management, some forty thousand acres. The enterprise found credit locally to buy the Kilbride ranch and Tom continued building their herd.

Their plans were rudely interrupted in 1921, in a year that brought with it hard times and toughening financial conditions and when the lending bank for the Kilbride wouldn't allow time to refinance, the Kilbride ranch became the property of the bank's principal shareholder. The Poole Cattle Company now concentrated on saving the Poole Ranch lands bordering the San Bernard River in Brazoria County, and they soldiered on.

In 1925, Tom's father wanted to bring his oldest son from his second marriage into the partnership to manage his one-half interest. His son Donald had married Marguerite Huebner from another ranching family and they agreed to make their home on the banks of the San Bernard River. To give Donald and Margurite title to the land where they would build a ranch home, Tom and his father deeded them 25 acres bordering on the river.

Tom's search for ways to overcome the financial difficulties brought on by the coming Depression, convinced him that tremendous gains could be put on steers by shipping them by rail in the spring grazing through the summer months on the strong, blue stem pastures in northern Oklahoma. Tom would need credit to buy steers for this new venture and Ed Pickering, a family friend and pioneer cattleman in Victoria, would introduce him to Victoria bankers who were cattlemen too. They understood what Tom wanted to do and were comfortable lending money on steers. Tom, having grown up around operations on the blue stem grasslands, was convinced that steers were a great alternative to the slow, tough business of developing cow herds and marketing calves. He planned to winter light steers in Texas then ship them North by rail in the spring where big steers would gain two to three pounds a day until shipped at their peak in September. Tom's uncle BR, still a major Kansas rancher, would find the land for Tom's summer range.

Ed Pickering, prominent Victoria rancher who arranged banking introductions to Victoria National Bank for Tom Poole Jr.

A factor that influenced Tom's thinking was an unusual winter storm in 1924 when an arctic "norther" killed cattle by the thousands along the Texas coast including the Poole Cattle Company herd. Driving icy rains froze to their backs and cattle with no sheltering woodlands were driven by the blizzard until they collided with barbed wire where they stacked up and perished. Total losses to the partnership are not known, but none of the coastal ranchers escaped the effects of the storm and for days afterwards cowhands were out skinning cattle for their hides to salvage what they could.

Tom was now ready to gamble on wintering steers for the Missouri markets; and, having grown up under the watchful eye of his grandfather, he was once again in familiar territory. He was certain that his Kansas connections would work for him and if he was right about the amount of rapid weight the steers would gain from April to September, profits could be sizeable. Armed with credit from the Victoria bank, Tom began to buy two-year old steers from every rancher within a hundred miles and crowding them onto winter salt grass pastures. For payment, the Victoria bank provided a single printed document designed especially for cattlemen called a "Draft and Bill of Sale." It described the cattle which served as a Bill of Sale to the purchaser and when it was returned for collection it became the bank's chattel mortgage and security over thousands of living and travelling, four-legged critters.

In the spring of 1926, as the spring grasses began to grow, Tom began loading steers onto Santa Fe Railroad cattle cars bound for northern Oklahoma, dependent now on summer rains and gambling that market prices would remain reasonably level. By the end of the summer of his first year, the light, Texas steers had gained between 350 to 450 pounds and when sold on the Missouri market the results confirmed his new direction and the coming years would prove to be extremely profitable.

When the full force of the Depression began with the crash of 1929, it was followed by years of new hardships to cattlemen everywhere but with the election of Franklin Roosevelt came new government lending programs for farmers and ranchers. In 1933, the Poole Cattle Company would take full advantage of government loans and to maximize the amount that could be borrowed by a single entity, Tom and his father partitioned the Poole ranch between them and applied for the maximum allowed by borrowing as two separate owners. The proceeds were used to pay their joint obligations and provide the working capital to carry on. As Tom's reputation as a steer buyer grew, ranchers from surrounding counties were finding him to be the market for their steers and began looking annually to sell to Poole Cattle Company.

Tom demonstrated his ability year after year to make substantial profits and the Victoria National Bank made available to him all the credit he needed. With this success he was anxious to find ways to increase the number of cattle handled and to add new territory for wintering steers. He removed the territorial constraints of his family partners' aversion to borrowing by leasing additional land for his own account. He added the adjoining Sargent to the west, the Allen Ranch to the east and the Rugely Ranch south of Bay City. Thereafter he routinely shipped from three to four thousand steers to summer range first in Osage County, Oklahoma, and later in the Flint Hills of Kansas.

Tom was not alone in this idea as other cattlemen began to see merit in the idea and soon thousands of steers were handled this way by a small fraternity of "steermen" pasturing cattle in eastern Kansas and northern Oklahoma. This small group of gamblers met every year during the fall shipping season at the Duncan Hotel in Pawhuska, Oklahoma, where they were joined by the commission company owners from Kansas City, St. Louis, and St. Joseph, Missouri. There they mingled with the cattlemen, vying for shipments to their respective companies and contending they would be best positioned to shape the cattle for sale to the packers. Every night would find the lobby and coffee shop of the Duncan Hotel full of these men, and Tom Poole Jr. was a charter member of this small fraternity of steermen.

When Tom's father died in 1938, his assets were distributed among the five children from his second marriage. Donald, already included in the partnership operations, continued operating one-half of the business for himself and his four siblings. From 1926 until the death of Tom Poole, Sr., the partnership had been in the business of shipping steers to Oklahoma and Kansas. Donald and his siblings were not willing to gamble on steers, preferring to limit the operations on their half of the ranch to raising cows and calves. Meanwhile Tom's half of the ranch, as well as adjoining leased lands now under his sole control, were dedicated to wintering steers for the Missouri markets.

After the death of his father, Tom continued to ship steers to Kansas for his own account and, to further expand his operations. In 1948 he purchased a ranch in Matagorda County known as the "Northern." It had been part of a canal and rice farming company owned by farmers from Minnesota, but the headquarters included several houses, barns, sheds, corrals and working pens suitable for handling large herds of cattle. The "Northern" was better suited for rice farming but Tom's interest lay in adding more steers to be shipped to Kansas.

To capitalize on the farming side, he formed a partnership with two experienced, young rice farmers, Oscar Rooth and John Dickerson. Under their business arrangement, Tom, as land owner, would furnish land, seed, water, and half the fertilizer, while John and Oscar would supply farm machinery, labor, fuel, farming expertise, and half of the fertilizer. They were two of the best farmers in Matagorda County and they farmed rice exclusively. When the harvest was sold, the profits were substantial and divided equally between the farmers and Tom Poole. Ironically, the "Northern" was less than ten miles from the site of the WBG Ranch on the Trespalacios where Captain Grimes and his son Bradford had started over 100 years earlier.

T.J. Poole Jr. shipping steers to Kansas in the 1940's. This photograph was taken by Humble Oil & Refining for its magazine *The Humble Way*.

On the "Northern" the farming partners planted 1,000 acres of rice each year and with Tom owning 3,400 acres, there was sufficient land to allow three years of crop rotation. Lands not under cultivation were dedicated to cattle operations and later Tom would add a feedlot and a mill to grind and mix a ration for fattening yearlings. Rooth and Dickerson expertly covered the farming side of the business and made profits from growing rice while Tom continued to ship steers to Kansas every spring.

After 1940, and for several years thereafter, Tom expanded in other ways by leasing ranches to the east and west of the main Poole ranch in Brazoria County and now could winter steers on some 40,000 acres. Every spring, Santa Fe Railroad cattle cars were loaded with between four to five thousand steers bound for Kansas.

The years after 1940 through the early 1950s were bountiful times for men shipping steers on the Osage in Oklahoma and the Flint Hills in Kansas. These deep-rooted, big blue-stem grasses never failed, year in and year out, to produce the gains anticipated. Round-up began in March and by April 1st of each year steers were on the train headed northward to the strong, rolling, blue stem pastures on a 12,000 acre ranch near Cedarvale, Kansas. These ranges were dependent on summer rainfall but in most years the rains came and cattle on these grasslands would gain until September when grass fat steers, in peak condition, would be rounded up and shipped to the Missouri markets. In today's market place, these steers would be considered organically raised on native pastures without hormones, corn, sorghum, or any other feed-lot type mixtures. People who still recall savoring range fat beef steak from those days remember it as being delicious and full of flavor.

During the heyday of sending steers to Kansas, Elmer Summers, an Editor for *The Houston Chronicle's Sunday Magazine* section, wrote a story on June 27, 1954, which lauded Tom Poole's prominence as a cattleman. About the time this story was written, an article on Tom's large scale steer operation was also published in *The Humble Way* magazine. The size of Tom's cattle operations had also attracted the attention of the Chemical Division of Humble Oil & Refining. They were routinely dipping cattle in numbers great enough to allow testing of Humble's chemicals for protection against flies and mosquitoes. The ranch dipping vats were ideal for this purpose and Tom was eager to try anything to give relief to the herds from the swarms of the greenhead flies and mosquitoes that tormented coastal cattle even in the winter months. Humble was welcome to come and charge the dipping vats with whatever chemical concoctions might improve the life of a cow.

1950 photograph for the *Houston Chronicle* article by Elmer Summers on Tom Poole Jr.'s cattle operation and his chuck wagon. Sessia Wyche, pictured far right, cooked for Tom Poole from 1912 until he died.

When Eisenhower was elected in 1952, these cattlemen dedicated to the steer business were unaware and unprepared for what the new administration had in store for them. Shocking change was about to come to this cattleman's way of life when a new Republican administration came to power and passed new laws bringing about regulations regarding the cattle business. The new regulations created a favorable advantage to the grain growers with feedlots which in turn proved an outlet for surplus of grain in the high plains states. Grain and corn would now be fed to cattle for the purpose of fattening them at an earlier age and new laws regarding the grading of carcasses would further encourage feedlotting. Under these laws, all of the packing plants were required to allow government in-spectors to grade and stamp each carcass in a system that forced large scale feeding of yearlings to be marketed to the packers after six months on a corn ration and killed at only 18 months of age. Feedlots were soon crowded with young-er cattle and the availability of older steers to be fattened on the grass lands of Oklahoma and Kansas vanished and the grass fat steer business was over.

By 1960 the Grimes legacy in Texas was nearing its end and, while Tom Poole continued his efforts to buy and winter older steers for the Kansas market, he was forced to dedicate his ranch lands once again to an all cow-calf oper-ation. In this operation he would winter cows and calves on the coast and then truck them to the "Northern" ranch for the summer months. It was a costly business and without the income once gained from shipping big steers to Kansas to fatten, the cattle business became less than profitable, and in the late 1960s, Poole elected to sell the "Northern" ranch. Now in his 80's the final blow was the death of Ses-sia Wyche, his friend, companion and chuck wagon cook for more than 50 years. When Sessia died he was heard to say: *"It's all over now."* Sessia had been an institution and had been with Tom Poole, Jr. since 1912.

In 1966, the *Cattleman* magazine honored Tom and Jessie Poole with an article entitled: *"Life Partners for Six-ty-two years."* Quoting from the magazine, *"It was natural that Tom Poole, Jr. would become a ranchman. It was in his blood. He comes from a long line of Texas cattlemen and in-herited their love and interest in cattle and ranch life."* That observation of the love of cattle and ranching being "in the blood" is easily proven by following the bloodline of the off-spring of William Bradford Grimes. The Grimes ranching industry in Texas is indeed, over, but the legacy lives on.

EPILOGUE

Tom Poole, Jr died in September 1969 and was praised in several publications. As a vice president of the Texas and Southwestern Cattle Raisers Association the following are quotations from the October 1969 issue of *The Cattleman* magazine:

"Thomas Jefferson Poole, Jr., outstanding rancher and cattleman throughout Texas, died September 2nd at the age of 85. He served for over thirty years as a Director of the Texas and Southwestern Cattle Raisers Association and was made an honorary vice-president of the organization in 1965. During his years as a director he served on several committees and at the time of his death was a member of the 1969 Legislative Committee. . . ."

The legislature of the State of Texas passed a resolution on September 2, 1969 honoring Mr. Poole which states in part:

". . . He was instrumental in the establishment and continued success of the Matagorda County Fair and Livestock Association, . . . chosen by the Chamber of Commerce as Outstanding Cattleman of Matagorda County in 1961, . . . was a director of the Bay City Chamber of Commerce from 1959 to 1964, serving as co-chairman of the chamber's Agricultural Committee, . . . was a member of the Presbyterian Church for over 60 years and served over half of those years as a church elder. He maintained a great interest in youth organizations, both in his church work and in civic affairs. . . ."

Although these accolades are noteworthy and certainly place Tom Poole above average, a simply written tribute in the Bay City First Presbyterian Church bulletin from

Sunday, Sept. 7, 1969, perhaps provides the best insight into what his life meant to the people who knew him best:

> *"Thomas Poole had invaluable qualities, an unfailing sense o truth in character, and a constant belief in life's essential goodness. To do what was expected was not enough; he was always prepared to do more. Over and over again in this man's life he showed us that character meant many things and one does not dodge profound experience however hard to bear. His faith had a discipline that made those around him braver for it. He was embedded with a deep resource of love, strong religious ties and beliefs in the future. A definite influence on all who were privileged to know him. To quote from Luke 16:10:*

> *'He that is faithful on that which is least is faithful also in much. He that is unjust in that which is least is unjust in much.'"*

Thomas Jefferson Poole, Jr., with the author around 1948

It is fitting that Tom Poole, Jr. in Texas and his uncles BR, Will and Dick, the grandsons of Captain Richard Grimes, all ended their days of open range cattle ranching of big steers on Kansas prairies, as that era was coming to an end. The scope of the saga touched many lives from Texas to the Dakotas and many points between, not only without blemish on their character or harm to others but with honor and praise from many.

The author with his grandmother, Jessie Logan Poole, at the Northern Headquarters circa 1950.

Jessie Logan Poole died on February 18th, 1972, and is buried next to Tom in the Grimes Family Cemetery on the Trespalacios River, near their early home on the WBG. Listed as a Texas Historical Cemetery it was recognized with a plaque, placed at its entrance by the Texas Historical Commission in June 2008, and its wording summarizes the significance of the burial ground. Among the markers is that of the Captain, the patriarch of the Texas branch of the Connecticut Yankee family that founded the family's cattle business. A few feet away from the Captain, the marker for a family servant and slave named Patience. Her marble marker leaves little doubt that even though a slave, she remained an honored member of the family long after her emancipation.

In 1970, I received a phone call from California advising me that Louise Grimes Darling, the last of the children born on the WBG Ranch, had died and that her ashes were being shipped to Texas for burial. She had requested that her remains be laid to rest in the ranch cemetery beside her mother, Maria Louise and infant twin sister Nellie who died with her mother in 1876. I had met her in the early 1950s when I was a young Navy pilot about to be deployed with my squadron to the Pacific. My grandparents Tom and Jessie and my mother Fannie Louise Davant drove all the way from Texas to California to say goodbye. While they were there, my grandfather suggested that we should visit his aunt Louise, the youngest child of William Bradford and Maria Louise, who was living in her home in Long Beach, California. Tom and his aunt Louise were children together—she was twelve and he was only five when he arrived in Kansas City to live. Their reunion marked the one and only time I had ever met her but I was happy to carry out her last wish.

The old Grimes cemetery was somewhat overgrown from neglect but I found my way to the lonely spot on the banks of the Trespalacios near the WBG Ranch headquarters from whence so many of the early cattle drives had started. The home and corrals were long gone, and I could only imagine the many round-ups, brandings and cattle drives North that started from this spot and ended up at Dodge City or Abilene. I easily found the grave of Maria Louise Grimes and little Nellie and without any final ceremony carried out my Great Aunt Louise's last wish, 94 years after her birth on this ranch.

Tom Poole, Jr. left Kansas with assurances from his

grandfather and was ready to carry on the Grimes tradition. With the blessing and kind encouragement of his aging grandfather, Tom had brought the WBG back to life. It was a different time with different rules but he would acquit himself well and give a good account of all he learned under Grimes' watchful guidance. Prior to his death in 1904, WB Grimes was well satisfied that Tom and all three of his own sons were well on their way to becoming successful cattlemen.

Bradford Robbins' biography speaks vividly of a life in the ranching business where he remained an active rancher until his death in 1948 and brought honor to the Grimes legacy and rich history.

Wm. B. "Will" Grimes, Jr. and his wife Blanche (Lackey) who was raised on a ranch near Ashland, Kansas, made their home in Dodge City. Later they acquired a ranch near Minneola, Kansas, where they raised six children. Two of their boys, Siegel and Lindsey, were cattlemen in eastern Colorado. Their daughter Helen married rancher Marion Rankin and all of their children were in the cattle or livestock business. The third son, George Robbins, "Bub," a graduate of Kansas University and Colorado State University, raised cattle on a 2,300 acre ranch west of Fort Collins, Colorado.

Richard, "Dick," the youngest surviving son born on the WBG Ranch, was schooled in Kansas City and in 1899 married Katherine Thomas. From 1905 to 1923 they ranched near Ashland, Kansas and he continued to work with his brothers Brad and Will in their respective cattle operations. He and Will also formed an Electric Power and Telephone Company in Great Bend and eventually formed the Grimes Electric Company in California. Dick's son Leland raised cattle near Oldsburg, Kansas, and also operated a dairy farm. Leland's son Greg worked as a dairy farmer as a young man but later began a career as a meat inspector. In retirement he is once again raising cattle and enjoying country living.

In 1967, the United States Fish and Wildlife Service of the U.S. Department of the Interior purchased substantially all of the Poole ranch lands in Brazoria County, Texas, and created a wildlife refuge there. Ranching operations through leasing land back from the U. S. Department of the Interior allowed ranching on the refuge to continue for several years beyond the death of Tom Poole, Jr. His youngest twin daughters, Jessie and Jeanne, continued in the cattle business into the 1980s at which time they elected to sell the cattle and dispose of the remaining ranch lands.

Jessie Poole Davis, Daughter of Tom Poole, Jr., branding steers bound for Oklahoma around 1970.

SOURCES AND BIBLIOGRAPHY

A Texas Cowboy, by Charles A. Siringo, 1979 edition, University of Nebraska Press.

Brokenburn Journal, Kate Stone, LSU Press

Canebrake Settlements, 1822-1870, by Mary McAllister Ingram, 2006.

Cattleman Magazine, various articles on Tom Poole, Jr.

Cattle Kings of Texas, by C. L. Douglas

1830 Citizens of Texas, by Clifford E. White.

Comanches, The History of a People, by T. R. Fehrenbach.

"Cotton on the Border," *1861-1865*, by Ronnie C. Tyler, *Southwestern Quarterly*, April, 1970.

Demings Bridge Cemetery, by Ruth Pierce.

Eighteen Minutes, by Stephen L. Moore, Republic of Texas Press, 2004.

Fire and Blood, A History of Mexico, by T. R. Fehrenbach.

Historic Matagorda County, Vol. I and II, compiled by Matagorda Historical Society.

Houston Chronicle Magazine, "Chuckwagon," by E. Somers on T. J. Poole, Jr.

Images of America – Matagorda County, compiled by Matagorda Historical Society.

Indianola: The Mother of Western Texas, by Brownson Malsch.

Indianola and Matagorda Island, 1837-1887, by Linda Wolff.

Indian Depredations in Texas, by J. W. Wilbarger.

John Brown's Body, by Stephen Vincent Benet.

Lone Star, by T. R. Fehrenbach, Tess Press, 2000.

Lone Star Nation, by H. W. Brands.

Memory, Texas Revolution and Secession, by Andrew Lord, Southwestern Quarterly, July, 2010.

Oak Leaves, Biographical Sketch of B.R. Grimes, Matagorda County Genealogical Society.

Riata and Spurs, by Charles A. Siringo.

Samuel Maverick, Texan: 1803-1870. A collection of Letters, Journals and Memoirs, edited by Rena Maverick Green, San Antonio, 1952.

Shanghai Pierce, A Fair Likeness, by Chris Emmett.

Sothwestern Historical Quarterly, various articles.

Spanish Texas: 1519-1821, by Donald E. Chipman.

Texas Forgotten Ports, by Keith Guthrie.

The Cowboys and Longhorns, by Eva May Bird.

The Devil's Triangle, by James Smallwood, Kenneth W. Howell and Carol C. Taylor.

The History of American Sailing Ships, by Howard I. Chapelle.

The History of Ancient Wethersfield, Connecticut, by Sherman Adams and Henry R. Stiles.

The Raven, A Biography of Sam Houston, by Marquis James.

The Texas Rangers, A Century of Frontier Defense, by Walter Prescott Webb.

The Trail Drivers of Texas, by J. Marvin Hunter.

The Wire That Fenced the West, by Henry D. and Frances T. McCallum.

Two Years Before the Mast, by Richard Henry Dana, Jr.,

War of a Thousand Deserts, by Brian Delay.

Wethersfield and Her Daughters, by Francis Wells Fox.

ACKNOWLEDGMENTS:

The material for this book would not have been available without the contributions of Jessie Poole Davis, who so carefully kept the diaries, letters and memorabilia of Captain Grimes and his descendants. Much additional material was provided by other descendants of the Captain.

My special thanks to Greg Grimes and his wife Ardie of Baldwin City, Kansas, who provided the inspiring 1857 diary of Frances Charlotte Bradford Grimes, the Captain's daughter. Georgia Robin Grimes Lyle of Cortez, Colorado provided so many original letters about life on the ranch in the beginning.

Robin spent countless hours carefully reading family correspondence, which tells much of the story of the early development of the WBG Ranch. Special mention is due to Robin for her final selection of family correspondence and journal excerpts from the 1830s through the 1880s, and for her historic reflections and introductory narratives in respect of the material contributed by her. Georgia Robin (Grimes) Lyle is the great-granddaughter of William Bradford and Maria Louise (Robbins) Grimes.

Greg, Robin and the author are all direct descendants of the Captain. A diary written by Fannie during and after the Civil War was in my possession and a third diary was provided by Robin. None of these diaries has ever been published.

In her diary of 1857, Fannie wrote a detailed account of early life on the WBG at the dawn of Texas cattle ranching. The diaries, letters written by this pioneer family and the memoir of Bradford Robbins Grimes, reliving his 1876 cattle drive to Dodge City, all fit together to complete the Grimes legacy.

Special acknowledgments for contributions to this work go to Pauline Wilbraham, who revised so much copy; to Patricia English, who did much of the research related to the deadly Gulf storm of 1837 designated the "Racer"; to Robert Clough, whose efforts were invaluable in delineating the boundaries of the Grimes cemetery, procuring its status as historical and qualifying the cemetery for its historical marker; to Helen Cates Neary for her invaluable encouragement and help with the history of the Holt and Kilbride families and old Matagorda; to Jennifer Rodgers, keeper of the Matagorda County Archives, to Rev. Jack Lancaster, Reverend Emeritus of First Presbyterian Church in Houston, who in his youth was Tom Poole's minister. He most graciously gave of his time at the dedication of the Grimes Historical Marker; his remembrance, friendship and admiration of Tom Poole, Jr. were most appreciated. My sincere thanks to all of you.

CPSIA information can be obtained
at www.ICGtesting.com
Printed in the USA
LVOW10s104060917
547657LV00006B/17/P